FRANK AUERBACH

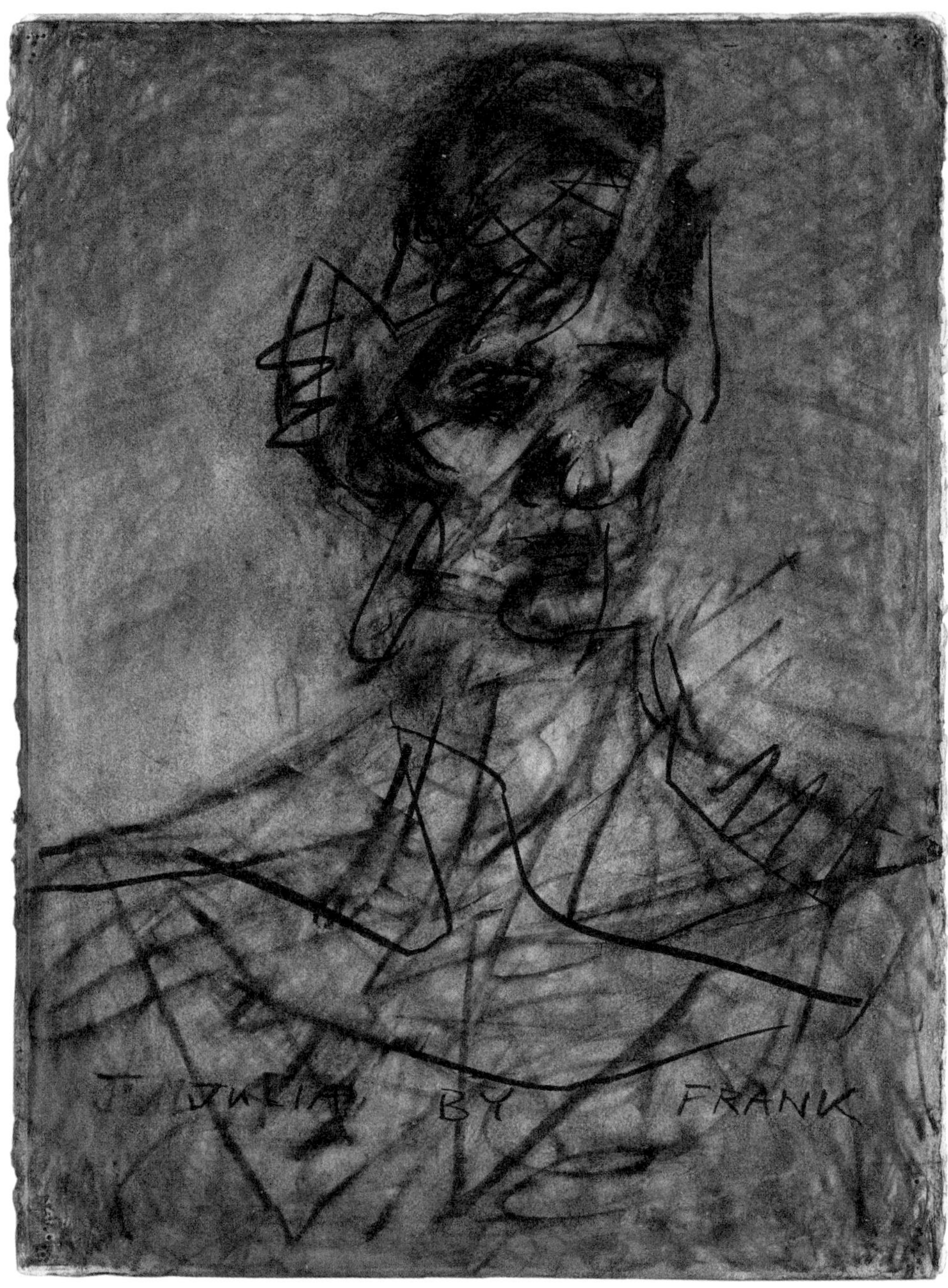

JULIA BY FRANK

Catherine Lampert

FRANK AUERBACH

Speaking and Painting

With 100 illustrations, 78 in colour

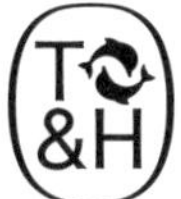

Frontispiece: *Head of Julia*, 1981

First published in the United Kingdom in 2015 by
Thames & Hudson Ltd, 181A High Holborn, London WC1V 7QX

First paperback edition 2019
Reprinted 2024

Frank Auerbach: Speaking and Painting
© 2015 and 2019 Thames & Hudson Ltd, London
Text © 2015 and 2019 Catherine Lampert
Works by Frank Auerbach © 2015 and 2019 Frank Auerbach

British Library Cataloguing-in-Publication Data
A catalogue record for this book is available from the British Library

ISBN 978-0-500-29399-7

Printed and bound in Italy by L.E.G.O. SpA

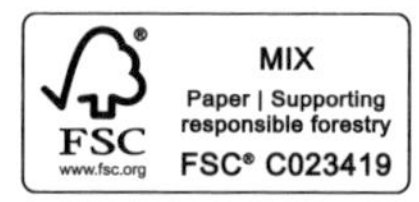

Contents

Preface

For the first few years I was sitting for Frank Auerbach it was hard to reconcile listening to someone so knowledgeable, so gifted in expressing his thoughts and memories, with the person who spent nearly all his time concentrating his whole being on a very messy, physically as well as mentally arduous process that took place in a cramped room. This painter not only resisted public obligations or any appointments, but also rarely socialized and almost never travelled, and then for only a handful of days.

When I was a student at University College London and the Slade, the paintings I saw in the Auerbach exhibition at the Marlborough in January 1967 made an indelible impression on me: the channels and skeins of paint marked a radical departure from representation, but the human subjects suggested complicity and the human imprint on the landscape was made visible, airlifting the viewer back to the life pulse of places and people. We met some ten years later when I was assigned as the exhibition organizer for the Hayward Gallery retrospective of the artist's work that opened in London in May 1978, and I began sitting for him that month. Recording and editing a conversation for the catalogue, it was then that I began to see how Auerbach's candid and uncompromising statements and his use of analogies provide a guide to the way he thinks, especially as he has never wanted to demystify art. For example, 'There's a phrase by Robert Frost about his own verse, I don't know what it means about verse, and I really barely comprehend what it suggests about painting, but it seems to me to be absolutely true. He said, "I want the poem to be like ice on a stove – riding on its own melting." Well, a great painting is like ice on a stove. It is a shape riding on its own melting into matter and space; it never stops moving backwards and forwards.'

Frank famously resists any invasion of his private life. Apart from several pages in the catalogue of the Royal Academy of Arts retrospective

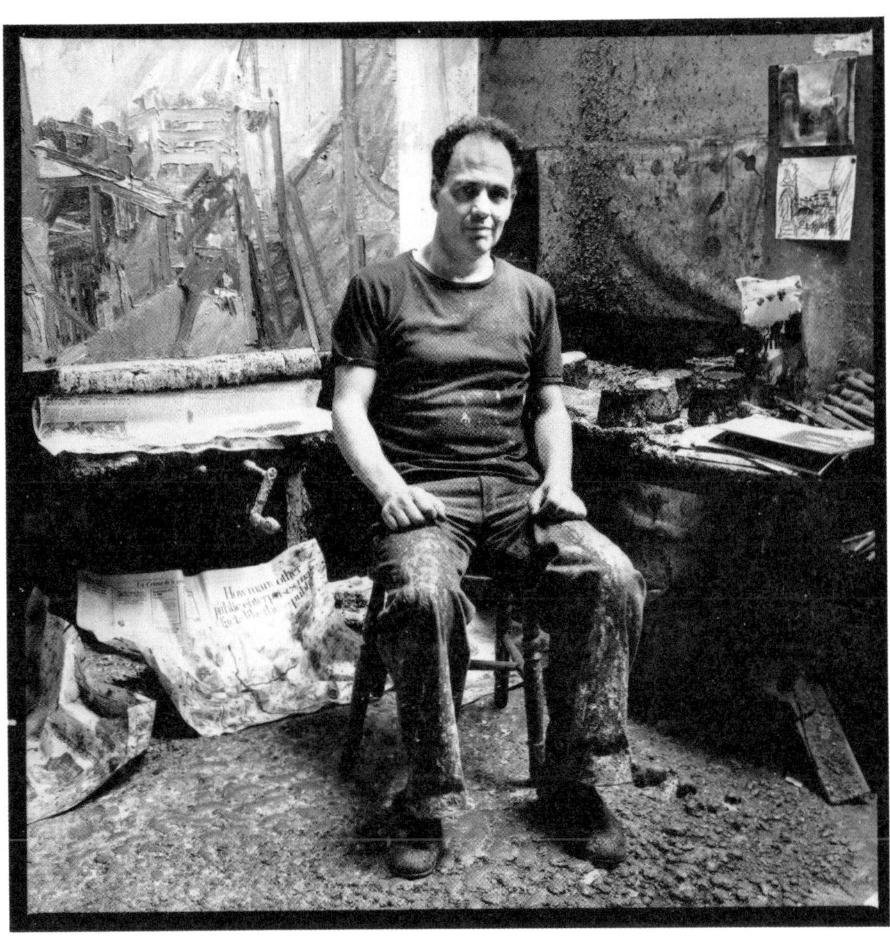

MARC TRIVIER, Frank Auerbach seated in his studio, 1982

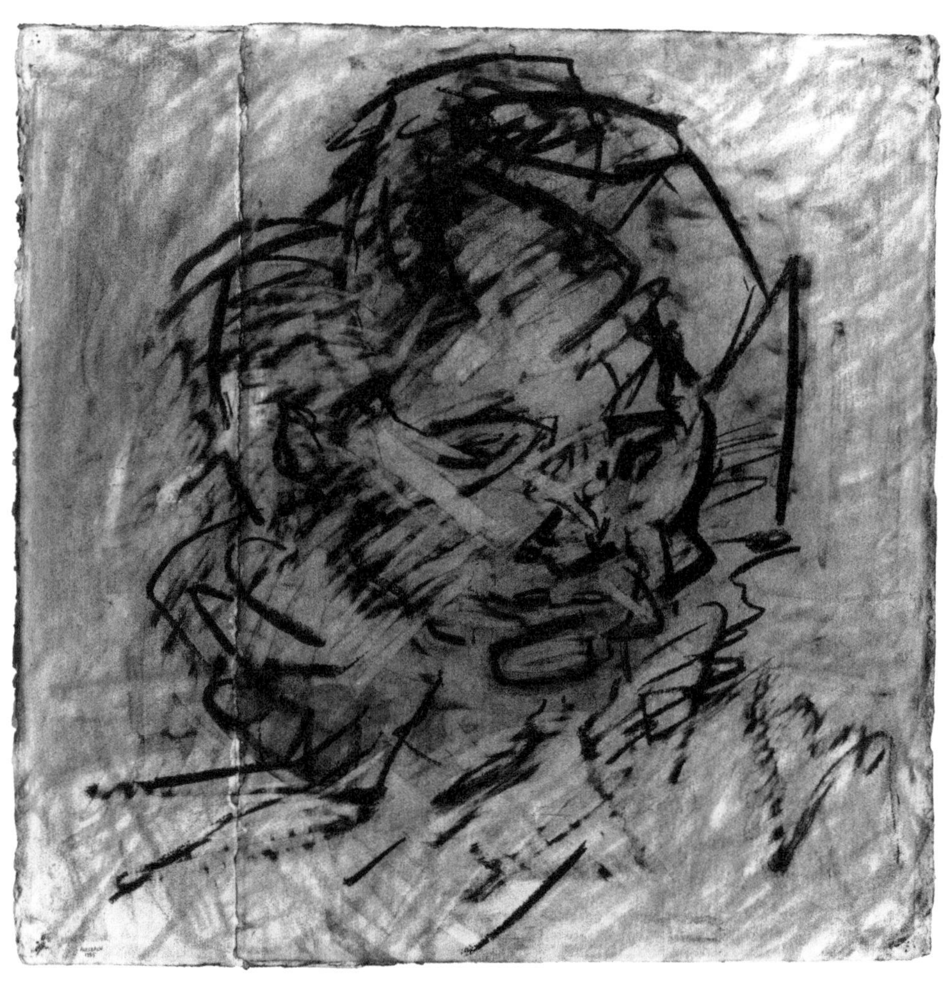

Head of Catherine Lampert, 1985

of his work in 2001, the published chronologies of his life and career in various publications consist only of bare facts. The usual terse second line, '1939: Arrived in England', is no doubt a result of his defence against insistent curiosity during interviews about the experience of being a Jewish child dispatched from Berlin in the company of strangers, and who lost his parents in the Holocaust. One reason for trying not to impute the significance of relationships and feelings is that, as he says about his own recollections, 'it is impossible to be certain of what goes on when people forget themselves'.

In writing about Auerbach, a biographical approach is not really appropriate, apart from in chapter 1, where I discuss his early years. Another consideration (besides his studio-bound life) is that the subjects of his paintings have been virtually unvarying – urban landscapes or portraits. Since he does not make plans or work in series, even discussion of 'development' is fairly artificial. Every painting is meant to be as different as possible from the last. If you ask him about his intentions and approach you are likely to get an answer such as this: 'I can't talk a great deal about the look of my paintings because they are really on the other side of the footlights. I find it somehow fruitless and it makes me self-conscious. Painting for me is a set of connections, a set of sensations of conflicting movements and experiences, which somehow, one hopes, has congealed or cohered or risen out of the battle into being an image that stands up for itself. I don't spend a lot of time looking at my own painting.'

For these reasons, this is a book arranged by topic and theme, with the chronology of the sections sometimes overlapping. The emphasis, as indicated by the book's subtitle, *Speaking and Painting*, is on Auerbach's professional life, working methods and views, as conveyed by, or implicit in, his own words. In this endeavour, I have been fortunate in being able to draw not only on my own notes and unpublished recordings of conversations with Frank, augmented by his vivid recall, but also his turns of phrase and observations in a rich assortment of interviews, some now difficult to access, as well as material in the archives of his gallery, Marlborough Fine Art. Clearly the book is underscored by intense admiration for his great achievement as an artist and is meant to complement, instead of being a substitute for, the experience of standing in front of one of his paintings.

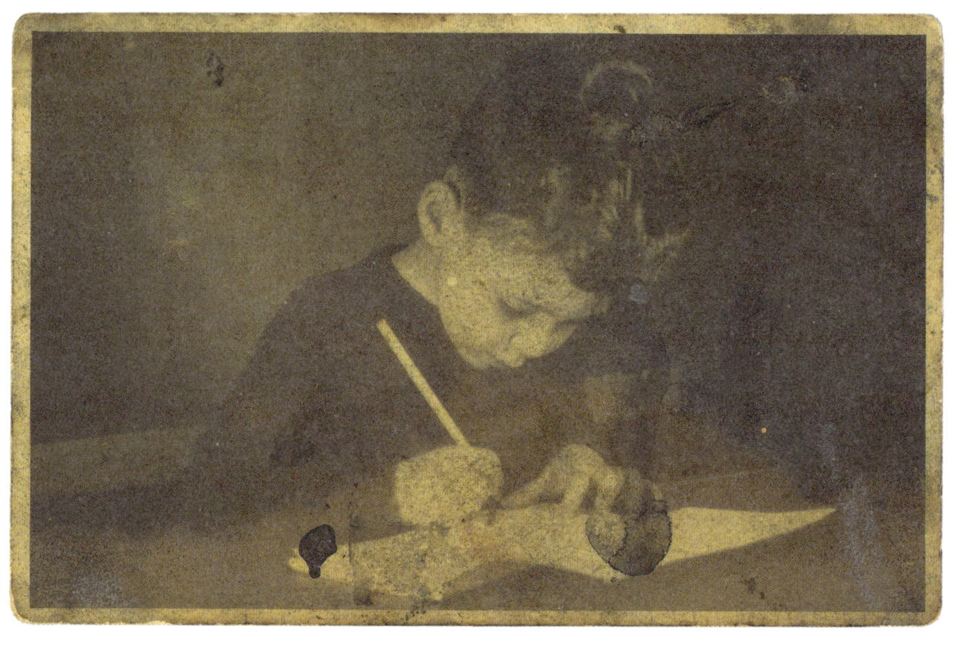

Frank drawing, Berlin, *c.* 1935

Finding a Home in England

Berlin childhood

Born on 29 April 1931, Frank Helmut Auerbach, an only child of older parents, recalls being coddled in a way that even at a young age felt suffocating. This stemmed not only from the memory of being dressed in a blue velvet suit but also from the fact that his daily life was rather isolated from other children, with little freedom to play unwatched. The flat where he lived with his parents, Max Auerbach (b. 1890) and Charlotte Nora Borchardt Auerbach (b. 1902), was in a tall building with a large courtyard at 49 Güntzelstrasse in Wilmersdorf, a middle-class area of Berlin.[1] A brass plate at the entrance announced his father's name and credentials: he was a patent lawyer specializing in engineering and had his office at home. He had served in the army during the Great War and been awarded a medal of distinction. Pudgy and blond with glasses, Max Auerbach was descended from a long line of rabbis, including his father, Mannheim. Frank's mother's family, also Jewish, came from Lithuania; she was a dark-haired woman with a fine figure, although her jaw, like that of other Borchardts, protruded somewhat. Charlotte had studied art as a young woman and had been married before.

The family lived in comfortable circumstances, milk and fresh rolls were delivered daily to the door. Frank's parents seemed to get on, although his father was more relaxed and indulgent than his mother. 'One of the few sort of tags of memories is of him buying a particular sort of bun for me and sitting opposite and seeming to take pleasure in the fact that I was

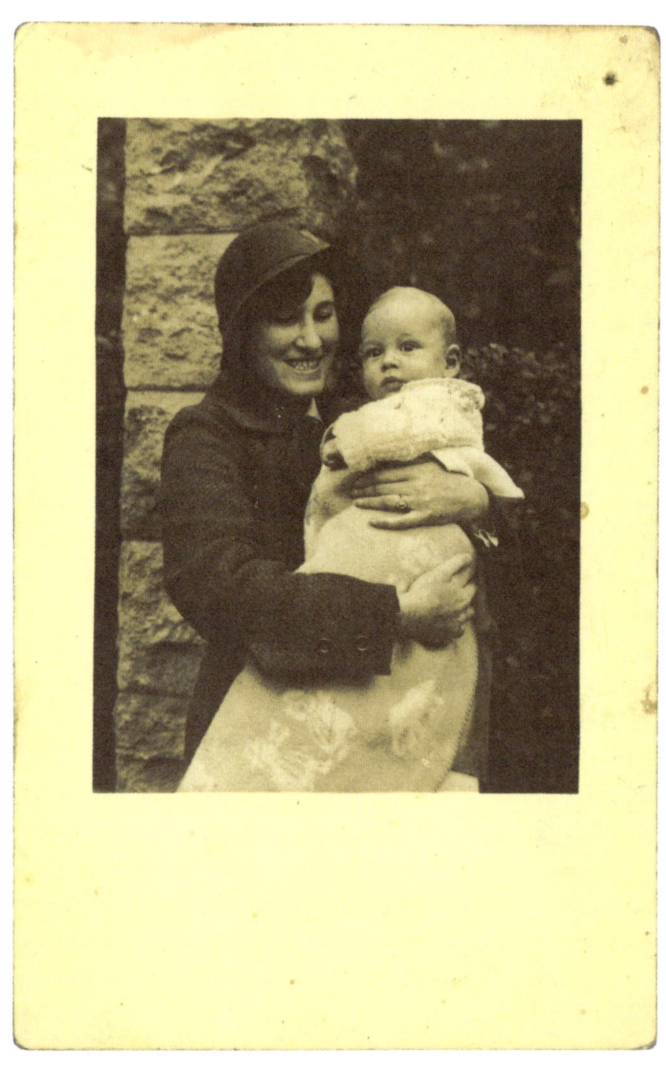

Frank with his mother, Charlotte, Berlin, *c.* 1931

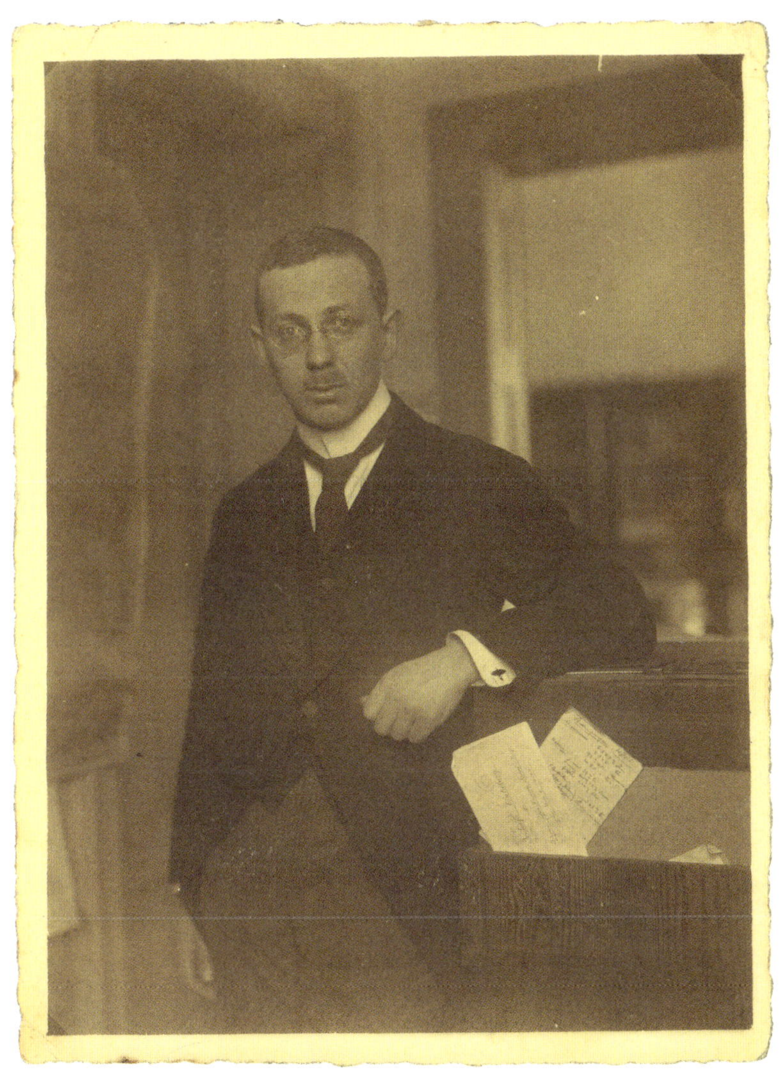

Max Auerbach, the artist's father, Berlin, *c.* 1932

greedily eating it.' Objects on his large desk, especially a blotter and paper punch, amused his son. Other recollections are telling, such as the gift of a paint-box. 'I remember vividly putting a wet brush for the first time onto a cake of watercolour and I think one of my tricks, like you get a dog to roll over, was that I did little drawings, and in my case they were of Red Indians on scooters, which I was asked to draw. I can't have been more than three or four.'[2] Among his books, *Kai aus der Kiste* (1926) by Wolf Durian was a favourite. It was 'about a German boy who stowed away, in a wooden box, for America. He had a great success in the States by devising ever more amazing advertising stunts.'[3] In conversation, memories still occasionally surface, as when I described going to the Turbine Hall at Tate Modern in 2013 to watch Kraftwerk perform. Mentioning their nostalgic song of 1974, 'Autobahn', Auerbach commented that when one of the first sections of the Berlin ring road opened in 1936, taking a drive was a popular diversion. The family stopped at the observatory just off the motorway, and the five-year-old impressed the grown-ups by coming out with the word 'meteor'.

The rise of the Nazi party and the appointment of Adolf Hitler as chancellor in January 1933 were a cause of anxiety and, already nervous by nature, Frank's mother was fearful of the mounting anti-Semitism. On one occasion, when the nanny took Frank to the park, he was given a sweet in the street and, hearing of this and alarmed that someone had been trying to poison her son, his mother put him to bed so she could watch for tell-tale signs. As time went on, the restrictions on Jews increased, particularly after the introduction of the Nuremberg Laws in 1935 that defined who was Jewish, and when the licences of Jewish lawyers were revoked, the plate at the entrance had to be changed to 'Max Auerbach, Engineering Graduate'.

Uncle Jakob, his father's older brother, was also a lawyer. His partner, Dr Altenberg, retired to Italy in 1938. There he met the wealthy Anglo-American writer Iris Origo, who was to provide a lifeline for Frank. Iris, who had grown up in Fiesole, had married a minor Italian aristocrat, Antonio Origo, in 1924 and the couple then devoted their lives to improving the poverty-stricken estate of La Foce that they bought in the Val d'Orcia in southeast Tuscany. Origo had started a school for the children of local peasants, most of whom were illiterate.[4] This led her to correspond with Anna Essinger, a German Jewish educator who had opened her own school,

Landschulheim Herrlingen, near Ulm in south Germany in 1926. The teaching was informed by Essinger's studies at American universities, and especially by her identification with Quaker principles. She embraced the educational philosophy known as *Reformpädagogik* whereby pupils and staff were considered equal and everyone was responsible for the common good of the school.[5] By 1933, the pupils in Ulm were exclusively Jewish and, concerned about the Nazi threat, Essinger transferred the school to England. She rented, and later bought, a Georgian house, Bunce Court, near the village of Lenham and not far from the town of Faversham in the North Downs of Kent, where existing and new students were offered places. Unsurprisingly, the demand from Jewish families rapidly escalated as the Nazis' racial laws tightened. Origo arranged with Essinger to sponsor six children to attend Bunce Court; those selected included Dr Altenberg's nephew and niece, as well as Frank.

Auerbach's parents had hoped the persecution of Jews would get no worse, but facing the reality of the situation, they had acceded to Dr Altenberg's plan. Shortly before Frank's eighth birthday they took him to Hamburg, where on 4 April 1939 he boarded the SS *Washington* in the company of three people he had never met before: the Altenberg children, Heinz and Ilse, and their nanny. The four shared a second-class cabin. This temporary home offered a rather special playroom on their deck with a rocking horse; Frank remembers this and the stale odour on the ship. When it docked first at Le Havre, he saw, with horror, carcasses of meat covered in black flies hanging in the butchers' shops. Arriving in Southampton, the group boarded a train to London and were met at Victoria station by someone from Bunce Court, who took the children down to Kent; the nanny returned to Germany. Frank's suitcase contained his clothes and on the larger garments his mother had stitched a red cross to indicate they were for later use; on items such as tablecloths and sheets intended for when he was grown up, two red crosses had been sewn in a corner.

Bunce Court

The atmosphere at Bunce Court was unlike anything Frank had encountered in his previous life, yet instead of feeling abandoned he felt curiously at home, in the sense of liberated. Frank remembers being locked in a shed by two boys on his first afternoon, yet the experience 'somehow didn't depress me'. Later he got into a fight with another boy, and turned to a bystander to say, 'I think I might get on a bit better if you cheered for me.' His supporter, Michael Roemer, three years older, became a friend and the two are still close. In the nine months from December 1938 to when the war started in September 1939 a number of the other pupils at the school arrived in Britain unaccompanied on the *Kindertransport* organized by the Refugee Children's Movement and World Jewish Relief.[6] The student body was not exclusively Jewish, however. Bunce Court advertised in the *New Statesman* and other left-wing papers, and English couples, perhaps going through a divorce and finding it awkward to look after their children, might send them there. Bruce Bernard, later a friend and a remarkable photo editor, together with his brother Jeffrey, a famous journalist, attended the school in 1936–37.

The staff, who were all devoted to the students, consisted mostly of refugees. Joined by British conscientious objectors once war broke out, they ranged from the unqualified to the overqualified. Essinger, known as Tante Anna, frightened many students, although a few, such as Roemer, were unruffled by her manner. After Frank had been at the school for about three weeks, the younger children were moved to the junior house, called Dane Court, a half-timbered Tudor building at Chilham, some ten miles from Bunce Court. The house-teacher was Gwynne Badsworth (later Angell), an attractive, sympathetic woman, who was 28 when Auerbach arrived. 'She didn't have any of this nonsense about not speaking English, so within three or four weeks we all were able to communicate in English. We were enrolled as Wolf Cubs or Brownies and did country dancing in the hall. And so, without any conscious effort we were anglicized.' In an interview with a Kent newspaper shortly before her death in 2014, Badsworth recalled that 'Every night I would read the little ones bedtime stories. I became a mother to them,' and she remembered Frank as shy.[7] Auerbach agrees: 'I was a rather quiet and nervous child … my respect for the way she dealt with the uprooted children has grown over the years.' One of the memories of the school that Frank shared with Bruce Bernard was of being given baths by the lovely Badsworth.

Bunce Court mirrored a kind of 'real', grown-up life, albeit in a place 'a bit like a closed religious community'. There were 'duties' for all, such as

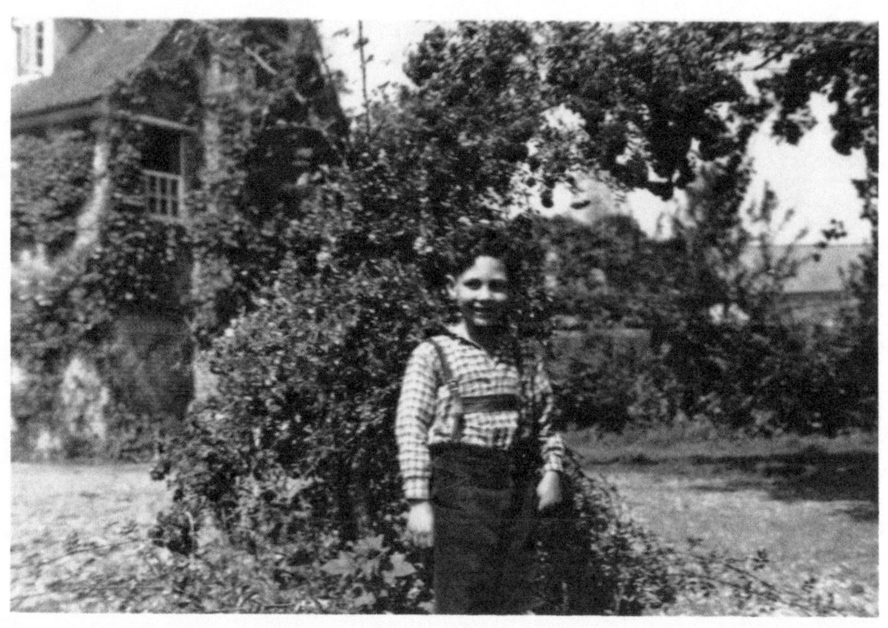

Frank at Bunce Court, 1939

scrubbing the kitchen floor or gardening, and the older boys were asked to sift the coal to find big lumps that would stoke the boiler. Occasionally they worked on neighbouring farms, digging up potatoes, and so forth. The deprivations of wartime rationing underpinned the austerity. The cook, Gretl Heidt, called Heidtsche, was an amazingly competent German woman, briefly interned as an enemy alien, who invariably provided nourishing and attractive meals. The students were fed six times a day, which for the older children included a snack of dried fruit and cocoa before bedtime.

Art was taught by the mathematics master and later by a pipe-smoking lady who worked with batik. Frank remembers 'being stirred' by a reproduction of J. M. W. Turner's *Fighting Temeraire* in Arthur Mee's *The Children's Encyclopaedia* and a poem on the opposite page. Later, when he was a bit older and ill in bed, he pored over R. H. Wilenski's *Modern French Painters* (1939); the book served as a window to what Frank called 'such a variety of styles'. Tante Anna had a Michelangelo print on the wall of her office and there were Brueghel reproductions over the dining tables, yet, as Auerbach recalls, the ambience was not art oriented: 'You know, there are arty schools where children are encouraged to express themselves – we weren't encouraged to express ourselves, we were encouraged to be part of a community and to have community spirit.'[8]

In June 1940, as the threat of German invasion increased with the fall of France, the army requisitioned Bunce Court and many Germans over the age of 16 living in Britain were interned. Tante Anna had to find replacement premises, and after a three-day search secured Trench Hall in Wem, Shropshire. This house where Frank lived for five years has stayed in his memory; it was grand enough to have a circular drive and a ha-ha, and inside a green baize door divided the living area from the servants' quarters where bells once summoned staff to the various rooms. When he became an 'older' boy, Auerbach slept in the stables, which were fitted out with five bunk beds in two rows with a stove between. He and his lively Polish girlfriend, Peppi Unger, contrived to meet at night in adjacent barns; after they received their School Certificates in the summer of 1945, she left for London. Later Peppi emigrated to Israel and married, but for many years she kept in touch.

Once the war was over, the school returned to its former premises in Kent. However, the situation was different and, with its refugee function finished and Tante Anna almost blind, Bunce Court closed in 1948. She died in 1960 and the building was sold, but over time the school's founder, teachers and students have become something of a legend. The memories of alumni, many returning for reunions (although not Auerbach), have fed articles that tend to focus on the nurturing effects of the teaching and on pupils who achieved public recognition. They include Leslie Baruch Brent, a distinguished immunologist; Helmut Sonnenfeldt, a foreign-policy expert known as Henry Kissinger's Kissinger (his fixer); Harold Jackson, the *Guardian* journalist and White House correspondent; and the musician and humorist Gerard Hoffnung.[9] Just three students remained friends of Frank's. Frank Marcus, the theatre director known for his play *The Killing of Sister George* (1964), Michael Roemer, who went to America after leaving school and became a filmmaker – his *Nothing But a Man* (1964) was unusual at the time for having a cast of largely black actors – and the flautist Rainer Schuelein.

By the early spring of 1943, when Frank was nearly 12, his parents' twenty-five word, censored letters, forwarded by the Red Cross, stopped coming. At no point in the months that followed did he find himself 'shocked or overwhelmed; it was gradually leaked to me they were dead, taken to a camp and killed'. Some of the Jewish residents of 49 Güntzelstrasse had been moved temporarily to other addresses; in 1942–43 all were cleared. The eventual deportation of twenty-one residents is now commemorated by *Stolpersteine*, brass plaques set in the pavement outside the front doors of the last residence of choice of victims of the Holocaust. The birth dates identify them as adults and along with the Auerbachs the names include Elise Bloch, Erika Blum, Leopold Cohn, Emma Friedländer, Carl Stern, Georg Stodola, and couples such as Siegfried and Lucie Zehden, all of whom died in Theresienstadt, Auschwitz, or other locations in the east. Charlotte and Max Auerbach were deported in early March 1943 aboard a transport to Auschwitz; the date of Charlotte's death is given as 30 June 1943, Max's as simply 1943.[10]

Auerbach has never enquired about what happened to his parents in the final year and last months. I think of parallels to Vikram Seth's intimate and respectful book *Two Lives* (2005), the story of his Indian Uncle Shanti and his German wife Aunt Henny, whose family, like the Auerbachs, were also assimilated Jews. Henny had escaped to London before the war with help from her fiancé's father, leaving behind in Berlin her mother and sister.[11] Seth takes us through the oppression that goes with the restrictive laws and persecution of Jews as they are banned from public transport, subject to curfew, and more and more confined to the homes that are steadily confiscated. When he seeks material in the archive at Yad Vashem in Jerusalem about Henny's mother and sister, Gabriele and Lola Caro, he finds evidence the older woman was taken to Theresienstadt. On a list compiled with 'methodical categorization of special circumstances' there are also notes of those who, like Max Auerbach, received medals for military service during the First World War, which might have delayed their deportation. Lola, born in 1907, is one of four hundred people sent in May 1943 on an *Osttransport* (East-transport) straight to Auschwitz-Birkenau. After the war, when Henny learnt details about the fate of her mother and sister, she wrote candidly to a friend: 'you can imagine how sad, how unendingly sorrowful I am, and I will never get over it. Sometimes I am so overcome that I don't think I can go on.'[12]

Frank, for his part, concedes: 'I think I did this thing which psychiatrists frown on: I am in total denial. It's worked very well for me. To be quite honest I came to England and went to a marvellous school, and it truly was a happy time. There's just never been a point in my life when I felt I wish I had parents.'[13]

On the other hand, there were teachers whose high standards and empathy made a lasting impression on Frank, offering guidance and comfort, as they did for other Bunce Court students. For him, the most significant was Wilhelm Marckwald, who had acted, directed and produced plays in the late 1920s and early 1930s at the Stadttheater Koblenz and the Deutsches Theater Berlin. Fleeing Germany in 1933, he went to Barcelona where he made films, but left Spain at the outset of the Civil War in 1936 and had an emigré existence in Sweden and France before arriving at Trench Hall in 1942. There he was employed as the boilerman and gardener and, more significantly, directed the school plays. Pilar, his Spanish wife, was very pretty, short and good humoured, and students remember her in the kitchen needing to stand on a stool to stir the porridge.

Marckwald worked with the school theatre group in a very thorough way; there were rehearsals every afternoon for months. 'We did *Twelfth Night*. But it wasn't a school play in the usual sense. We worked over each theme and by the time we had finished rehearsing we hadn't got to the point where Fabian [Frank's part] enters – so that was that. But the next play was *Everyman*, which isn't a long play, and we managed to do the whole thing, and I was Everyman. I remember a rather heady moment. We worked in this man's painstaking way to get everything right and to understand. Then we came to a point where Everyman finally realizes how wrong his life has been, and says: "I will make my testament Here before you all present." This speech hadn't been rehearsed. And I did it, it was only about eight lines, and he [Marckwald] said: "Sometimes one does get it right without the rehearsal." I think, because of all the training, I had perhaps managed to make some sense of it.'[14]

With hindsight, the story reads like a blueprint for creating something unforeseen that is rigorously true: the repeated study of the script, the striving to get things right and then the moment of abandon. There is a remote analogy with painting one subject for many months and years: as the person moves around during breaks, Auerbach might begin to see other things that wait to be portrayed; as he repeatedly draws outdoors from a fixed position, he gathers information and atmosphere. While painting, all of Auerbach's energies are engaged with the formal and 'truthful' possibilities that have arisen, as he does nothing but observe and paint; for several hours he is immersed in the effort of making a unity of the forms. The analogy to acting goes further. 'What I have in my mind is, as it were, the lump of the subject, the three-dimensional entity which I somehow try to inhabit and become – in the way that an actor would don a character or become a part – and to make statements about it from inside.'[15]

Moving to London

Towards the end of the war Auerbach stayed in London with his much older cousin Gerda from his father's side and her husband, Gerd Boehm, for part of the holidays, burying himself in books borrowed from the library on Keats Grove in Hampstead; during the rest of the time he remained at Bunce Court. Leaving there in the summer of 1947 with his Higher School

Certificate and a document of naturalization, which he received on 16 July 1947 in Faversham, he was absolutely determined not to end up in an office or a bank. Without Latin his choice of university was limited, but no advice or effort was made to place him where he thought he might thrive – in an art or drama school.

A few surviving relatives were able to offer a bit of support for the 16-year-old orphan. His Uncle Jakob, who had escaped Berlin through the Netherlands and arrived in London after the war, his mother's brother Uncle Hans Borchardt, who had fled to Buenos Aires, and cousins living in the United States joined together to provide a stipend of £4. 10s. a week for a year or so. Moving into a room in Pond Street in Hampstead, which he shared with Schuelein, who had left Bunce Court at the same time, Auerbach enrolled in art classes at the Hampstead Garden Suburb Institute. Despite the teaching seeming rather amateur, the instruction in how to handle materials proved quite useful. 'There was Mr Oliver, a calligrapher. He did the lettering for the Stalingrad Sword, and he not only taught calligraphy but also employed students as calligraphers to do memorial books for churches and chapels – for which, of course, there was a big demand after the war.'[16] Auerbach proved too clumsy for this task: 'I think they regarded me as far too rough, foreign, modernistic, incompetent and hopeless.'

At Bunce Court he had tried out a few 'modern' idioms, that of Paul Klee being the easiest to master. Now, he read James Frazer's *The Golden Bough* (1890) with the idea of attempting mythological subjects; Frank's versions imagined a penny on the eyes of a dead man, and sailors who tied knots in sails so they could be let out if becalmed. He made a Crucifixion scene in the style of Edward Burra. In the summer holiday of 1948 Frank returned to Bunce Court and painted a picture a day. A few staff remained and 'no one had the heart to say to me what right have you got to be here, or told me I couldn't stay there. It was really home and gave me as much confidence as a family would have done.'[17]

Apart from wanting to make art, there were opportunities to continue acting. Two school friends, Frank Marcus and Herman Essinger, a nephew of Tante Anna, had joined the International Theatre Group, which was the Kensington branch of the left-wing Unity Theatre based in St Pancras. Writing in the *London Magazine* in 2000, Patrick O'Connor, a former member of the ITG, placed the company in a historical context, explaining that Marcus had 'challenged the dogmatic hierarchy of Unity Theatre and broken away'.[18] O'Connor helped to convince the others that it was a good thing that someone with contacts, Marcus, was willing to take on the responsibility of being director. Marcus began by 'introducing to the company a retiring young painter called Frank Auerbach ... He also played Pantalone and used the stage name of Frank Ashley in *The Servant of Two Masters* by Goldoni. He would do the decor. We would be on a sharing basis, also using serious drama students.'[19]

One venue they had an opportunity to use was the Torch Theatre on Wilton Place in Knightsbridge. Although it seated less than one hundred, it was a fully professional theatre and was known as a 'shop window' to the West End. A small bar at the top of the stairs served as a club; Auerbach remembers seeing the actors Michael Wilding and Laurence Harvey around. In the evening various groups performed their plays, some featuring members of the cast of the wildly popular BBC radio programme 'Dick Barton – Special Agent'. In 1948, most likely in September as O'Connor remembers coming there at the end of a summer-long heatwave, they began rehearsing Peter Ustinov's play *House of Regrets* (1940). Frank's role as Strukhov, the elderly batman to the even older General Andrei Cherevenko, was rather testing. In spite of having only a few lines, he was required to be on stage a lot of the time, waiting to say, 'Dostoievsky writes very clearly ... I find that he frequently makes people speak who live so clearly that I often feel that they might walk in through the door.'[20] The rehearsals went on so long Frank sometimes slept in the theatre at night, under the seats. Most significantly, this was where he met Estella West, another member of the cast, who was to become a vital part of his life.

Auerbach also acted in plays at the 20th Century Theatre in Westbourne Grove and at the New Lindsey in Notting Hill. These were proper fringe theatres, and although the activity for this young student was an evening one, he remembers that 'the people I worked with were almost all trained actors'. He joined the Tavistock Theatre in Islington for a short while and had a couple of minor parts, one in *Beggar on Horseback* by George F. Kaufman and Marc Connelly: 'I think that was because when I filled in the form, I said I could do an American accent – which was stretching it a bit.' On another occasion, Auerbach answered an ad in the *Stage* and went to Ireland for a week to work for a stock company until he was sent back on account of having a foreign accent and resisting the advances of the actor-manager.

The subsequent plays Marcus directed with the ITG cast notable actors, and attracted sought-after critics, including Beverley Baxter, who was in the audience when they were playing at the Chepstow Theatre in Notting Hill. O'Connor recalled that Baxter's 'presence was due mainly to the machinations of Jacqueline Sylvester [who later married Marcus], sister of [the aspiring art critic] David. She had erupted into one of our readings, a wild gamine look about her, hilarious after a party, dressed like a gypsy, her black hair disarranged, delivering *bon mots* to right and to left. Deflating the more pompous members, she was the Anna Magnani we lacked, winning all our hearts. We cast her as the vociferous hoyden in *The Broken Jug*.'[21]

The example of David Bomberg

At the beginning of 1948, the artist Archibald Ziegler, whose wife had been a teacher at Bunce Court in the 1930s, arranged for Auerbach to have an interview with the principal of St Martin's School of Art. He was accepted for September, but impatient to begin studying art at a place more challenging than the Hampstead Garden Suburb Institute, Frank walked around other London art schools with his portfolio under his arm. Arriving at the Borough Polytechnic Institute located on Southwark Bridge Road, he met Mr Patrick, the principal of the art school, a cake designer and a kind man, who agreed to admit him immediately. Founded in 1892, the college had a mixture of part-time and full-time students who crossed generations and classes; many had been in the Forces and were, as Auerbach put it, 'actually serious about life'. In keeping with the postwar mood of egalitarianism, here and elsewhere, there was a feeling that everyone had the right to an education. As well as its mainstay trade courses, the Borough Polytechnic had a good reputation for art and employed, for example, the designer Tom Eckersley and the painter David Bomberg as teachers.

Bomberg had established his reputation as an artist associated with the Vorticists (who in turn were close in their modernist idiom to the Cubists and Futurists). One of Bomberg's early masterpieces, *The Mud Bath*

(1914), was a painting based on what he remembered of Schevzik's Steam Baths in the East End of London, in which the figures were reduced to blue and white angular forms apparently climbing in and out of a red basin. Bomberg was, for Auerbach, 'by far the most talented of people who worked in that neo-Cubist idiom'. Nonetheless, he later became 'an extremely adept landscape painter of very, very topographical landscapes – marvellously done in Palestine in the twenties. So this wasn't a man who had some sort of single mission.'[22]

Mr Patrick put together a timetable for Frank. 'I think I'll put you in for a day with David Bomberg', as if to say, 'Well, Bomberg's a bit dicey, but you never know – you might get on with him.'[23] Bomberg had caused controversy while he was still a student at the Slade in 1911–13. Although proud to have made a copy from a Holbein early on, he eventually reacted against both what was taught there and the emphasis on winning prizes for draughtsmanship. He was thrown out for his rebelliousness; the Slade was perhaps worried that his attitude would spread. While Frank concedes that Bomberg was 'difficult', and that 'what he taught wouldn't have equipped any of us to pass any exam, and there used to be art exams ... He had this sort of idiom that allowed one to go for the essence at the very beginning ... it was an experimental journey and this was not what was taught in art schools.'[24]

Bomberg's life class occupied a former engineering workshop, which Auerbach vividly recalls: 'It had vastly high ceilings, tiled walls, and a curious metal structure holding up various skylights and angles in the roof; and a door that, when you opened it, kept on swinging like a bar door in a Western saloon for about five minutes after you'd entered.'[25] Bomberg taught one day and two evening classes. Auerbach remembers that in the day session there was a Polish girl who painted waves for months on end and scraped off what she did with a circular tool. There were two other Polish girls who were very giggly and three former GIs who focused on picking up girls. A more serious student was Richard Negri, who was studying stage design and went on to a distinguished career at the Royal Court and in Manchester, as well as becoming a teacher at Wimbledon School of Art.

In the first term, Auerbach was asked to square up a part of a drawing and to enlarge that area. His offended expression (now he regards the

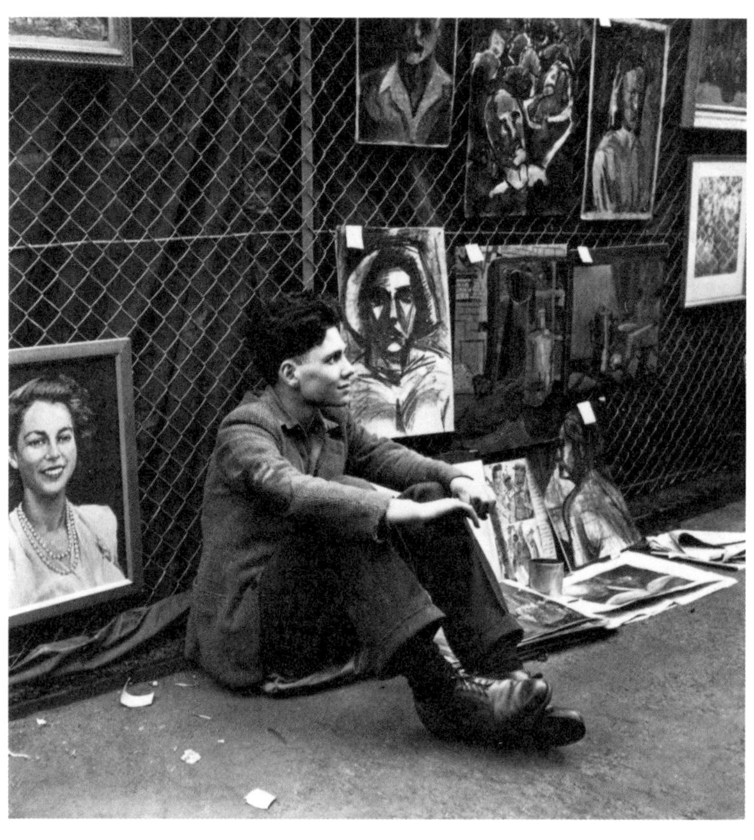

Frank at the LCC 'Open-Air Exhibition', Embankment Gardens,
London, July 1948

exercise as a very intelligent one) led Bomberg to ask, '"Oh, so you think I'm a silly old idiot don't you", or something like that, and I said, in my 17-year-old arrogance, "Yes, I do". He was delighted and I didn't realize that I had met with probably the most original, stubborn, radical intelligence that was to be found in art school ... For me, very few works that could be described as works of art were produced there, but anything that seemed artificial or concocted or sort of false sauce or gravy on an insufficiently vital fact would be rejected by Bomberg. On the other hand, something which contained simply the tiniest hint of a personal distinction, it might be accepted. The result was that people would produce these anonymous cloudy pieces of paper which had absolutely nothing cheap or nasty about them and which would, to the sympathetic eye, have an adumbration of something rather grand and organic and particular. But, in competition with the great paintings of the world, which also have a vitality of a cutting image like superb posters, these drawings would seem like defenceless molluscs'.[26]

Rather than instruct young people as if they were mere students, part of Bomberg's message was that if 'what you're doing is to have any validity at all; it's going to be on the level of these Masters that we admire'. Auerbach remembers looking at a reproduction of El Greco's *View of Toledo* (1629) and Bomberg explaining how the scene was inaccurate compared to what Auerbach regards as his teacher's equally thrilling, more descriptive approach to depicting the same town.

It never occurred to Bomberg to suggest a subject as he assumed everyone had one. For him, it was necessary for artists whatever their age to be determined and ambitious. Students tended to draw in charcoal on large sheets and paint with large brushes; the same model continued to pose for an entire day or evening (contrary to the practice of short poses in other classes). Bomberg's ability to demonstrate something to a student by painting or drawing rapidly and with great facility on the work in progress was breathtaking and formidable. 'He came up behind you and said, look at the model, it's doing this, it's doing that – I suggest this and so on. So it was a practical course of instruction which actually took up most of the time.'[27]

At the London County Council (LCC) 'Open-Air Exhibition' in the summer of 1948, Auerbach decided to try selling works by hanging his own pictures on the railings of Victoria Embankment Gardens, not far from where the much more mature Borough Group's were showing. The impetus for that group, which included Cliff Holden, Peter (also known as Miles) Richmond, Len Missen, Dennis Creffield and Dorothy Mead, derived from these older students. They formulated manifestos and showed together, so there was a certain doctrinaire tendency within the art school. As Frank observed later: 'Like every religious order, I suppose, like every innovative movement in art and ideas, what was actually an improvised, energetic, fresh leap into the unknown has been turned into orthodoxy by followers.'[28] Neither Auerbach nor Leon Kossoff, who from 1949 attended Bomberg's evening classes, became members of the Borough Group, or any movement; it was the contact with Bomberg and the freedom to work from the model outside the conventions of art school life-rooms that brought them to south London.

Another very independent-minded student of Bomberg's, also a refugee from Nazi Germany, was Gustav Metzger. Born in 1926, Metzger was conditioned by disturbing images from childhood. 'My parents lived just off the main road between Furth and Nuremberg. Thousands of people would march along that road to the Nazi rallies. I was frightened.'[29] In 1948, one of Metzger's paintings, an oil on metal, was shown with the artist's collective, the London Group. Auerbach recalls the forms, looking like three eggs, a bit like one of Robert Motherwell's elegies to the Spanish Republic. Later, Metzger eschewed painting and brought in anti-establishment ideas. In the 1960s, as an advocate of the auto-destructive movement, his application of acid to painted nylon during performances was intended to mirror the arms industry's obsession with obliteration via nuclear weapons. Themes that surface in Metzger's later installation work, particularly the materiality of nature and a desire to provoke a visceral experience on the part of the spectator, perhaps relate to what both he and Auerbach took away from Bomberg's own traumatic experience as a soldier in the trenches in 1914–16, in particular their mentor's insistence on working from life and rejecting style.

The rhetorical side of Bomberg's teaching is associated in most accounts by students and art historians with a particular phrase, 'the spirit of the mass', but taken out of context it can be misleading. It was intended to describe the subject as a three-dimensional entity; Bomberg 'didn't believe in modelling the thing up artificially to give it weight. Weight was something you *felt*.'[30] Such an intuitive, explorative approach made reference to Bishop Berkeley's philosophy of seeing. Writing in the eighteenth century, Berkeley maintained that sight is connected with the experience of the physical world gained by experimentation with touch and the other senses. Auerbach paraphrases Berkeley's ideas as follows: 'If you have a spoon and you look at its back, on the convex side, you get your image. If you look at the front, the concave side, you get your image upside down. Exactly the same thing happens to the retina: on the back of the retina we get a reverse image, so that the newborn infant will reach down for something that's up and up for something that's down. It's only by crawling across the floor, touching things, judging distances *haptically*, that the child will relate the sight of what he sees to the physical world.' This process transfers to the artist in the studio who comes to understand the architecture of a building or a person and in a rather mysterious way ingests the whole. Looking back, Auerbach concludes that what Bomberg meant by 'the spirit of the mass' was to do with adding to the sense of three-dimensional architecture something very particular and exact. As he puts it: 'You find yourself making gestures that imply legs and breast and so on; you begin to imply a sense of mass on the paper or on the canvas simply because you felt it.'

In 1986, when the New York-based critic and historian Robert Hughes was preparing a monograph on Auerbach, the artist extended the comparison of Bomberg and Berkeley to F. R. Leavis, the Cambridge academic who insisted that literature came from an indwelt identification with words and experience rather than from learnt concepts. 'You can tell a piece of Leavis, with its peculiar grinding cack-handedness and heaviness of syntax, almost anywhere – partly because he was chewing out his own definitions.' Auerbach went on to say that Bomberg's conversation naturally seemed 'fairly impenetrable to outsiders unless they had patience with him or, as in my case, were young enough to have become habituated to it. He spoke on his own terms, and didn't take anything over from other people without examining and remaking it.'[31] Frank drew a series of simplified diagrams of birds to illustrate his point. 'If you have two lines that represent a bird's mouth, you could do a thousand drawings on a piece of paper and each of these birds would have a different expression. That one is obviously a more jokey bird than the others, and so on. Well, in that sense, this being the simplest possible combination of directions, there's only one exact and direct expression for yourself of the mass in front of you. There are a million ways of *not* getting it right … you're most likely to get it right when you're least self-conscious, when you've given up any hope of producing an acceptable drawing or painting … because then you're permeated wordlessly by the influence of the thing you're painting.'[32]

Robert Hughes regarded Bomberg as an exemplar for Frank and in his book (published in 1990) he outlined some of the qualities and positions that link Auerbach to his first real teacher: 'much of the younger man – his empiricism, his scorn for modernist conventions, his impatience with theory and ideology, his reverence for the past and his determination to paint as though there were no breach between it and the present – was there in the older.'[33] Perhaps the most important conviction they shared was that, in Auerbach's words, 'visual art is made with resistant matter and comes up against awkward rebarbative obstacles'.[34] Auerbach explained to Hughes that Bomberg's insistence on never borrowing anything from others without examining it and remaking it for oneself also made a deep impression, but 'the deep necessity that I have to actually get profoundly involved with the subject is something I certainly didn't learn from Bomberg. He often painted things that meant a great deal to him. But a large part of the time he was like a tourist painter. He would move from place to place, paint the landscapes where he saw them, and be able to make original and profoundly stated images with a subtext of philosophical enquiry and grandeur.'[35]

In his interview with Hughes, Auerbach also placed emphasis on the difference between working from a model in a class and doing so on one's own. 'There was an idea of quality and lack of fear in those classes, but their actual productions and the mere fact that they were the productions of a life-class, which has always seemed to me to be an artificial situation unless it's acknowledged in its artificiality, made them, for me, fall short of any sort of ambition that I would have. I think I really only found what I wanted to do when I recorded something that was intimate enough to me to be worth recording,' and, having in his mind equally impersonal classes at the next two art colleges he attended, he continued, 'a life-class where one sees a stranger naked and draws her, well, although I think it's the only training-ground, it doesn't seem to me to be the situation in which one makes an image'.[36]

St Martin's School of Art, 1948–52

Auerbach acquired a copy of Alfred H. Barr, Jr.'s monograph on Picasso soon after it was published in 1946, and it was, and has remained, a stimulating source. While working he kept the page open at various pictures then captioned *Head (Femme au nez en quart de Brie)*, 1907, and the *Girl with Dark Hair (Portrait of D.M.)*, 1939. 'It seemed to present the artist as an extraordinary fertile conjuror. I think I once thought I was that sort, wanted to be that sort, of artist; it was only in the act of working that I discovered I wasn't that kind of painter at all.'[37] But, what seems self-effacing can be misleading. For example, in the exhibition of the wartime works by Pablo Picasso and Henri Matisse that opened at the Victoria & Albert Museum in December 1945, one of the paintings there, Picasso's *Woman with Green Dress (Femme en vert)*, 1943, still looks relevant to Auerbach's art. The strong rhythmic definition of the seated figure and the quirky spiral patterning within her dress is reminiscent of the bold drawing with liquid paint and the moment of lightness that sometimes guides much later work by Auerbach, as well as the triangular or loopy cipher inserted into a portrait and the skewed posture that is factual.[38]

In the summer of 1948, before entering St Martin's, Auerbach went to Paris for a few days with his cousin Gerda Boehm and he returned there briefly in *c.* 1951 with three other St Martin's students. He found himself disappointed on both occasions by the works on display, for example, at the Maison de la pensée française, Picasso's owls and kitchens, by Matisse's cutouts at the Musée d'art moderne, which he didn't rate – then, rather than now – and by weak works from the Ecole de Paris, such as those of André Lhote. In comparison, walking around London galleries was definitely exciting and Auerbach took a keen, temporary interest in an exhibition of Ivon Hitchens's paintings at the Leicester Galleries. The National Gallery was in close proximity to St Martin's and he began making drawings there on a regular basis (and continued to do so until the 1980s when the bus service deteriorated and consulting the old masters no longer seemed relevant).

Auerbach was supported by a LCC grant of £120 a year, and, as he was only 17, was still entitled to free milk. The St Martin's course was closely tied to exams, which were linked to prescribed exercises, such as accomplishing a drawing in a day and a life-painting in a week, and at the end the successful students were awarded a National Diploma in Design. The Borough Polytechnic course had given Auerbach limited exposure to illustration, poster design and clay modelling in the courses taught by various instructors other than Bomberg. At St Martin's in the beginners' (first) year there was antique drawing, costume, art history and various other related subjects, as well as life drawing, and in the intermediate (or second) year they took life and costume drawing, composition, art history, architecture, perspective and anatomy. Building on those broad foundations, students in the third and fourth years studied life painting, pictorial composition, methods and materials, and submitted a short 'thesis'. Teachers had some leeway in how they taught; for example, in the first year Clifford Webb took the students to the London Zoo in the mornings to draw and asked them to paint from what they brought back in the afternoons (Frank remembers painting a tiger, a rhinoceros and a fruit bat).

John Wheatley, a Royal Academician who trained at the Slade, gave a lecture on Walter Sickert every year as part of his methods and materials course. Auerbach reflects that 'I was not particularly interested then, but in retrospect, the account by Wheatley, who had been his student, of Sickert's routine is intriguing. He worked on his paintings in sequence (perhaps thirty), all numbered on the back, over perhaps many months, drawing in the evenings. When a painting was finished, he started another from his stock of squared-up drawings. Of course, Sickert was volatile and *often* changed his ideas and his way of working.'

Frank resisted the idea of painting genre scenes or narratives: 'When I was a student many of the students around me were doing paintings of nudes on iron bedsteads [*à la* Sickert], and I thought of that as a cosy, domestic let-out. My vision of painting, the picture I had in my head, was of some clearly formal statement; an explosion; and I thought there was something too domestic and whimsical and Impressionistic about Sickert. I remember reacting with considerable scepticism when Helen [Lessore] said he was the best.'[39] More than his painting, Sickert's critical essays,

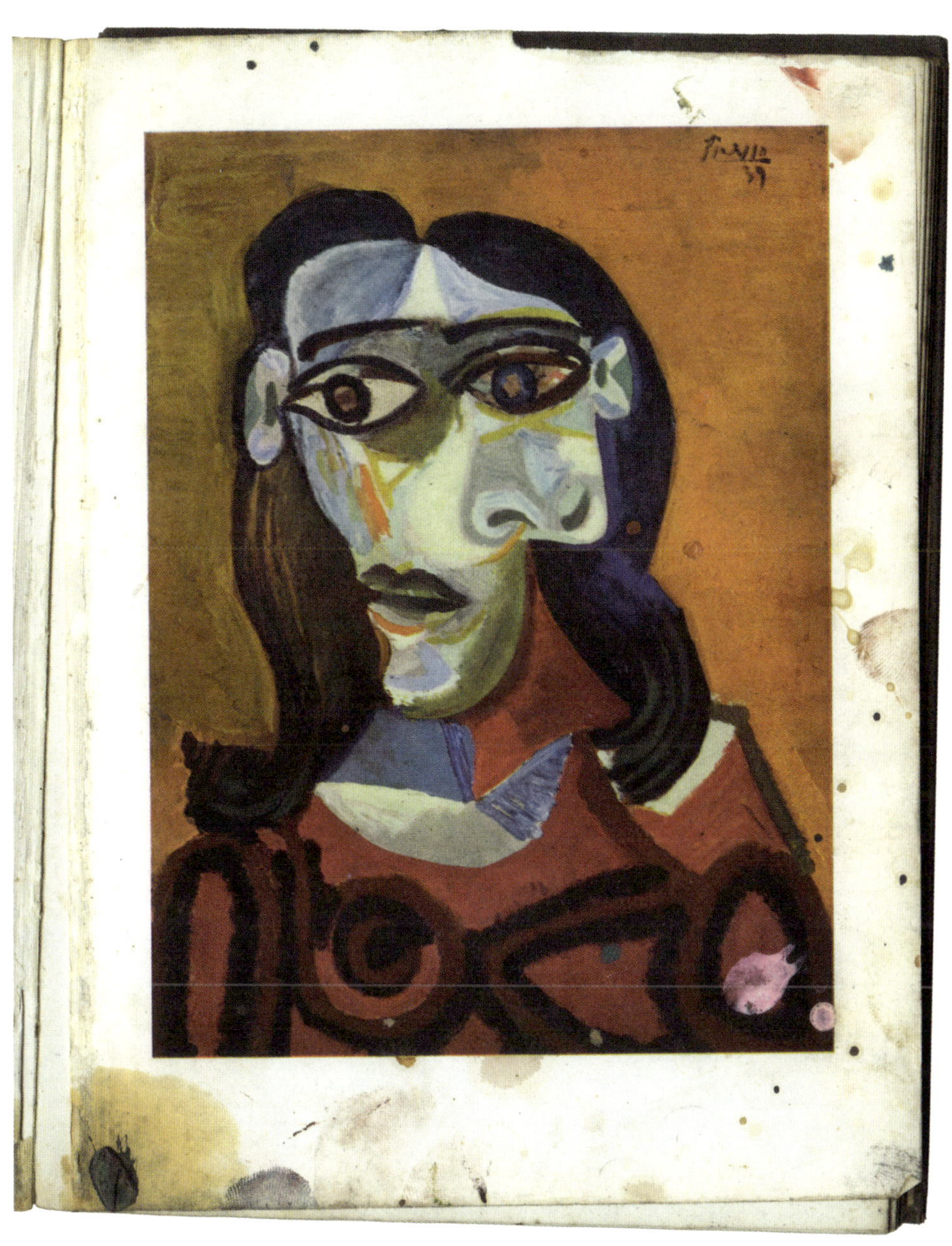

PABLO PICASSO, *Girl with Dark Hair (Portrait of Dora Maar)*, 1939, in Frank's
copy of *Picasso: Fifty Years of His Art* (1946) by Alfred H. Barr, Jr.

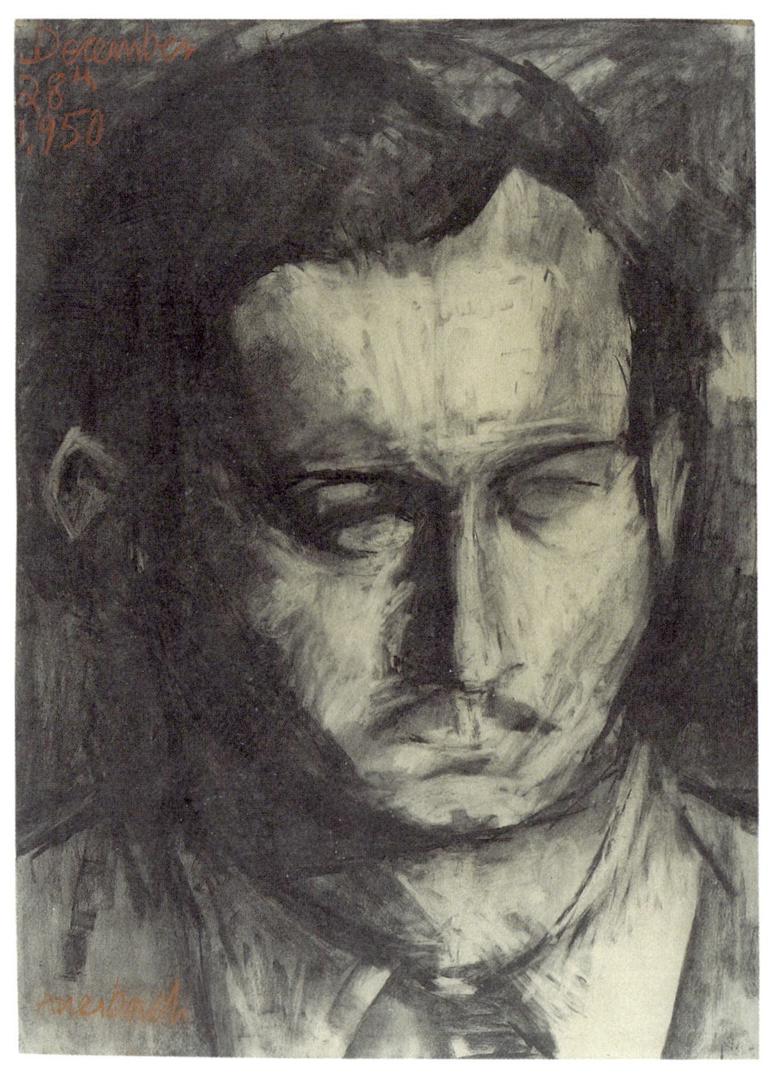

Portrait of Leon Kossoff, 1950

published as *A Free House!* (1947), and later the collected writings, became and have remained a great stimulus. 'I read his writings when I was a student. They worried me; I didn't think it proper to be reading them ... perhaps one should be reading Apollinaire instead? But his energy and wit, and the optimism, and the considerable profundity in odd places just got through to me. I loved the book and I still do. When I find myself very tired of an afternoon I sometimes pick that book up and go to a page and read it, and I find it works for me – I just want to go on working. It's a matter of the man's all-round worth.'[40]

The 1948 intake at St Martin's was comprised of an unusually large number of students who became well-known artists: among others, Joe Tilson, Donald Hamilton Fraser, Jack Smith, Peter Kinley, Bernard Cohen, Peter Coker, Michael Fussell, Anthony Hill and Sheila Fell. Again, their backgrounds were diverse. Tilson, for example, had come up from the suburbs, trained as a carpenter, worked in the building trade and had done his National Service in the RAF. He arrived for classes at St Martin's on a motor scooter with a blonde girlfriend and knew about Soho life. Auerbach's relationship with Leon Kossoff began when they met at St Martin's. Leon, Phil Holmes and Frank went around as a kind of trio. When feeling a bit flush, they ate upstairs at Shearns, a vegetarian restaurant and health-food shop in Tottenham Court Road. On occasion they watched T. S. Eliot, a poet they much admired, poke a camembert before buying it.

Kossoff, who was to become one of the important painters of his generation, was born in London in December 1926. He had attended St Martin's during the war, then spent the years 1945–48 in the Royal Fusiliers attached to 2nd Battalion Jewish Brigade before re-enrolling at St Martin's in 1949. One day, Kossoff expressed his admiration for a drawing Auerbach was doing in the antique room and not long afterwards the younger student suggested that Bomberg's class, which he was still attending in the evenings, might suit him. Kossoff came along and the two became close, having in common a resistance to compromise and a more rebellious temperament than the other students; Kossoff found it impossible to conform to the exam requirements. Looking back, Auerbach explains that compared to him Kossoff had a much clearer sense of who he was and what he wanted to achieve in his work. In 1949, Kossoff made a painting of a coal man, in

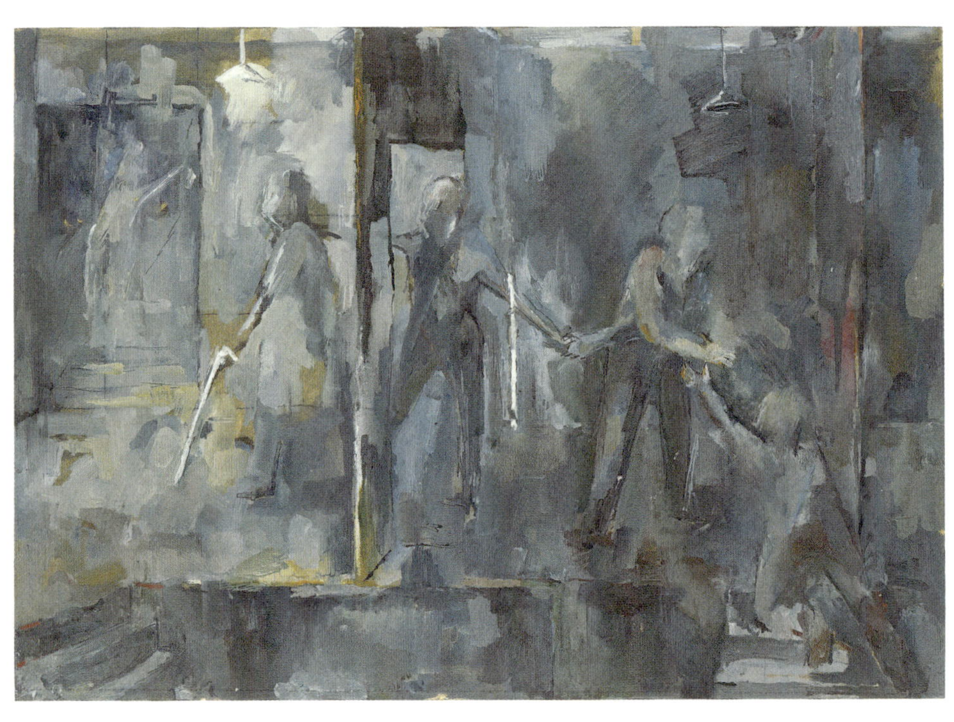

Three Blind Men, 1951

the days when they still used horses. It stays in Auerbach's mind as being exceptionally raw and large-scaled; when the intermediate-year compositions 'were meant to be 15 × 22 in., this was 20 × 30'. They began to pose for each other over the Christmas holidays in 1950–51, initially in a room Auerbach took in Palace Gardens Terrace, Kensington. There are two finished charcoal drawings by Auerbach from this period. In the summer holidays they went to draw on Hampstead Heath.

Auerbach found he was doing one sort of drawing at St Martin's and another in Bomberg's classes. However, this is now hard to judge since most paintings and drawings made while he was student were destroyed and those that survive are undated. Auerbach points out that for *Birth, Marriage, Death* (1949), a triptych 4 × 6 feet made while at St Martin's, he used his own body for some of the figures, as well as drawing a girlfriend called Lesley. Other group scenes still exist: *All Night Party 1* (1950) and *Three Blind Men* (1951).

Drawings and paintings done in Bomberg's evening class, as Auerbach once recalled, were 'quite remarkably like some of those pictures produced in New York at about the same time, also by painters working in total obscurity. Nobody at the Borough Polytechnic knew about the American painters.' In preparation for this book, I asked Frank what might have happened if he had emigrated to the United States and his first contact with professional artists had been at Hans Hofmann's School of Fine Art at 52 W. 8th Street in New York. His reply was, 'It would have definitely made a difference. There is a certain sympathy between the way Hofmann's students painted – that is, of finding the very lively formal essence of the material – and the way Bomberg's students thought. It is true Bomberg's teaching was closer to Hofmann's than, for instance, what Albers taught, which might suit some people.' From Auerbach's perspective, Josef Albers, another native of Germany, who taught at Black Mountain College, North Carolina, from 1933, and later at Yale University, operated in a rather different area, abiding by a consistent 'schema', which from 1951 was his homage to a square, and this kind of established system reassured his followers.

Frank went on to say, using as comparison his own experience as a visiting tutor, 'Painting can't really be taught. All you can do is get people to where they jump in and swim. Hofmann had his own language, push and pull, which meant something specific to those in his classes. Bomberg had his own language which meant something specific to the people in his class. People hope to get students to the point where they can involve themselves in the painting, which is what people at the beginning can't do, and so they find more extreme and recondite ways of entering the formal content of the painting.'

A breakthrough, summer, 1952

'I remember the breakthrough, the point at which it seemed to me that I started making my own pictures. It's very vivid, very specific, in the summer of 1952.' These paintings that Auerbach claims are true to the subject were provoked by a feeling of crisis. 'I'd been in institutions for five years, which seemed a century to me. I felt I would be doomed if I went into the army. I also felt I would be doomed if I went to the Royal College and just became an art student for another three years.'[41] That summer, to his relief, he managed to fail the army medical, which meant he was excused from doing National Service. Meanwhile, he had a good job helping a girlfriend of Phil Holmes's who ran a bagatelle stall at Battersea funfair, where he was paid 30 shillings a day by the boss and 30 shillings by her out of the fiddling. Frank was copying drawings of bicycles from a British catalogue, placing three to a page, so that his employer, a Nigerian, could duplicate them and offer the bikes to clients in his home country. He did this from four to six in the morning in order to have the rest of the time free for painting.

It was then that 'two things happened'. He was working from Stella (Estella Olive West, or E.O.W.) and she was someone he was involved with, not a professional model, 'so the whole situation was obviously more tense and fraught. There was always the feeling that she might get fed up, that there might be a quarrel or something. I also had a much greater sense of what specifically she was like, so that the question of getting a likeness was like walking a tightrope. I had a far more poignant sense of it slipping away, of it being hard to get. I'd done the painting for some sittings in a relatively timid way; that is, I'd tried to do one part and then another part, and save a bit. Then I suddenly found in myself enough courage to repaint the whole thing, from top to bottom, irrationally and instinctively, and I found I'd got a picture of her.'[42] The nude of E.O.W. does not appear conventionally resolved, one of her legs is tiny and the other big. 'It only seems an authentic

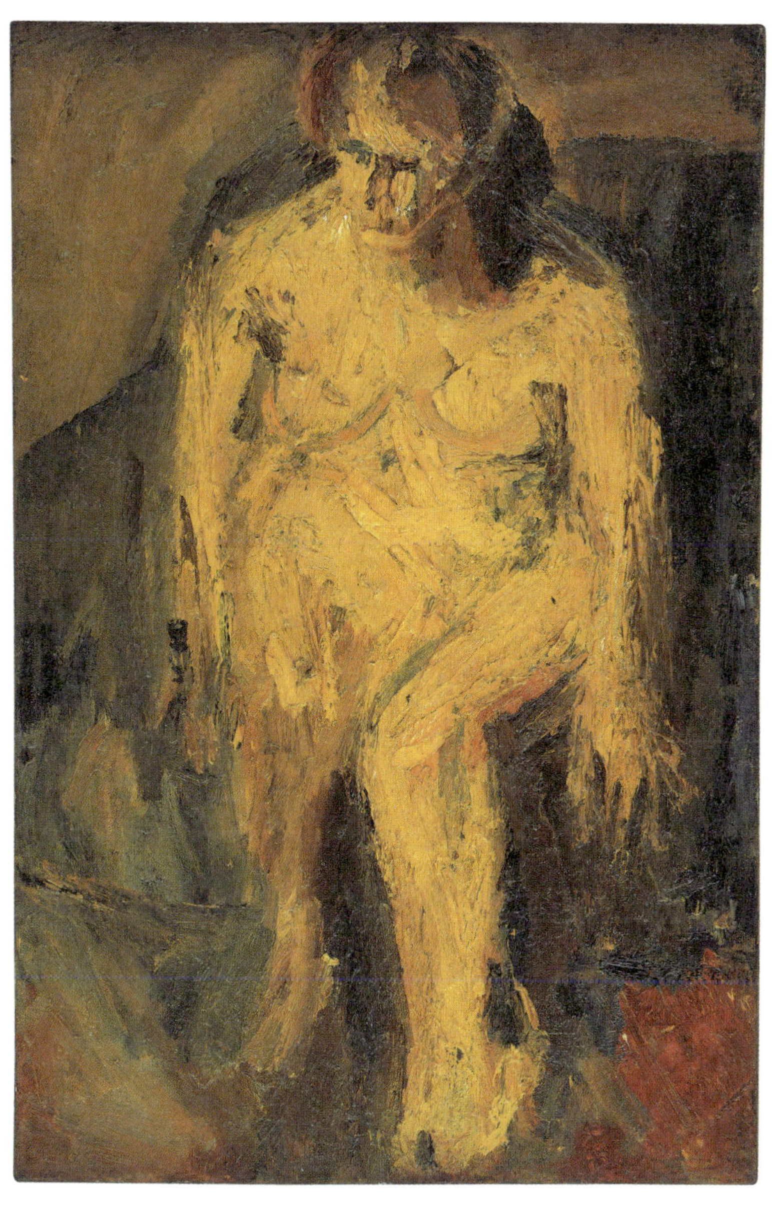

E.O.W. Nude, 1952

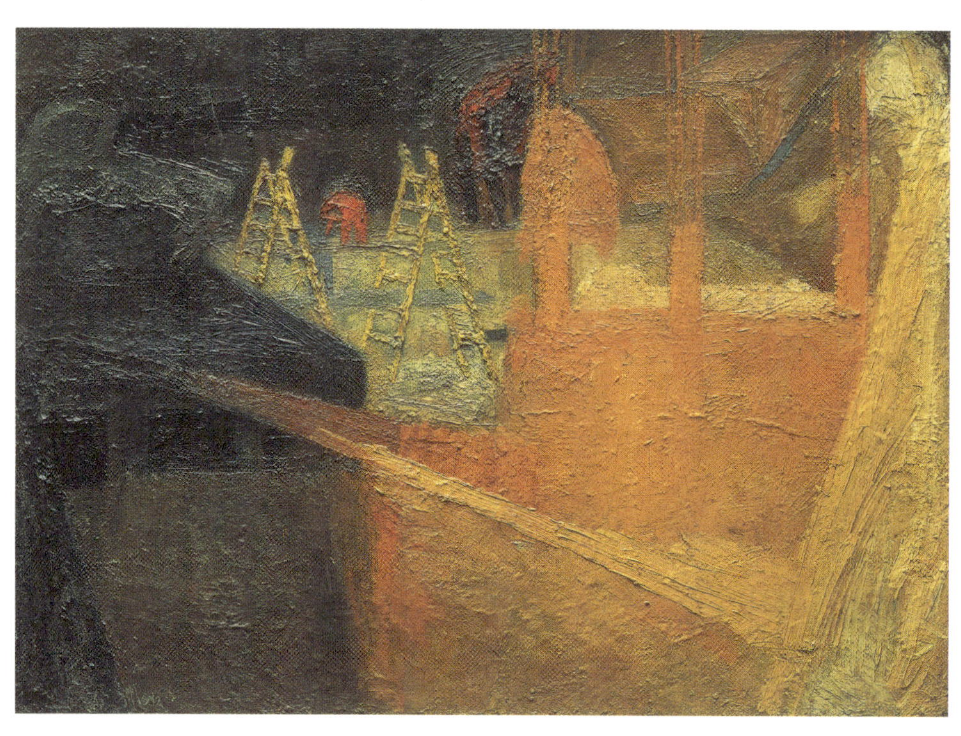

Summer Building Site, 1952

invention when I know that, however nutty it might look to someone else, that it is actually true, for me.'

The second and parallel act of desperation and epiphany transformed a building site that Auerbach passed regularly on Earl's Court Road. 'I went on doing drawings and trying to do this painting all summer, determined not to compromise.'[43] Arriving at the Royal College of Art in September, his sense of doubt about whether he should have enrolled to do an advanced degree was heightened when the new class was allocated six tubes of colour; it seemed ridiculously inadequate, even then when everything was rationed: 'I felt so disgusted entering an institution again, becoming a student again, thinking that I would have to conform in some way and compromise again ... I went home and in my anger finished the Earl's Court Road painting. Again, because of a crisis.' Our eye is led to the ladders, girders and construction workers, but it is the intensified sense of space and movement imparted by Auerbach's resort to amplifying some things and diminishing others, together with his use of bold, oblique strokes and orange and green blocks, that turn the street scene into a radical painting.

The Royal College of Art, 1952–55

The professor of painting at the Royal College was Rodrigo Moynihan, an artist who was part of the objective abstraction group in the 1930s and had returned to figuration when teaching at the Euston Road School. The first-year tutor was John Minton, who came over to Frank and said, 'You look as though you know what you're doing, I'll leave you alone.' Auerbach recalls him as nice, and a painter who made more authentic work than his 'neo-romantic' associates.

At the Royal College there were departments of illustration, furniture, stained glass and so forth. The fine-art course was not unlike that of the Slade, which was the other highly regarded college and a place Auerbach had thought of attending (he was accepted, but was wary of going to a school where the students seemed rather too sophisticated and genteel).[44] The atmosphere was less 'bohemian' and intellectual than the Slade, more down to earth, which is not to say that some of the painting students were not daring, extreme and inventive. In both colleges emphasis was put on drawing in the life-room, indeed, William Coldstream, professor at the Slade since the summer of 1949, had known Moynihan since their student days and the two spoke every day. Francis Bacon and David Sylvester were visitors to both institutions and the students met each other in pubs and at exhibitions.

Minton tolerated Frank's procedure of drawing from the model in the mornings, then returning home to do his painting. Once or twice in the life-room 'I told people to keep quiet because it seemed to me to be intolerable that people should talk in the room where one was trying to work.' One of his contemporaries at the college was Bridget Riley, and she recalls that they were the only students who persisted over the three weeks during which a particular model posed (Frank stood to work; she used a donkey easel to sit and balance her drawing board). The principal, Robin Darwin, suggested that Frank and Kossoff (he arrived at the RCA in 1953), who were known to be close, paint in the studios at the college instead of where they lived. But, after a brief compliance with Darwin's directive, they carried on as before.

Prior to 1954, the room Auerbach rented for the longest time was at 69 Anselm Road in West Kensington, near the North End Road. It cost 27s. 6d. a week. The location of *Building Site, Earl's Court Road, Winter* (1953) was not far from where he lived, and in retrospect that picture is also associated in Auerbach's mind with moving beyond a student's viewpoint and doing something more original. He arranged a saw, pincers and hammer in his room in the hope that shifting from doing drawings to a painting of this still-life grouping would help with the challenge of doing the same when faced with the ever-changing scene of men, angular steel elements and mounds of earth. 'It seemed to me that certain pictures that I had admired had done this and that the conflict between the slight sheerness and blandness that comes in working from drawings and the awkwardness and oddity that the objects in front of one have might make a more convincing image.'[45]

In a BBC radio interview in 2001, the journalist John Tusa asked Auerbach what he would say to a young artist starting out from art school and the answer pointed to the winter building-site work. It was important to begin with 'some experience that is your own and to try and record it in an idiom that is your own, and not to give a damn about what anybody else says to you ... I think that the key word there is subject – find out what matters most to you and pursue it.'[46] He has observed that 'style' is a sort of subject, a statement of your interests. This building-site painting seems to

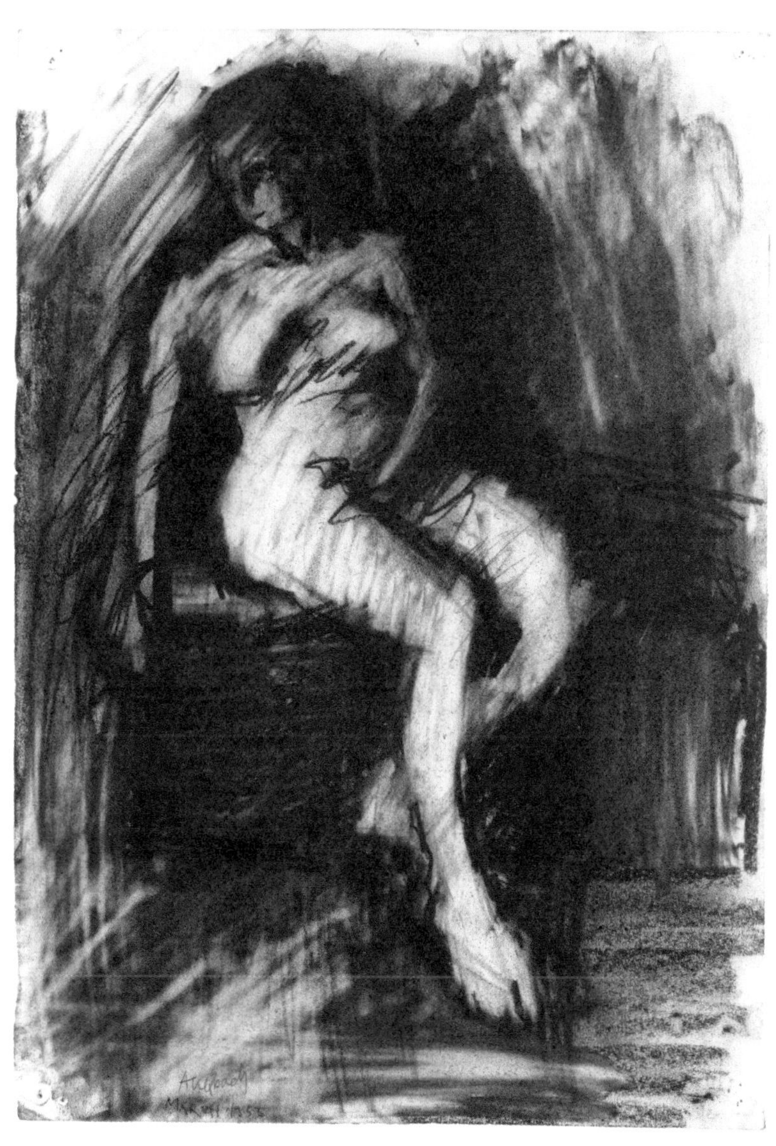

Seated Nude, 1955

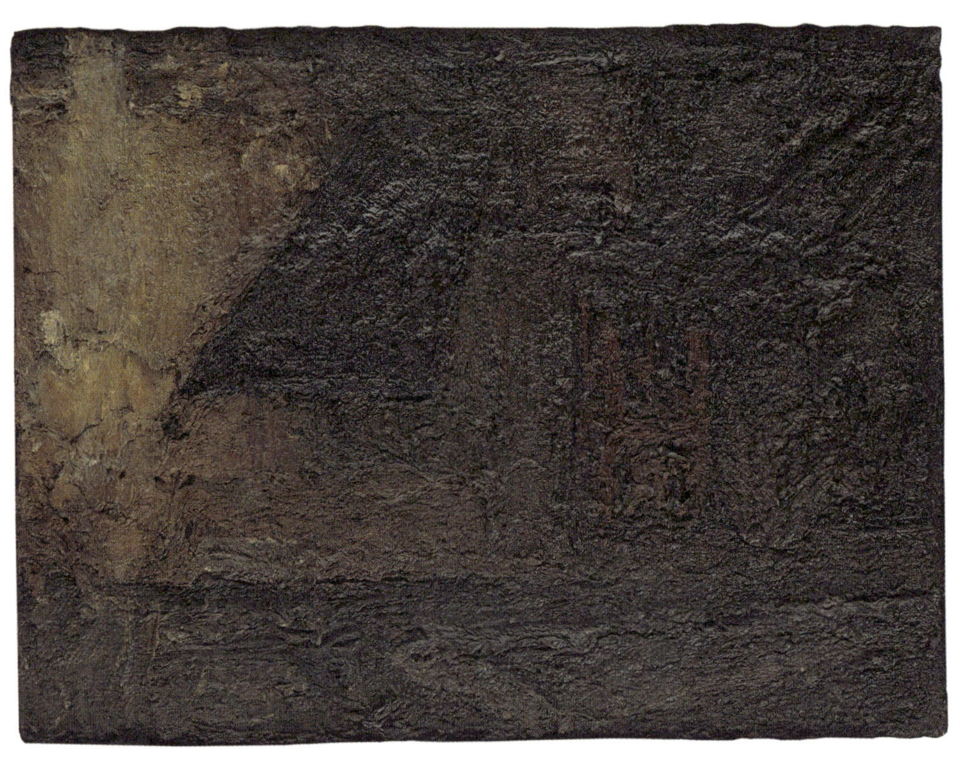

Building Site, Earl's Court Road, Winter, 1953

him 'to be a sort of remarkable object, and though nobody else may be aware of it, I am aware of the amount of painting experience that's buried under those heavy lumps of black and white and ochre.'[47]

Francis Bacon, without a secure studio, had occupied one at the RCA in 1950, then returned in 1952 when Moynihan lent him his own, which was the professor's room at the college. In his first year Auerbach became aware of this figure in a stylish French mariner's shirt, like those worn by sailors. By eleven o'clock the shirt was covered in paint stains. Bacon would sometimes briefly visit the students' sketching club and comment on what he saw. Born in 1909, he had only become established as a painter with the triptych *Three Studies for Figures at the Base of a Crucifixion* (c. 1944), shown in 1948, and through the remarkable exhibitions of his work at the Hanover Gallery. At the opening in December 1951, Auerbach thought the Pope paintings looked impressive because they were more painterly than the somewhat graphic run of English contemporary art, which he regarded as illustrative. Looking back in *c.* 1990, Michael Andrews, a Slade student who in the mid-1950s became a friend of Auerbach and Bacon, wrote: 'The supremely significant thing as far as I was concerned about Francis's pictures, when I first became familiar with them as a Slade student in 1949–53, was that they were of mature adults, responsible, culpable, corruptible, vulnerable men, and occasionally women – not boys and girls. And that together with the fact that if they had no clothes on, what was remarkable was nakedness rather than nudity – contemporary adults undressed. That's what struck me first and foremost, immediately, and still does.'[48] The critic John Berger put it another way in 1953, 'Bacon paints crime ... as though he were an accomplice.'[49]

The London art scene at this time was small and the relationship to modernism in flux. The West End galleries were full, as the artist and critic Andrew Forge put it, with 'the last dregs of neo-romanticism, decorative painting that exploited the nature imagery of [Graham] Sutherland, and every imaginable variant of a decadent synthetic cubism'.[50] A respected artist, Victor Pasmore, had moved from beautiful life paintings of his wife, Wendy, and a close relationship with other Euston Road School tutors, to abstraction, via a painting of a snow scene as a spiral in monochrome, shown at the 1951 Festival of Britain, before exhibiting his first abstract reliefs in

1953. When Bomberg's contract with the Borough Polytechnic ended in 1953 he asked Coldstream whether there were any vacancies at the Slade, reminding him that his own approach to drawing aimed at 'a fuller and more expansive delineation in the representation which is structural, taking no account of appearances', and thus closer to Cézanne and Michelangelo, who were 'builders of form', in opposition to the more usual representational art that was imitative and superficial.[51] One hears an echo in Auerbach's words of 1958: 'My attitude to form is conditioned, often, by an interest in the exact distribution of weight rather than in an exactitude of shape, in the true inflections of the masses in space rather than in the associations of particular colours or arrangements.'[52]

E.O.W. in Earl's Court, 1948–60

From the beginning of his time as a student, Auerbach was involved with Stella West (1916–2014), who he had met when they were both in Ustinov's *House of Regrets*. Stella described the much younger man she met in 1948 as a driven person looking more mature than his years. 'Frank always knew best, knew more.' Auerbach has said similar things in connection with his ambition as a painter: 'I was born old and I wanted to make a great dignified perverse image, a formal image.' After talking to Stella for more than an hour at her home in Malvern in 1986, Robert Hughes coaxed some deeper recollections from her: 'I haven't stressed enough that Frank was the most marvellous person at explaining things, as long as he wasn't personally involved. He would have made a wonderful teacher. He always knew the answers. He always had an explanation which was unexpected, surprising, bizarre, but he hit the nail on the head, always. Sometimes, when I was young, even though I was so much older, I regarded him as a sort of father-figure.'[53]

Stella thought of her childhood as difficult. She was the daughter of a 'gypsy' mother and the philosopher O. S. Wauchope, noted for his book *Deviation into Sense: The Nature of Explanation*, published by Faber and Faber in 1948. The book, indirectly imbued with an existential lack of emotionality, is still read; its language is plain and its focus on 'saying that is so'. His theories strangely accorded with work from observation and measurement and other ideas current in the visual arts, including those held by several artist friends he made. Among these were painters Auerbach admired, such as the talented, instinctive Gerald Wilde, a regular at the Fitzroy, a bohemian pub in Charlotte Street.[54]

In January 1947, Stella's husband, Dr Michael West, who had recently begun work at St Mary's Hospital, Paddington, drowned in a tragic accident in the Serpentine when he was walking home one night after a black-tie dinner. The 30-year-old Stella was left mother to two small daughters, Sarah and Julia, and pregnant with her son, Michael, born that October. Stella's beauty is evident in photographs; her broad forehead and slightly slanted mouth transfers to Auerbach's first drawings of her made in the early 1950s. Her friends urged her to get out a bit, so she joined a drama group, and this is how she came to be playing Madame Barinova, the frail Russian landlady in the 1948 production of Ustinov's play, set in West Kensington. As Stella told it, she became aware of Frank's attention soon after this, during an evening gathering of friends at her house. She was sitting on the sofa, wearing a fashionable off-the-shoulder blouse and a billowing bell skirt with a pattern of brown and green rings. Frank moved over and began removing hairpins until her abundant hair cascaded down.

Stella lived in a rather tall, thin, elegant house at 81 Earl's Court Road and as a widow was obliged to rent out rooms. Frank became a lodger in her basement and their relationship began a week later; soon he also became part of the family, an unusual role to fall into for someone only 17. Stella remembered him as being very poor: 'he used to walk around with bread in his pocket, with sixpenny lunch tickets [or vouchers], and a rail pass.' Nonetheless, he bought a black dog and hamsters for the children, and over a week in August 1949 he painted a long mural for the nursery: a fairground composition with the tent and acts described in cones and cylinders. 'As time passes I realize that in a way – a formal way – everything I have done stems from that.' The treatment of volumes and space is remarkably like that of the paintings he started making at St Martin's in 1950.[55] Frank and Stella attended variety theatres – the Metropolitan, the Chelsea Palace, the Hackney Empire – together in the last years of these dying institutions and saw not only George Robey and Max Miller, but also upcoming stars such as Harry Secombe and Michael Bentine. Her children were amused by Frank's own very good impersonations.

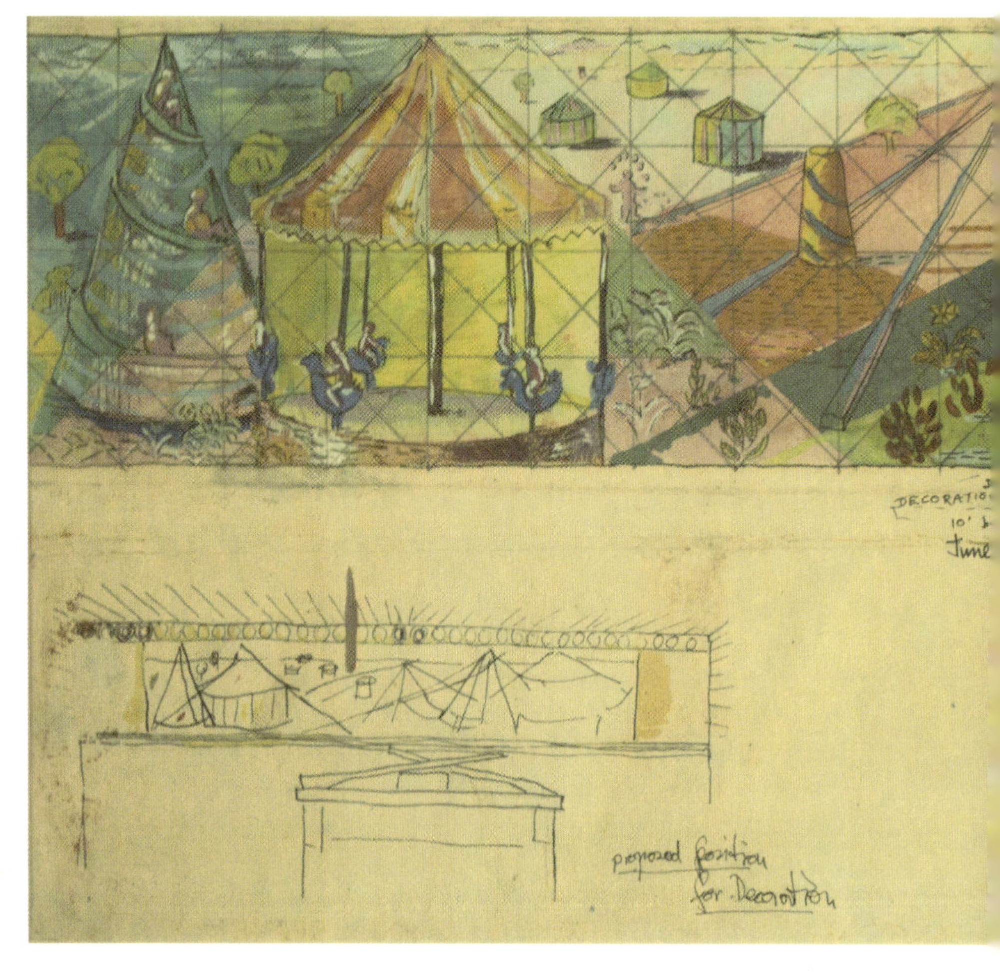

DECORATIO[N]
10' [b]
June
proposed position
for Decoration

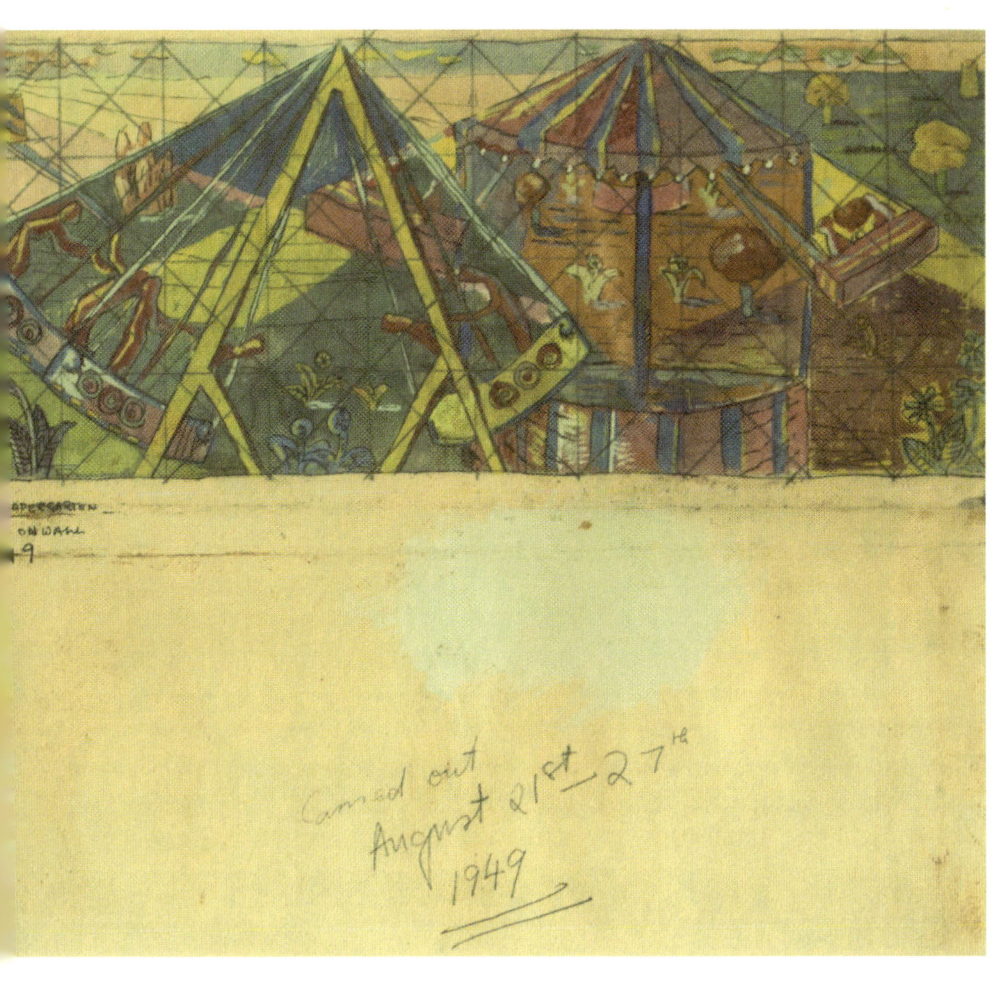

Study for fairground mural, summer 1949,
for the children's nursery in Earl's Court Road

In the years *c.* 1949–51, Stella sat for a few casual studies, one a head-and-shoulders portrait when she wore a favourite dark red corduroy house-coat. Using the room in the basement had its problems; some of the lodgers were always coming down and asking for things. Perhaps the most troublesome was the writer Len Deighton who helped himself to coal without asking and cooked smelly eels on the stove. In late 1950, Auerbach moved out and began the custom of spending Friday, Saturday and Monday nights with Stella, working from her three evenings a week. The routine was for Stella to return from her job as a social worker in the East End, put food in the oven, persuade the children to be quiet for a bit, and to start posing. They began first with an hour, with a five-minute break to see how the meal was coming on, followed by another hour. The sitting over, they would eat.

After she began posing nude, Stella became aware of the seriousness and the effort required. In the full-length 'breakthrough' painting of 1952, discussed earlier, which hung in her house for many years, she was comfortable with a Rubens-like quality in the body, but embarrassed by her legs. Auerbach, thinking back in 2012, recalled the circumstances of painting Stella for many years: 'Every single one of the paintings of Stella, totally without exception, was done with me on my knees, with the painting resting on a very, very paint-y chair, and with Stella sitting for a very long period of time.' In Earl's Court Road, Stella would either sit in an easy chair on one side of the fireplace or lie on a bed, with the pots of paint around Frank (after he moved out the paint had to be 'lugged' over from where he lived). Newspaper was spread on the floor to stop the paint getting all over, 'but it was still a pretty messy procedure and she was very tolerant for it to be allowed. After I had been drawing Stella in charcoal she put an embargo on charcoal because the whole house was covered in charcoal dust.'

Stella remembered that 'he was very violent and quite in a world of his own, and it was quite frightening in the beginning. But I got used to it after a time.'[56] Frank's recollections focus on the struggle to achieve an image, referring to the years 1952–58 when he could only afford earth colours and black and white, and was reluctant to scrape off expensive pigment and loose passages that worked: 'It may be that the reiteration of the effort and the fact that I could afford so little material played some small part in the look ... the thickness of the paint.'

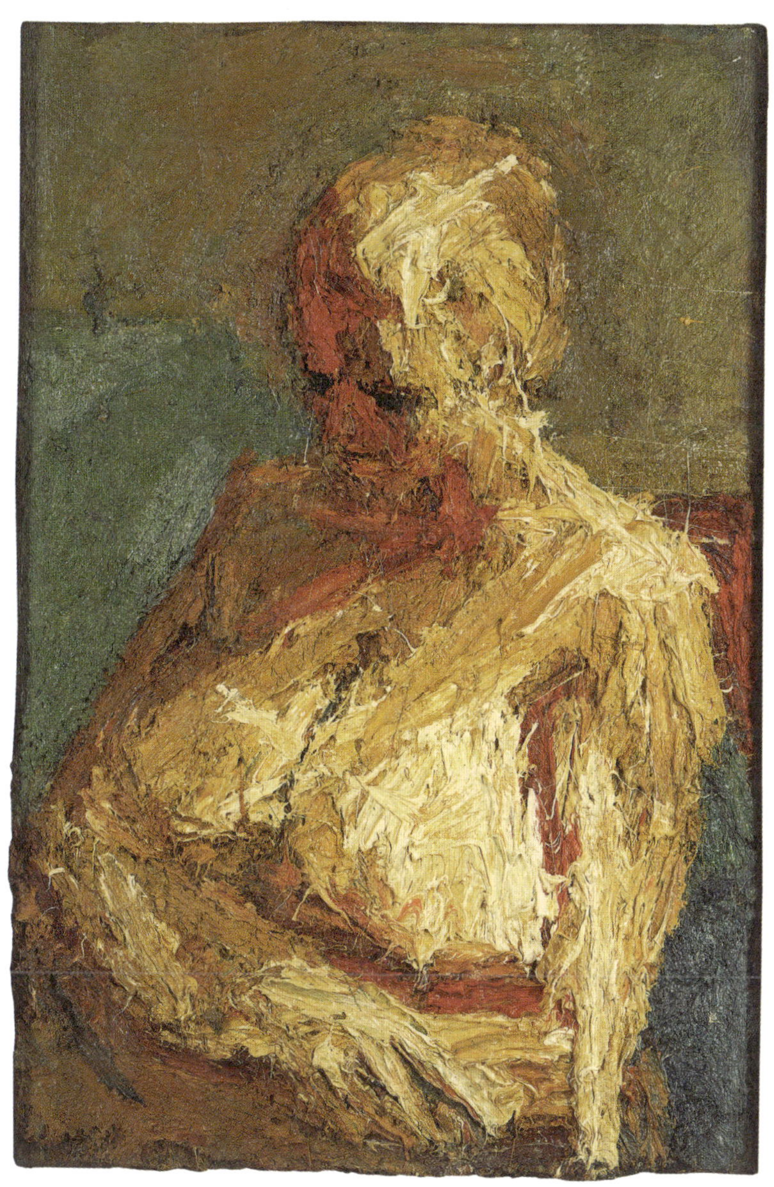

E.O.W., Half-length Nude, 1958

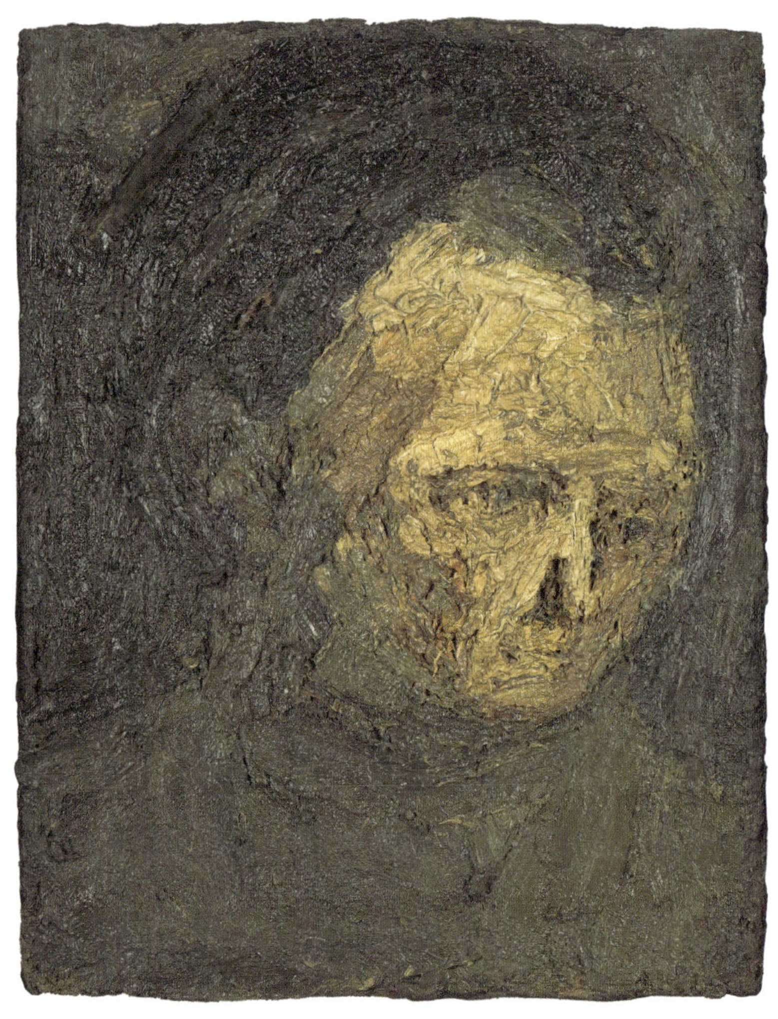

Head of E.O.W., 1955

Auerbach left the Royal College in the summer of 1955 with its degree, Associate of the Royal College of Art, with first-class honours, and a silver medal for painting. In the last term, a younger student from Yorkshire, Julia Wolstenholme, who had seen his drawings and thought them marvellous, asked if she could buy one. She went along to where he lived to have a look. She later recalled 'it was pretty clear that would be all right and he'd give it to me, and he did'. The two became involved and married not long before their son Jacob was born in March 1958 in Sheffield. Mother and son lived on Vincent Terrace in Islington, and working there one night a week Frank finished two drawings of Julia in 1960 (see p. 88). However, shortly after that they were no longer in regular contact, until they got together again in 1976.

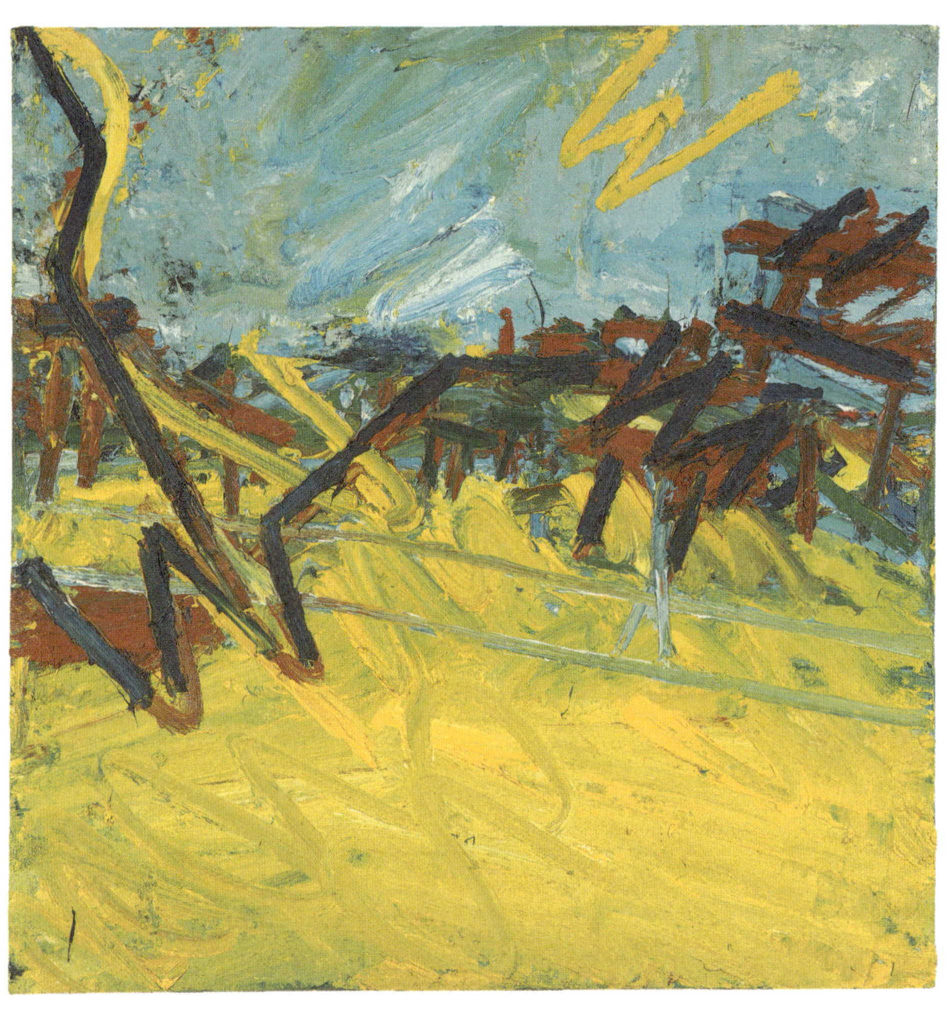

Primrose Hill, Autumn Morning, 1968

Forging a Reputation

'A secret internal geometry': Building sites, 1952–62

In an odd way being adrift in London after Auerbach left Bunce Court was preparation for the remarkable paintings he did of the city's postwar landscape in the 1950s and early 1960s. 'Being a solitary teenager in London, as I didn't have family or anything, at first I shared a room, then I had various rooms. But they weren't rooms that anyone would want to sit in. So my life was very much of the streets. I went around London, I took bus rides. This became one's physical and mental terrain, which stimulated me to try and paint it, slightly impelled by the feeling that gradually it would be tidied up and disappear.'[1] Recording the blitz-ravaged city had appealed to older artists; David Bomberg and William Coldstream in the period 1944–47 each made several panoramic paintings and drawings that featured the shells of famous churches surrounded by razed buildings in the City of London, with the features on the skyline relatively easy to identify.

Auerbach's paintings, on the other hand, began with the earth displaced during the excavation of the sites and engaged with the first stages of the new buildings. The earliest that survived, the 'breakthrough' painting of 1952 with the ladders and girders in Earl's Court was important, he explained, because he had cut through habits and reached a conclusion that remains an imperative, 'a clear expression – something that seems to lock like a theorem.' Auerbach and Leon Kossoff drew together around London and several of their paintings are of locations that were symbols of the city's resilience and renewal, such as the area adjacent to St Paul's Cathedral that had been razed during air raids in 1940 and 1941 and a new office block in

Victoria Street, near Westminster, as well as the transformation of the South Bank. Frank had no head for heights and remembers inching along planks where workers passed with wheelbarrows, trying to get a better view but scared to stand while drawing.[2] As Barnaby Wright, curator at the Courtauld Gallery, has written, 'He would visit a site perhaps five or six times over a relatively short period, usually at an early stage in the construction, capturing what he needed before the works moved on and the scene had changed completely. Throughout the process of painting selections of the numerous sketches remained pinned up on his studio wall and were a constant reference point ... Legibility was subject to sacrifice if it brought Auerbach closer to achieving what he describes as "formal grandeur" or "a secret internal geometry" which gradually emerged after months of labour and struggle.'[3]

Only a scattering of drawings survives but they are of several types. Some when pinned up together on the studio wall might have resembled a storyboard where one can identify men with shovels at the bottom of the pit, dwarfed by the machinery, and follow annotations there to remind the artist of colours. Other drawings are less explicit, the marks conjuring up the vaulted darkness within old master paintings and Piranesi's imaginary prison etchings, the *Carceri* series. Auerbach's *Study after Turner's The Parting of Hero and Leander* (c. 1953), which is a drawing based on a work in the National Gallery, puts emphasis on the grand buildings of Abydos, with spectators lined up on the dock, and on the storm over the Hellespont in which Leander drowned. A gridded building-site sketch on the verso curiously transports the eye into deep space; the ideal architecture and the lightning bolt in Turner's painting is here a diagonal stroke that we read as a huge beam being cantilevered into position.

Archive photographs of the Shell Buildings under construction and finished, normally empty of people, seem rather dull and inhuman in comparison to Auerbach's grand re-imagining of what he witnessed. Upon completion in 1962 it would be the largest office complex in Europe, occupying the riverside front from Waterloo Bridge to County Hall as part of the South Bank development. Soon two office blocks loomed over the Royal Festival Hall, one with an unprecedented 26-storey tower, both requiring deep foundations. 'The Shell site was extraordinary ... It was a vast building

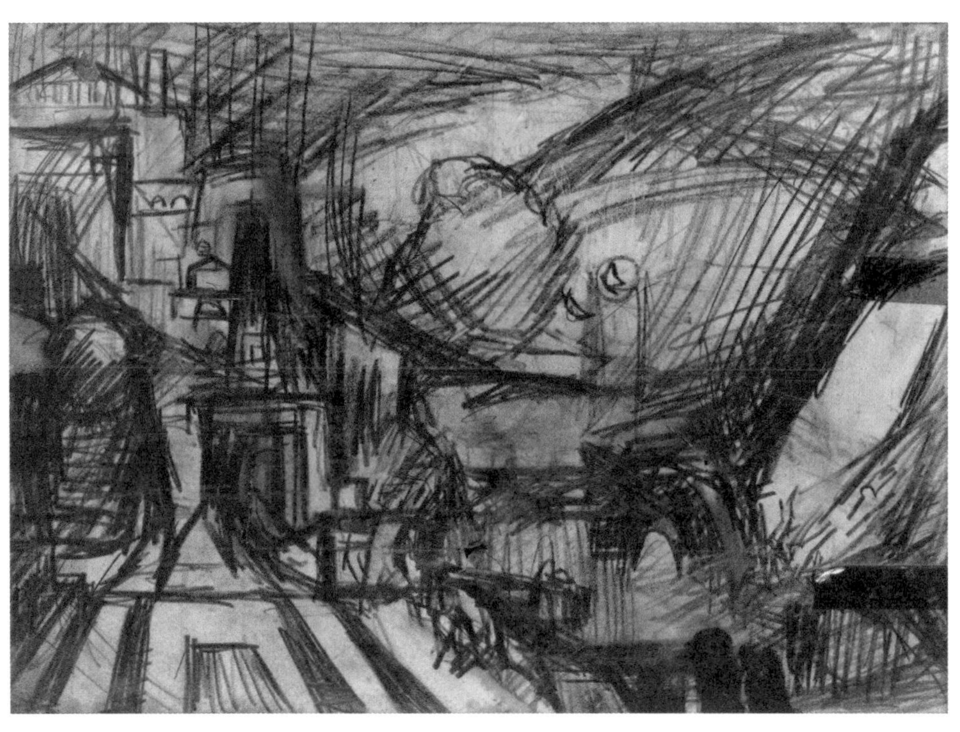

Study after Turner's The Parting of Hero and Leander, c. 1953

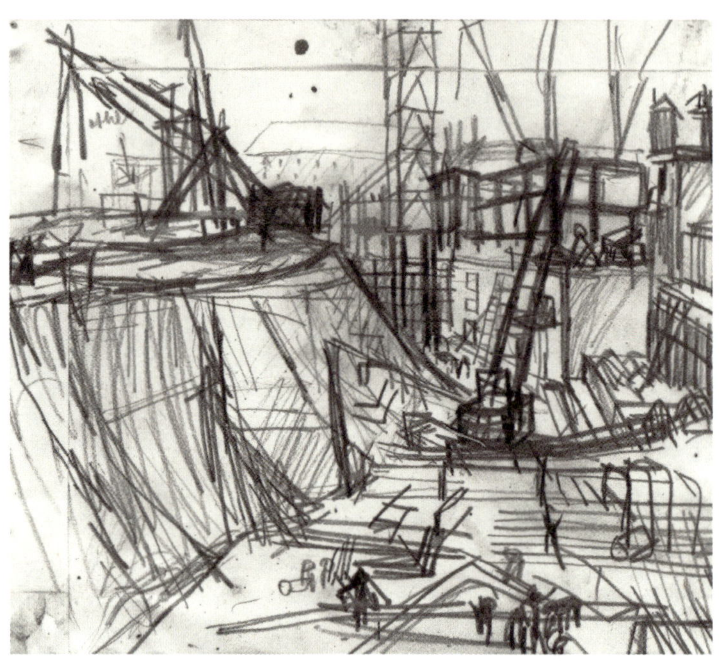

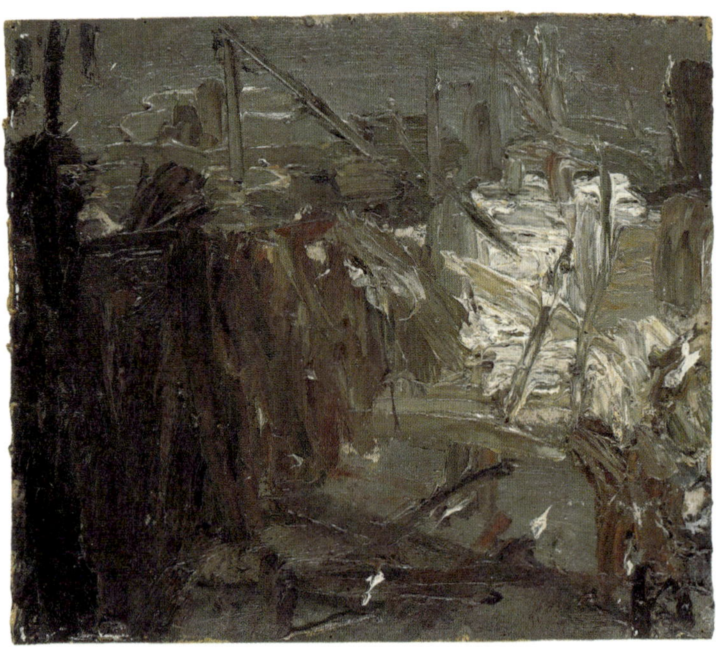

Top: Study for *Shell Building Site from the Festival Hall, c.* 1958–59
Above: *Shell Building Site from the Festival Hall,* 1959

site and it looked absolutely superb. It was like the Grand Canyon. I remember going there ... it was almost a gift ... you could have taken it and put it in a museum being what it is.'[4] In the two paintings approaching the site from the Thames, the viewer looks down on a golden void, with the lines of a crane, a boom and cables dividing the surface, in the distance Waterloo Station and below the stubby steel supports indicating the foundations for the new building. The oil sketch (opposite below) and a larger painting both subtitled *From the Festival Hall* describe a more recessional space, with the foreground punctuated by marks indicating steel uprights and in the distance the outlines of the new blocks.

When the fourteen building-site paintings, dating from 1952 to 1962, were gathered together at the Courtauld Gallery in London for an extremely well-received exhibition in 2009, Auerbach reflected on his state of mind in these years in the course of a conversation with the critic Martin Gayford: 'You know how when one is young everything has a very strong effect and one remembers much more of those years than one does of any other? I'm speaking here for a young man who no longer exists and of whom I'm a rather distant representative. I think there may be some feeling of that turmoil and freedom in those pictures that there was in London after the war. There was a curious feeling of liberty about because everybody who was living there had escaped death in some way. It was sexy in a way, this semi-destroyed London. There was a scavenging feeling of living in a ruined town.'[5]

For artists working in this period, an association with existentialism was inevitable, as the curator Paul Moorhouse put it in his essay in the Courtauld catalogue: 'The writings of Jean-Paul Sartre, Albert Camus and Simone de Beauvoir identified a world in which man existed in the absence of any divine plan,' and consequently artists could immerse themselves in 'a private quest' as they progressively restated an image.[6] Auerbach sometimes reflects on the mentality of the period. 'I very much liked the idea that you made your own justification for existence. I don't think I can exaggerate the degree to which consciously or unconsciously the atom bomb hovered over all our heads. Very few of us thought that we had many years to live. So what are you going to do? You live in the moment and you try to construct your own framework to justify this brief and instinctive existence.'[7]

The emphasis on the personal and the concrete is characteristic; it began with what he saw: 'A city fully functional is to me a somewhat formally boring collection of cubic rectilinear shapes, but London after the war was a marvellous landscape with precipice and mountain and crags, full of drama formally ... compost for images all around one.'[8] The shapes and relationships had to be regurgitated and made into something pictorially fresh and tangible; the surface might mimic earth with ruts and crusts; and the atmosphere was fuliginous. But this build-up was never created with the intention of conveying something primal; the texture was the natural result of the way Auerbach added paint, in these early years working without scraping and able to afford only earth colours. The criterion applied to every painting, then and in the future, was 'to catch something that is mobile' so that the marks and colours should 'reconstitute themselves if they're any good into a sort of experience that has very little to do with the paint'.[9]

At the beginning of the 1960s, Auerbach turned to the demolition of the Maples store on the Euston Road and the rebuilding of the Empire Cinema, Leicester Square. Meanwhile he introduced other very active and dramatic locations, such as the street in front of the Carreras cigarette factory across from Mornington Crescent Underground station and railway arches in Bethnal Green. In order to recall the activity of the porters carrying meat in Smithfield Market, he made a sequence of photographs, 'almost like a photo-essay', to progress the vertical painting finished in 1962. 'One gets involved with a theme and one just wants to do it. It's almost as though someone had challenged me to a duel with them and I can't back out!' His fascination with urban landscape was already matched by a need to go to open spaces with different rhythms; as soon as Frank moved to the studio near Mornington Crescent in 1954 he began painting Primrose Hill, a mound adjacent to Regent's Park twenty minutes' walk away. Auerbach said later that the close tones conjured up space for him. The terrain in these first pictures seems churned and dense; the furrows made by the brush relate to trees or paths embedded in the golden-greenish surface.

Over the years he continued to paint Primrose Hill (see p. 54); a city park crossed by paths and lampposts. It provided an 'antidote' to the hard, angular forms of buildings. Gradually, the area of sky grows and individual trees are described, the viewer feels the movement of wind in the trees,

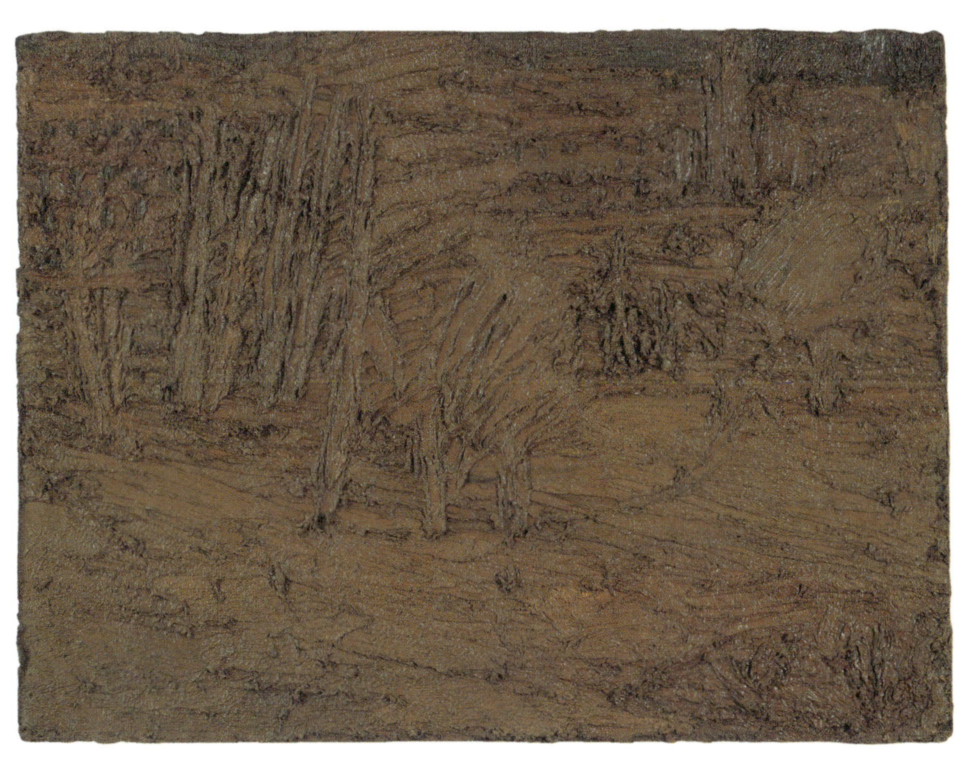

Primrose Hill, 1954–55

and takes in the profile of tall buildings in the distance. A connection to one of the artist's favourite painters, John Constable, another landscape painter, is inevitable. Auerbach says that like his predecessor he also became very familiar with his material and 'actually tried to convey within the forms how things interlock, even where you can't see them'. He drew from the work of a variety of artists, relishing, for example, the work of English painters such as Turner, Gainsborough, Constable and Hogarth, while not excluding minor ones such as Benjamin Haydon. 'I have hardly ever drawn from a modern picture – I know how it's made. When it is one by an old master, I know they are marvellous, but I can't see what is the secret that makes them so.' Interviewed at the Victoria & Albert Museum in 2014, when they presented 'Constable: The Making of a Master', his comment on *Salisbury Cathedral from the Meadows* (1831) describes his own work, then and now, as well as the drawings and etchings of this painting by Kossoff, in which the cart, man and three horses are very prominent. Constable 'always had to have something a little bit industrious in the front, evidence of work, even if it is only cows. It's like: don't believe that life is all going to be rainbows and heaven.'[10]

Not one without the other: Frank Auerbach and Leon Kossoff

'We were like two mountain climbers roped together.' At the dinner to celebrate an exhibition of Leon Kossoff's drawings in May 2013, I heard Auerbach borrow Braque's famous quotation about his relationship with Picasso in the pioneering days of Cubism. It was an analogy he had used before in connection with Kossoff, the implication being that during their student years and beyond as one artist managed to grasp what he saw and transpose 'the sense of corporeal reality', however laborious the process, on to paper or canvas, the other was challenged to do something even more extraordinary. They frequently worked in proximity. In 1950, Kossoff had taken over the purpose-built studio with north-facing light near Mornington Crescent from the previous occupant, Gustav Metzger. After Kossoff married and moved to Bethnal Green, the tenancy passed to Auerbach in March 1954.

Looking back, in 2012, Frank explained how they worked in the years 1954–57: 'I would sit for an hour and Leon would paint me, and then Leon would sit for an hour and I would paint him, and so we went on all day, turn and turn about. I've forgotten how long the process took and I've forgotten also how many days a week we did it, it may have been two days a week. It may have taken about two years for Leon to finish two paintings of me, one a half-length and one a head, and for me to finish two paintings of Leon.' *Head of Leon Kossoff* (1954), facing right, was finished first; for Auerbach it is the slightly more organic portrait, whereas the other one where the subject faces left he sees as oddly hieratic, with an Easter Island feel about it (see p. 64). 'Both were shown in the "Daily Express Young Artists' Exhibition" in 1955 where Lucian [Freud] won the second prize for the portrait of Caroline with her finger in her mouth in the Hotel Louisiana in Paris and Lucian, not a particularly good likeness, standing behind looking extremely troubled. The actual main prize was, I think, won by somebody who's since disappeared for a painting called the *Departure for Cythera*.'[11]

Auerbach went on to recall the circumstances of painting three tablet-sized portraits, which despite their scale took a considerable time to realize (see p. 65). This was in 1954–56. 'I did a few little paintings in Leon's flat, and I think once again it was turn and turn about. I had left the college and was in a fairly desperate state, not only as regards keeping alive, [but] also as regards affording a quantity of paint and I think that might have been an element at least in doing smaller pictures.' The works Auerbach made at the end of this exchange, in 1957, back in Mornington Crescent, were three very heavily worked charcoal drawings of Leon looking down, the lines in the surrounding space echoing those that shaped the round cranium and below the sharper lines of jaw and neck. 'I know Leon finished before me and he very generously went on sitting for the drawings after intervals to do with his own work. There is a sort of superstition that drawings have to be quick and paintings have to be slow but these weren't particularly quick, they took a number of sittings.' While posing, Kossoff had observed the way Auerbach rejected images that it was 'possible to preconceive', those that 'lied': his words in the catalogue preface to Auerbach's 1978 exhibition suggest Kossoff was speaking for both men: 'The only true guide in this search is the special relationship the artist has with the person or landscape from which he is working. Finally, in spite of all this activity of absorption and internalization the images emerge in an atmosphere of freedom.'[12]

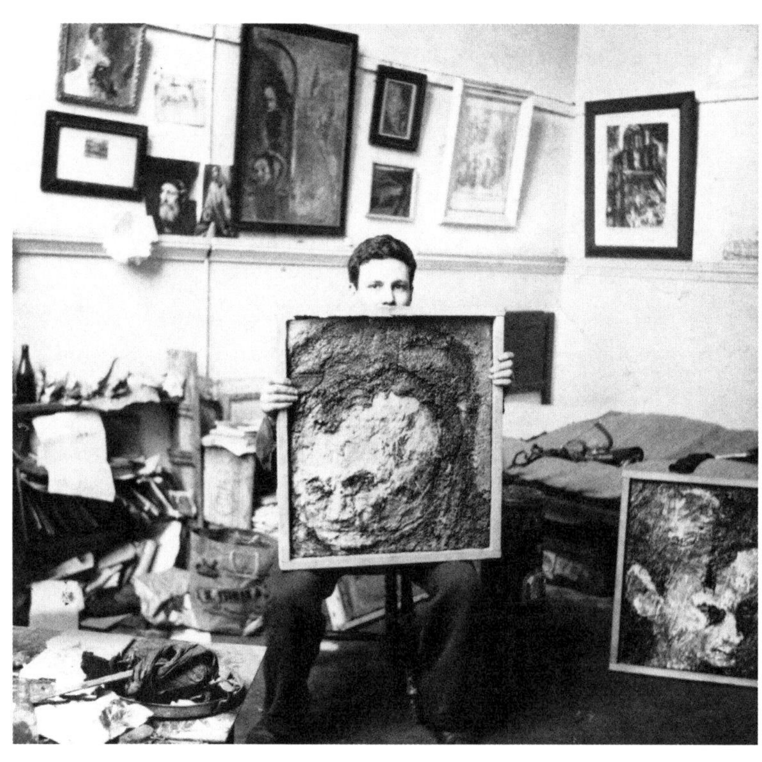

Frank in the studio with portraits of Leon Kossoff made in 1954, *c.* 1955

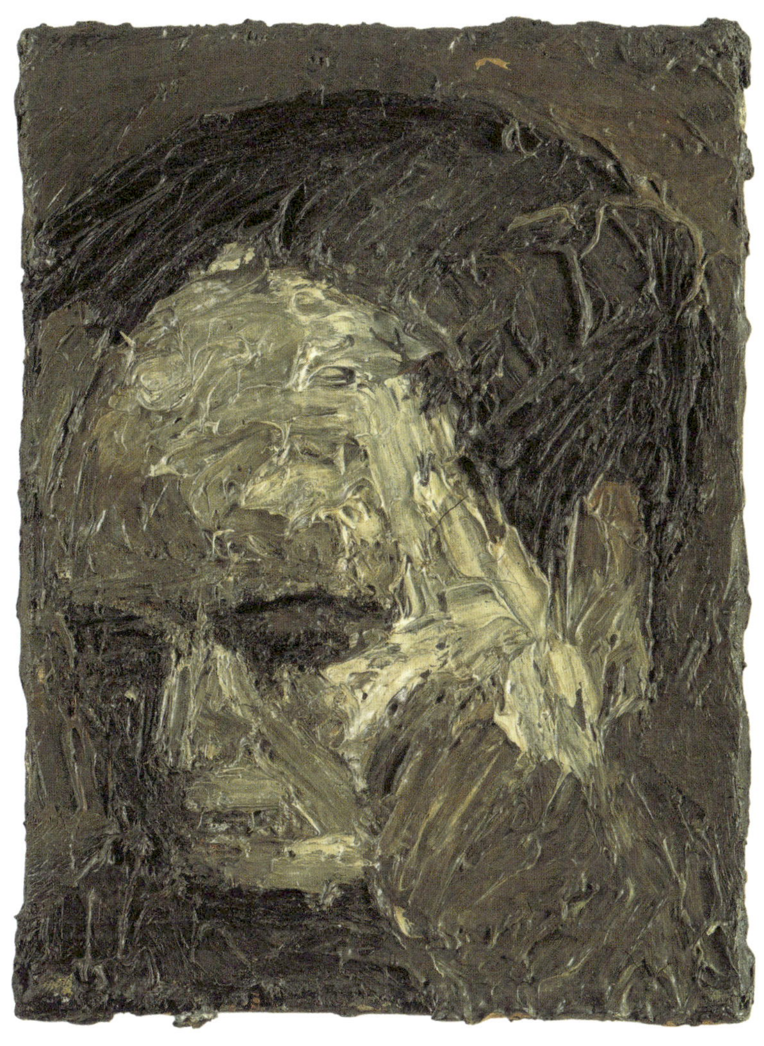

Head of Leon Kossoff, 1954

In 1998, the critic Michael Peppiatt pursued questions about the relationship between Auerbach and Kossoff and was told, 'We saw each other very frequently, and we saw each other's work as it was being produced and – I can't speak for Leon – but I was excited by what he was doing and felt that it was worth emulating the quality, if not the idiom, or the way of painting. We used to go over to each other's studios right through the fifties and into the sixties ... Then I think we became more private, as one does as one gets older and more mature and more ...' Peppiatt suggested, 'Oneself?' 'Yes, I think once one has discovered and defined, willy-nilly, the sort of person one is, then the battle becomes almost entirely one's own. One hopes to be stimulated by quality, but it's at least as likely to be by pictures in the National Gallery as by something remarkable being done while one lives.'[13]

Helen Lessore and the Beaux Arts Gallery

'I think that between the years of say 1952 and 1956 I was working at my own frontiers. I mean, I don't think that there was an ounce of attention, energy, commitment, or courage to spare that wasn't devoted to my painting.'[14] Auerbach's first one-person exhibition at the Beaux Arts Gallery opened in January 1956 and contained the remarkable results of this intense and experimental period: twenty-four paintings, of which eight were urban landscapes, ten heads and four nudes of E.O.W., two heads of Leon Kossoff, plus eight drawings from life models and a set of five drypoints.

The work made an immediate impression among artists and critics. David Sylvester in the *Listener* thought the Primrose Hill and Building Site paintings 'must be the heaviest paintings in existence, for the paint has been put on so thick that they resemble relief maps of mountainous regions'.[15] Critics, then and later, made a comparison to two current movements, Art Brut and Art Informel, as exemplified in the work of Jean Dubuffet and Jean Fautrier, but there was nothing 'naïve' or process-led about Auerbach's approach; he went on with each work for a long time until 'they looked banally true to me'. To Sylvester, gazing at one of the portraits 'gives a sensation curiously like that of running our fingertips over the contours of a head near us in the dark, reassured by its presence, disturbed by its otherness'.[16]

Auerbach's association with the Beaux Arts Gallery came about after its director, Helen Lessore, visited an exhibition of five graduating painters at the Royal College in the summer of 1955: Joe Tilson, Anthony Whishaw, Mike Pope, Keith Cunningham and Frank Auerbach. She invited each of them to send a picture to the summer show she planned for her Mayfair gallery; Auerbach contributed two nudes of Stella.[17] Soon after, another gallery approached Auerbach, so he wrote to advise her of this. In October, Lessore hurried to the studio to see his new work, 'and she said, almost tearfully, but *I* like it', proving her commitment by immediately buying six pictures for £60 while rightly suggesting the other offer was suspect: 'No serious gallery will give you a show that quickly.' Lessore responded especially to the paintings of E.O.W.'s head in profile and those of her extended body; to her it was 'as if the planes were carved out of a stubbornly resistant rock-face of grey stone', like a low relief.[18]

Sylvester went so far as to judge the inaugural exhibition an event: 'As to Auerbach, he has given us, at the age of twenty-four, what seems to me the most exciting and impressive one-man show by an English painter since Francis Bacon's in 1949 ... these paintings reveal the qualities that make for greatness in a painter – fearlessness, a profound originality: a total absorption in what obsesses him; and, above all, a certain authority and originality in his forms and colours. Here at last is a young painter who has extended the power of paint to remake reality.'[19] Most of all, other artists took note. Francis Bacon encouraged his friend Lucian Freud to come to the opening. Fifty years later, when the V & A staged a joint Auerbach/Freud exhibition, Frank reminisced, 'I remember Lucian making a very ceremonious bow at the end when he left the gallery.'[20] Richard Cork turned to Freud to record his initial impressions of Auerbach's work, 'I remember thinking what a lot of paint! When you're an artist yourself, you are always very aware of the technicalities. They were all heaped with paint, and done on board.'[21]

Although Lessore sold only a few small pictures from that exhibition, Auerbach's relationship with her survived, not least because this dealer was distinct from the others. For a start, she herself had studied art at the Slade in the 1920s and had continued to paint after she found a job at the Beaux Arts Gallery. Lessore had married its proprietor, a much older artist, the sculptor Frederick Lessore, brother of Sickert's third wife, Thérèse. After he died in 1951 she was obliged to run the gallery to support the family, moving with her two sons, Henry and John, into the separate flat on the ground floor of this collection of small buildings on Bruton Place, near Bond Street.

The Beaux Arts Gallery had a reputation for seriousness, as was conveyed by Andrew Forge in a catalogue introduction written three years after it closed for the group exhibition 'Helen Lessore and the Beaux Arts Gallery' that Marlborough Fine Art staged in 1968: 'You came off the street up a dark staircase and straight into the upstairs gallery. It was like entering an attic. The first things you saw were floor-boards and a floor-level view of the pictures. The floor-boards creaked and the place always smelt of the paraffin stoves that were standing around (there was some inadequacy in the wiring). Through the top gallery you came to a balcony hanging out over the large gallery below, just as it might over the squash court which the lower space resembled. On the balcony to the right was Helen Lessore's desk and she was almost always there, pale, beaked, a melancholy bird. To your left, a precipitous iron staircase took you down into the large gallery. A door opened straight on to the pavement of Bruton Place. Mrs Lessore's shoes would watch you go. More than anything else it was like a studio, an *atelier de peintre* spruced up for visitors, and it was this – that the gallery itself seemed nearer to the painting end of pictures than to the merchandising end – that gave it its inimitable, irreplaceable quality.'[22]

Auerbach had annual exhibitions at the gallery – a small display of drawings in 1957, paintings in 1958, with a larger show of paintings and drawings in 1959 – continuing through to 1963, the final show before he moved to Marlborough Fine Art in the spring of 1964. Professional achievements that suggested his reputation was growing were mentioned in the rather basic catalogues: for example, Auerbach's inclusion in the Pittsburgh International Exhibition, 1958, and the purchase of *E.O.W., Nude on Bed* (1959) by the Chrysler Art Museum of Provincetown, Massachusetts. Michael Roemer, Frank's school friend, was the first to buy, and kept doing so; for twelve years he paid in monthly instalments of $5. The poet and civil servant C. H. Sisson purchased a sketch for the *Oxford Street Building Site* (1960) and *Nude on Bed IV* (1961). Six works were sold by Lessore to the actor Laurence Harvey, and after Auerbach joined the Marlborough he continued acquiring works; the collection was begun while Harvey was starring in box-office hits such as *Room at the Top* (1959) and *The Alamo* (1960). The Tate, Arts Council,

Whitworth Art Gallery in Manchester, Ferens Art Gallery, Hull, and the Contemporary Art Society bought as well. In 1961, after five years of modest sales, Lessore was able to offer Auerbach a contract that promised £1,500 annually so that buying enough quantities of paint and being able to afford brighter colours, reds and vivid greens, became more feasible.

David Sylvester was invited to select Arthur Tooth & Sons' fourth Critic's Choice exhibition for the summer of 1958. He began by defining what was British. 'The sensible formula seemed to be the one adopted when Rothko and de Kooning are claimed as American artists while Lipchitz and Gabo are not: artists from abroad were considered ineligible if their artistic formation had preceded their settling here, and eligible if it had not.' Taking an age limit of 50, in the first room he hung works by William Coldstream, Francis Bacon and Victor Pasmore, the trio described collectively as 'profoundly individualistic, idiosyncratic – in a way that is peculiarly English. I do not mean by this that these artists are in the tradition of English eccentric painters: on the contrary, whereas eccentrics are innocent about problems of style, these painters have a highly self-conscious, fastidious, sense of style. Neither does the fact that they are "originals" make them isolated figures: each has numerous followers and imitators.'[23] At one point Sylvester considered inviting another recent graduate, Michael Andrews, to show work. However, settled into a residency at the Digswell Arts Trust and engaged on painting a local gardener, he was unable to deliver in time. Auerbach was the alternative. In the second room, four paintings, *Primrose Hill* (1954–55), the ochre ground *Primrose Hill* (1958) and two heads of E.O.W. from 1957–58, hung adjacent to sculpture by Kenneth Armitage and Eduardo Paolozzi.[24]

Many viewers at these early exhibitions found it hard to locate features in the thickly painted works and were troubled by the churned impasto. In 'A stick in the dark', a review in the *New Statesman* of Auerbach's Beaux Arts exhibition in 1959, the critic John Berger recognized that the 'thick, uneven, turgid' paint would always seem inadequate given 'the richness of life and the poorness of art'. However, he detected a thrilling new achievement, not least because Auerbach had avoided the perils of imitation and subjectivity. 'The inert deadness of the mud in Auerbach's earlier paintings becomes eloquent now about the weather and the depth dug in the building sites,

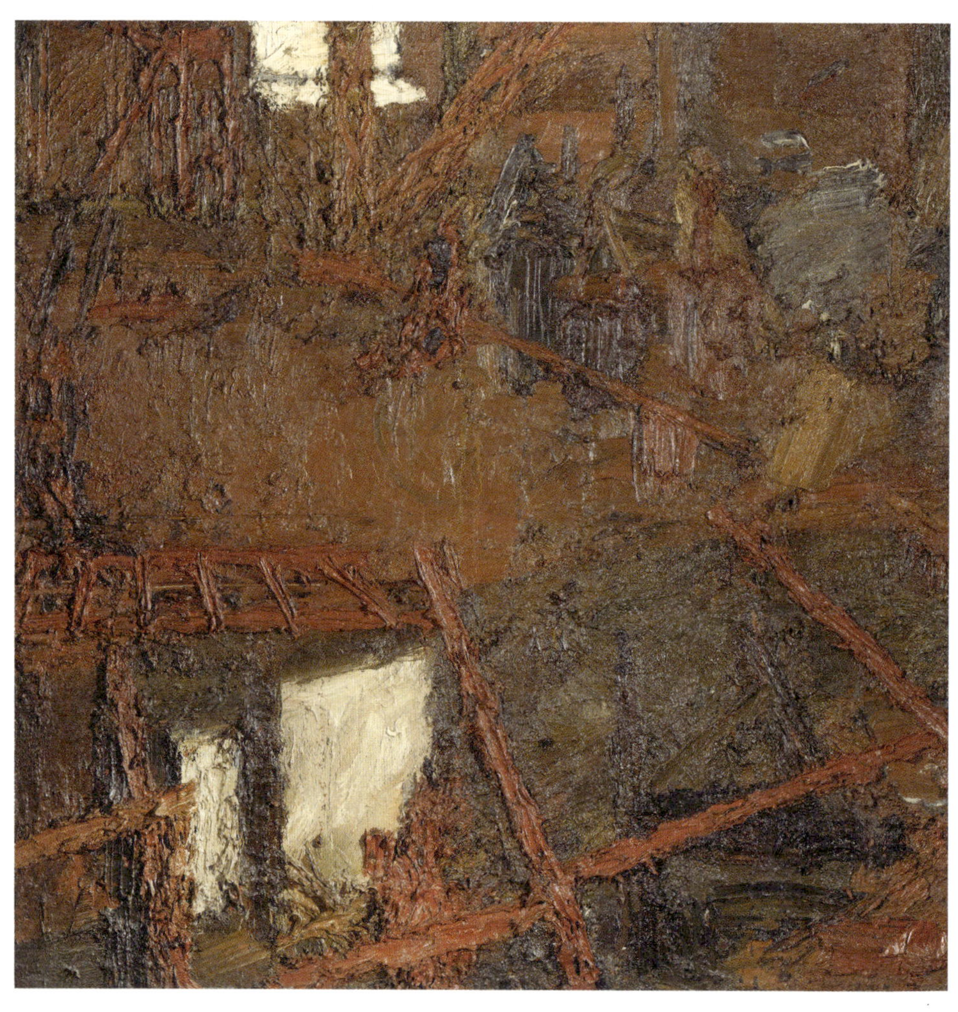

Rebuilding the Empire Cinema, Leicester Square, 1962

just as in the nudes it becomes eloquent about the substance of flesh.'[25] One painting, *Shell Building Site: Workmen under Hungerford Bridge* (1958–61), 'with its almost purple bloom upon it', was commended by the *Times* critic for its extended range of colour. Nevertheless, after the exhibition closed this painting was returned to Auerbach's studio because he realized it needed to be reworked: 'I must have had some brandy because I remember drinking and repainting the whole thing in black and white from top to bottom.'[26]

In 1962, works by the Swedish painter Evert Lundquist, Kossoff and Auerbach were hung together in a Beaux Arts summer exhibition. In the *Sunday Times* Sylvester, who loved to rate everything – artists, works of art, carpets, food, women – made another claim: 'Today we make heroes of painters still at art school, but there's only one postwar painter in this country, Frank Auerbach, who in my view has gone as far as Bacon and Coldstream before reaching 25.'[27] One critic identified a 'head-on clash between American-influenced abstraction and a Bomberg-inspired realism'; the author of this opinion, Alan Bowness, art historian and later director of the Tate, compared Auerbach with Soutine, both were 'expressionist painters', while regarding the artist's new interest in the 'spatial setting', and the black and white pictures in this exhibition, as a positive sign.[28] Andrew Forge, writing in September 1963, insisted the commentary about Auerbach should go beyond the repetition of subject matter and the thickness of the paint, which he considered just a 'conversational handle', to look harder at the real and 'extreme demands he places on the paint' as surface and as image. 'The closer the circle tightens round him and his model, the smaller the field within which spontaneity is possible – and the more desperately necessary spontaneity becomes ... He insists that "distant" does not feel the same as "near", that things are changed by their position in space, that his pictures include the eye's swoop across a yawning excavation or into the hollow of an eye. He rejects the Cubist conventions. He wants the movements into his pictures to be swift and deep and ample, as they are in Rembrandt.' The 'object-character of the picture', against what it represents, is an extreme position to take and is used 'to smash the familiar features and replace them with raw material ... sometimes one feels that they [these pictures] are like the most rigorous demonstrations of the mysteries of the painted surface.'[29]

Teaching and surviving

Whereas a number of artists leaving college had help from their parents, or perhaps income from a building society account, Auerbach after he left the Royal College in June 1955 was on his own. Initially he survived by doing odd jobs, including working part-time packing in a frame moulders and for a year helping on Sundays in the branch of the Kossoff bakery shops in Brick Lane. (He served bread while Leon handled the cakes, manned the till and phoned the head bakery if they were running short of bread.) His first part-time teaching appointments in the autumn of 1955 were as a supply teacher at a boys' school on the City Road and a day a week at a girls' school, Langford Grove, at Barcombe Mills, near Lewes in Sussex. There he replaced the painter Edward Middleditch (and before him Denis Wirth-Miller and earlier Helen Lessore). The headmistress, Miss Curtis, an eccentric lady, regularly invited him to share a lunch of scallops and gin, and at the end of the day threw down the stairs a cheque for three pounds. In 1957, Auerbach began teaching three evenings a week at Ealing School of Art.

The loss of time to paint meant these interruptions were dispiriting. At the Royal College he disdained to write a clever thesis, and he has insisted that words exist around the periphery, protesting when questioned too deeply that 'painting is a dumb activity' and pictures embrace 'many elements not to be comprehended in any coherent verbal theory'. Nonetheless, Auerbach's growing ability to articulate his experience, to offer 'loose ends which lead back to the central activity', happened in tandem with the early years of talking about drawing and painting as a visiting tutor.[30] 'I think it would now probably seem limited, but this [verbal] invention actually sustained me in my work and there were phrases that I found myself saying to students because I found it intolerable to be in a room with unambitious or insensitive work.'[31]

Former students remember how he spoke to them as if future artists. Early on, this assumption created problems when he began a part-time job at Sidcup School of Art in 1957. The college is known for its connections with the music scene. The rather rough R&B band Pretty Things was formed there in 1963 and played at a club nearby, Chislehurst Caves. It was a school of commercial art and Auerbach recalls that the students were supposed to be inferior because they had not passed GCEs, but in his view 'they were far from inferior, they were lively, and they started wanting to paint'. One, Rosemary Bridger Leith, remembered that Auerbach was always encouraging and endlessly patient, impressing upon the students 'that a painting must "come forward" and be strong and bold in the foreground!'[32] Very soon the growing taste for painting in the students supposed to be entering design studios alarmed the administration and he was sacked. Keith Colburn, principal of the affiliated Bromley College of Art, heard from a student about this effective teacher and decided to hire him straightaway. As Frank recalls, 'there was an element of sort of slightly gleeful politics' about his being re-employed.

Bromley College of Art, before the merger of three schools and re-naming as Ravensbourne College of Art and Design in 1962, was housed in a Victorian building on Tweedy Road in the centre of Bromley, Kent. Over the three years Auerbach taught there two days a week, 1958–61, several students left a lasting impression on him. One, Joe Keys, came from a very poor background; when he went home in December his father said he would have to pay for his share of the Christmas dinner. On the basis of a self-portrait, he was admitted to the Slade where Frank observed that he rather fell under the influence of Art and Language, the collaborative practice that began in 1968 with the intention of challenging both the fashionable and too often doctrinaire espousal of conceptual art and modernism, although their own ideas and texts were sometimes as impenetrable. Keys eventually moved to Ireland and made a life as a painter. Another interesting student for Auerbach was Raymond Atkins who went on to make large, rugged scenes of Cornish quarries and scrapyards, working in the open air.[33]

In an article published in 1959, Auerbach detailed something of what he could hand on without suggesting there were shortcuts and secure ways of moving forward. For him, the impulse to paint begins with an extreme situation: 'One's got to make a new problem, to make it one's own – the identity is new, that is one of the points about it. All important discoveries are made in the course of autobiographies.' He insisted original painting has to be relevant to the moment and that reworking brings unforeseen solutions: 'One tries to do what one can't do – painting is a very specific thing, even the painting I've done in the past is impossible to do. In the act of trying – the new look – it sometimes happens by opposites ... bright colours suddenly look brittle, so one tries to push it further – strongly divided in black and white ... suddenly turned the brown to yellow ... destroy it, and so on. But it happens in specific ways – by a hair's breadth (these are windy running words), but I think one should never *try* to do anything new. Big words – all they can do is stir one's conscience.' Painting is an artificial activity, which he later compares to scientific experimentation, then finishing this passage by reminding himself and others that, 'Without discipline, rigours, rules, the discovery wouldn't mean anything at all'.[34]

Teaching naturally offered contact with other up-and-coming artists working in various idioms. In 1958, Auerbach took on a part-time job at Camberwell where Robert Medley ran the painting department. There he made lifelong friends with the painter R. B. Kitaj and the art historian Michael Podro. Two other artists, Euan Uglow and Patrick Symons, who also taught on Wednesday evenings, went with Frank after class to various well-known restaurants, such as Overton's opposite Victoria station, or Rules in Covent Garden, or sometimes to cheap cafés. Many of the students were inclined to attempt William Coldstream's 'objective drawing' procedures as if it were a safe idiom, but without really looking at the forms. Auerbach pushed them to look longer and harder and to try to make a form that encapsulated their own experience.[35] George Rowlett, who had come down from Grimsby School of Art, is known today for his landscapes done in the open air. Many of his locations are around his home in Rotherhithe near the Thames; working with spatula and fingers, the facture of his paintings brings back the light and chaos of the scene. John Kiki and Tom Phillips were two other interesting Camberwell students who have stayed in touch.

In 1961, Auerbach suggested to Coldstream that he might have something to offer the students at the Slade and was invited to address the sketch club; in October 1963, he took up a part-time post, a day a week in charge of a life-room and tutor to around eighteen students (this continued until June 1968 when he felt able to survive without this income). Several members of the painting staff and visiting tutors at the Slade in the mid-1960s worked from concrete subjects, among them Michael Andrews, Patrick George, Euan Uglow and Jeffrey Camp, but there were also artists with opposite positions. For example, Harold Cohen pursued a cerebral abstraction and after moving to California in 1968 invented AARON, a computer program designed to produce art autonomously.

Approaching a student, Auerbach would ask, 'Do you want me to talk with you or do you want to be left alone?' Only Matthew Spender, attending a life-drawing class, replied 'Yes, I do want to be left alone.' In subsequent years Auerbach kept in touch, mainly by letter, with several former students from the Slade and other colleges, among them Mike Knowles, Peter Prendergast, John Wonnacott, Christopher Stein, Ray Atkins, Christopher Couch and John Virtue.[36] Auerbach associates each with their strong points; Peter Saunders, for example, was admired for the real subjects he found, like the tea dancers in Covent Garden and South Bank skateboarders.

John Wonnacott describes Auerbach coming into the Slade life-room armed with catalogues and books. Paradoxically, 'part of the importance of Frank's teaching was that he not only opened our eyes to the rich complexity of the visual world, but at the same time convinced us that the intrinsic value of the images he most admired had little to do with their historical or cultural provenance.'[37] There was no need to feel under an obligation to be avant-garde, nor to revere artists, although the great painters such as Rembrandt and Velázquez set standards. Auerbach would say something along the following lines to the students, as given in a 1971 interview: 'You have the greatest painting in the world in a room and look around you ... at the chairs, the tables, and the people moving about ... in some way they always seem more alive, more exciting, more extraordinary and more odd than the picture – than the greatest painting in the world – *Las Meninas* or a great Rembrandt or a great Matisse, or anything. There would be no motive for painting if the painting did not somehow conquer the existing world. So one tries to catch hold of the world of fact and experience at some point at which it hasn't been caught hold of before, so that one remakes it in a sense which speaks to oneself directly – so that every mark, proportion and weight in some way conforms to one's deepest desires without betraying it's essence or identity – so that the stress of the real world and the stress on the newness of the painting are really a stress on the same thing ... not the sort of painting which simply evolves from painting which already exists.'[38]

The exceptionally open atmosphere at the Slade emanated from Coldstream, an artist Auerbach regards as one of the most remarkable

English painters of the last century (L. S. Lowry, Gwen John and William Nicholson are other slightly unfashionable artists whom he rates). Coldstream's tense, careful, delicate, underrated work emerged from the man's strong response to his subjects. As Frank remembers it, Coldstream drank half a bottle of whisky daily, the first shot to calm his nerves, and meanwhile managed to handle the Slade administration with a singular clarity. Auerbach was exempted from going to meetings.

Sometimes conversations that he and 'Bill' Coldstream shared come to Frank's mind. One day in the autumn of 1966, when they were having lunch in the University College refectory, they both expressed their admiration for Marcel Duchamp. An extensive selection of Duchamp's works had been shown a few months earlier at the Tate, culminating in *The Large Glass*, which Richard Hamilton had re-made for the occasion. Auerbach then and now regards the idea of the readymade and the actual objects and drawings Duchamp selected and created as 'so exquisite and specific'. Frank said to Coldstream that having ideas might for him function like beginning a painting with pictorial scaffolding; when the 'house' is built, you can take it down. The sculptor Reg Butler passed by and overheard the name Duchamp. As Auerbach remembers, Butler interjected, '"Charlatan was a great man," and bounced out. After he left, bemused, Bill said, "Reg always has a good reason for what he does. In winter, because his life takes place in dark enclosed spaces, he sculpts metal boxes – one cannot look into them, but he says that they contain secret objects [pause] ... his seems a democratic art ... I think I could make quite a good box!"' Implicit in such memories of conversations with artists is Auerbach's horror of art becoming democratic, therapeutic or indeed respectable; to him, art should be 'distrusted by all sensible orthodoxies and moralities for who knows where it will lead?'[39]

A famous cousin and some family history

It has never been easy for Auerbach to shake off interest in his life story, but his determination is no doubt linked to a parallel refusal to be obliged by domestic commitments, property or anything that represents distraction from painting. The basic nature of the Mornington Crescent studio is consistent in a paradoxical way with his manner of dealing with the Auerbach relations in the years when he was becoming recognized and some were putting down roots in London. 'I don't keep anything. It may be due to my background. I absolutely believe that you keep forging on, forwards, and that if you look back you turn into a pillar of salt.'[40]

For a start, Frank reminds us these family members were encountered afresh. 'I didn't see for many years anybody I'd seen before so it was like being picked up and transported into a different world and if there are no attachments, if there are no associations, then one doesn't remember.'[41] Nevertheless contact began in the late 1940s and, as it happened, by the mid-1960s one of his older cousins, Marcel Reich-Ranicki (1920–2013), was becoming well known. His fame rose after 1973 as a controversial literary critic writing for the *Frankfurter Allgemeine Zeitung* and as a regular broadcaster on radio. His autobiography, *Mein Leben* (1999), number one on the German bestseller list for fifty-three weeks, deals with family history in a minimal amount of space, but it is telling, and as Marcel describes the Auerbach family, one gets a sense of sophisticated, assimilated Jewish professionals attuned to the arts and literature.

Marcel's mother, Helene, an older sister of Frank's father, Max, was one of seven children of Rabbi Mannheim Auerbach, who died in 1937 at the age of 88. She married David Reich, a Polish businessman with an affinity for music, who brought her to the city of Poznan where their three children were born, Gerda in 1907, Herbert in 1911 and Marcel in 1920. When Reich went bankrupt in 1929, the family was obliged to move to Berlin to live with Rabbi Mannheim, by then a widower, and to seek help from Uncle Jakob, the lawyer whose partner arranged for Frank to be sponsored by Iris Origo and sent to England. He was 'a sought-after, almost a prominent, attorney and notary, and proud of his very remarkable success. His brothers, too, were well off, living in an affluent style, but he alone was anxious to demonstrate his social rise.' Jakob owned horses: 'Every morning he would go riding with his wife in the nearby Tiergarten, as was the done thing. The neighbourhood in which he had settled was, at least in his opinion, aristocratic.'[42] Reich-Ranicki focuses on the music room in Uncle Jakob's spacious apartment: 'On a wall in this room, among many other paintings, there was a picture of a woman in oriental attire lying on the floor. She was gazing, longingly and challengingly, at the face of a man whose head lay on a silver salver. Later my girl cousin informed me, not without pride: "That's Mama as Salome." Aunt Elsie had been an actress in her native Cologne.'[43]

Uncle Leo, the youngest brother of Frank's father, was 'a handsome, elegant man, in the opinion of some of the family a little too elegant and something of a show-off. He was an attorney with an office on Unter den Linden, which the family regarded as inappropriate, as a sign of his hubris. He had broken the mould in two respects. He had a weakness for horse-racing and his bets occasionally landed him in serious financial trouble.' A lawyer for casino owners, Leo escaped Germany for France before joining the Foreign Legion (where he was put in charge of the library). When he returned to Paris after 1944, his future wife, Ingrid, who claimed to be from the celebrated aristocratic Richthofen family, 'had had her head shaved and possessed jewelry', gifts from German soldiers. In his twenties Frank remembered seeing Uncle Leo a few times at birthday dinners for Uncle Jakob, who arrived in London in 1948. At one occasion at Kettner's in Soho, Ingrid dropped a knife and as Frank bent to pick it up, she said, 'Don't bother; it's the waiter's job'. In the 1950s, Leo settled in Frankfurt and continued gambling. Another of Max Auerbach's sisters married a Polish dentist and they lived in Washington. Their son served in the US army and had come to see Frank twice during the war, bringing with him American newspapers with enticing comic strips and a book of Karl Shapiro's poems.

Marcel's account of his early years includes two references to Frank and his parents. Uncle Max is identified as a 'cheerful patent agent'. On the morning of 28 February 1933, Marcel remembers a telephone call: 'He had an irresistible urge to give us some sensational news. It was not "The Reichstag is on fire", but "The Nazis have set fire to the Reichstag."' Uncle Max 'never ceased to believe that the Third Reich would shortly collapse.'[44]

As a teenager Marcel enrolled in the Fichte-Gymnasium in Berlin-Wilmersdorf in 1935, by which time he was already obsessed by the theatre and by literature, and he was very pleased his uncle Max owned books by the most exciting banned authors. 'I often had an opportunity of making use of this gold-mine. My uncle had a delightful young son, then about five years old, and I was frequently needed as a babysitter. Those were wonderful evenings: I not only amused myself with countless books but was also generously recompensed.'[45]

The husband of Marcel's sister, Gerda, Gerhard, or 'Gerd', Boehm, received special praise: he was described as a not very successful export merchant, a short man and a tall story teller, a likeable person, intelligent and articulate. 'He was extremely well versed in literature, especially in the new German literature ... He loved Kurt Tucholsky ... More than once he quoted to me the ancient dictum *Primum vivere, deinde philosophari* [First live, then philosophize].'[46] Gerd instructed Marcel about communism and Soviet art, about Lenin and Trotsky. Much later Marcel learned his brother-in-law had worked in the political resistance in Germany in the 1930s.

The Boehms arrived in London in the spring of 1938. Looking back, Auerbach sees the short periods he spent with the couple in the school holidays at the end of the war were in some ways 'very beneficial to me because I led this extraordinarily cloistered life at a Quaker boarding school in the country ... there were certain conventions and we seemed to be different from the rest of the world and had never quite caught up with the twentieth century ... certainly Gerda Boehm and her husband were very much the opposite of that.' Although the marriage was not a success, the experience of living in cosmopolitan Berlin in the 1930s had 'somehow imparted to Gerda a desire to dress well and cut a figure in the world, and an appetite for going out.'

Five of Marcel's Berlin cousins managed to leave Germany to attend schools in England, whereas his own family lacked the money to guarantee costs. In October 1938, the holders of foreign passports (his was Polish) were expelled, so he joined his mother in Warsaw, and in September 1942 his parents and other Jews living in the Warsaw Ghetto were ordered onto the transports to Treblinka during the *Grossaktion*. Marcel, with his hastily married girlfriend Teofila (known as Tosia), survived another six months in the ghetto before escaping, and from June 1943 until the end of the German occupation they were hidden in the house of a working-class typesetter on the outskirts of Warsaw. At night while they all rolled cigarettes to sell, Marcel entertained the poverty-stricken couple with stories from classical literature. After the war, he came to London as the Polish consul but when anti-Semitic prejudice re-emerged in Poland and he wished to turn his back on the communist world, Marcel and his wife managed to move to West Germany in 1958. Their son Andrew, educated partly in England, became a distinguished mathematician and academic, settling in Edinburgh. In the year before he died Marcel was regarded as so much part of German national life that he was invited to address the Bundestag on 27 January 2012, Holocaust Remembrance Day. At his death the German Chancellor Angela Merkel paid tribute to a lifetime dedicated to interesting a larger public in reading: 'We lose in him a peerless friend of literature, but also of freedom and democracy. I will miss this passionate and brilliant man.'

One can hardly imagine Auerbach exposing his life and feelings so explicitly as Marcel did in the autobiography, much less tolerating official attention. Several of his contemporaries accepted knighthoods and higher honours; Auerbach has avoided anything that sets him apart from other people living in London or which places him in the role of an exemplar. He reminds us that during the German occupation, Maurice de Vlaminck published articles deploring the 'foreign' influence on French art – meaning, presumably, Picasso, Chagall, Mondrian, Kandinsky, Miró, Soutine, Gris, etc. Picasso found this attitude disgusting and declared, most likely in jest, that collaborators should be executed and that in the case of Vlaminck he would be prepared to carry out the execution himself. Although the inhumanity of the Nazis and of war criminals such as Adolf Eichmann strikes Auerbach as unpardonable, he has commented that no one can be sure how the British, including painters, would have behaved if Hitler had occupied the country. He has avoided 'all that gnawing at the past'. 'I just think one plays the cards one is dealt, and that's it. I've been aware of what happened all my life, and as luck would have it I found myself in the situation of being the "innocent party". If I had not been Jewish who knows what I would have done or felt. I was also lucky to be young enough not to come with a lot of emotional baggage.'[47]

A painting that might consciously or unconsciously relate to death and religious persecution is Auerbach's version of Rembrandt's *The Lamentation over the Dead Christ* (c. 1635) in the National Gallery.[48] Rembrandt's *Lamentation* is twelve inches high and Auerbach's 1961 version is over six feet. A bleak, monochromatic picture, the structure resembles the pictures of the Shell Buildings site from 1959, which have a similarly illuminated central area. Here, in an echo of the features in the Rembrandt painting, the ruined city is in the background, and the three crosses, with the two ladders

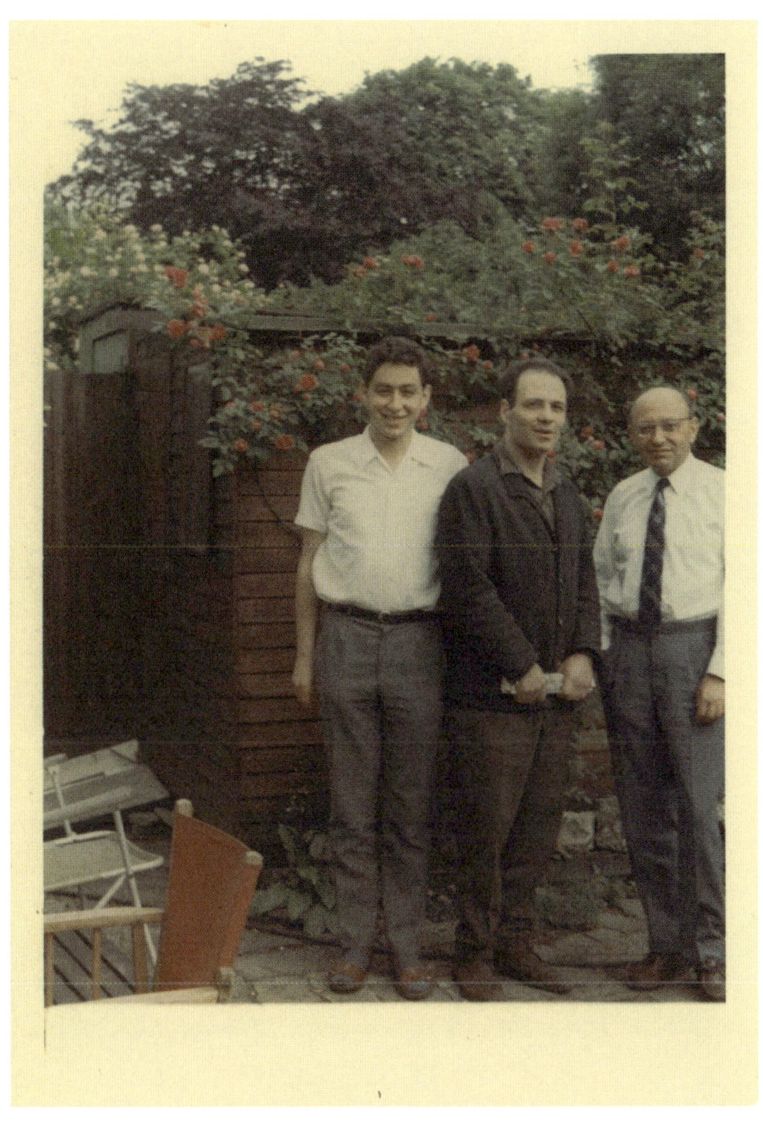

Frank (centre) with his cousin Marcel Reich-Ranicki (right) and Marcel's son
Andrew Ranicki (left) in Hampstead, 1970

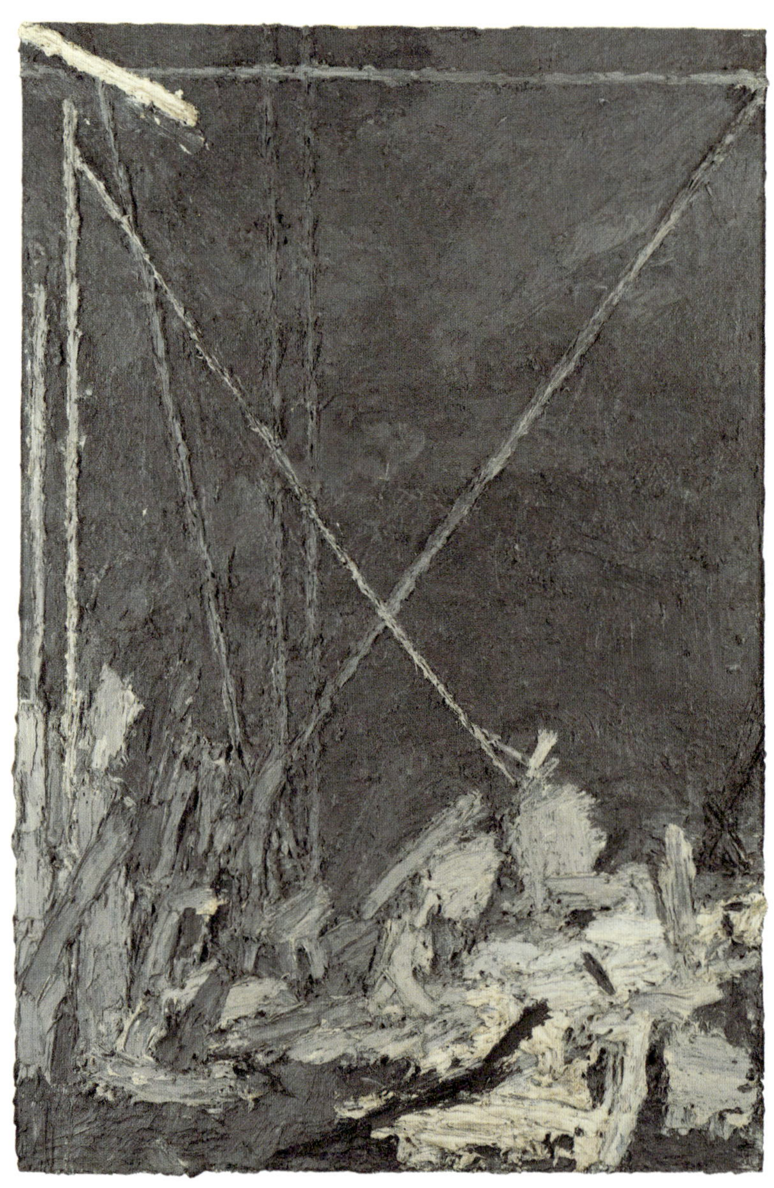

Study after Deposition by Rembrandt II, 1961

to bring down the bodies, are transposed into triangular shapes dividing the picture plane. Asked for more information in 1995, the artist replied, 'I find it as difficult to read now as anybody else would, because it was done such a long time ago.'[49] Rembrandt's small painting, on the other hand, rekindled a response: it seems to be 'so charged with feeling, with extraordinary detail of drama, with compositional invention, with sophisticated storytelling, that I couldn't possibly have dreamt of making a small version of this vast idea on a small panel ... it is just such a highly charged little picture, it's a miracle.'[50]

The curator Colin Wiggins, writing in the catalogue *Frank Auerbach and the National Gallery: Working after the Masters* suggests that the deeper meaning of Auerbach's work is conveyed in the facture: the painting is a modern statement about state murder. 'Rigid and severe, it becomes a symbol of the torture and death of Christ, who seems to be the only figure who is still recognizable. He is differentiated from the rest of the figures by being represented in a lighter tone, his face and twisted legs picked out carefully in black. The other, grieving figures sacrifice their individual identities and become fused together in one living and tragic mass.'[51]

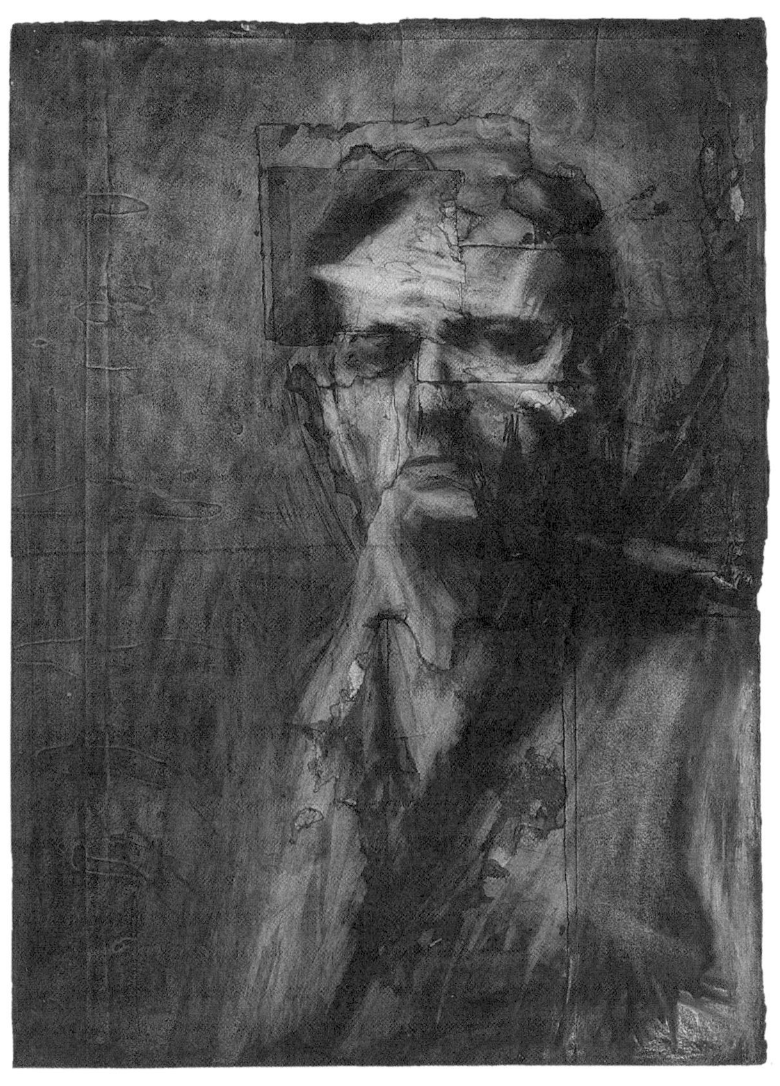

Self-Portrait, 1958

'Painting is My Form of Action'

Painting from life in the postwar years

In 1968, Andrew Forge reminded his readers that in the 1950s artists who worked 'with any vitality and independence in a figurative way' had needed to accept that they were 'swimming against the tide', and while it was difficult to define a commonality among those shown by Lessore at the Beaux Arts Gallery, he praised Auerbach, Kossoff, Andrews, Uglow and Craigie Aitchison, mentioning 'their corresponding acceptance of the ethical content of painting'. As an example, he cited 'Euan Uglow, whose timeless indifference to the dialectic of style is as radical and challenging in its way as the obsessive reiterations of a Kossoff or an Auerbach.'[1]

The dominant mode in Britain was still hidebound representation, as espoused by the majority of Royal Academicians, and an illustrative, rather thin neo-romanticism; whereas European Modernism was becoming orthodoxy in spite of such British exponents as Ben Nicholson, Barbara Hepworth and Henry Moore. William Scott shifted from making rather gritty still-life paintings of fish in frying pans to a distillation of floating shapes and open ground 'abstraction'. A slightly younger artist, Peter Lanyon, thought the polemic that distinguished representational and abstract art was misguided and, instead, attempted to capture in paint the air, movement and forms experienced moving around his native Cornwall; after 1959 looking down from the perspective of a glider. Jack Smith and Prunella Clough, who had once focused on industrial and domestic subject matter, retained their characteristic emphasis on shallow space when they went abstract, while other artists such as Gillian Ayres, Robyn Denny and John Hoyland who exhibited in the 'Situation' exhibition of 1960 claimed their work was 'without reference to the world outside the canvas'.[2]

Auerbach views such claims and labels as essentially meaningless; for him, where figurative art excels, if it is any good, is in what is abstract within the painting and the concept. The forms one engages with, and invents, will have a plastic character and individuality unconnected to their names. In his experience, work that does not 'go to the beginning where the thing is everything but art' is likely to add to 'the boredom of the world'. Implicit in an interview with John Christopher Battye in 1971 is his impatience with those who try to define polarities and identify a current mode. 'People paint hard designs, shapes and the great revolutionary spirit makes everything massive, messy, chaotic and anonymous; then the named and the labelled become the general movement and the whole thing goes on like a pendulum ... I mean if you look at Mondrian and you start off with the chrysanthemums and the landscapes and the still lifes and the self-portraits you see this extraordinarily patient and touching and dedicated process of Mondrian trying to extract from this material what it is in it which is fact and not art, and you see him arrive at these – which are not marks on canvas, but notations of a sense of space, tension and movement in the world of fact. The difference between that process and the process of somebody getting out of Swiss Cottage station and arranging a red square, a black line and a blue square on a canvas in some way that they think has to do with designing or dividing the canvas, is not the same sort of process done at a lower temperature – it is an entirely different process.'[3]

Auerbach's own development was evolving by way of very subtle changes in subject matter as well as facture. As the range of sitters became wider, he was challenged to react to each person differently; this becomes patently evident in the very austere, resonant – and large – charcoal drawings made between 1958 and 1962 where the aura of the individual, and their relationship to Frank, extends into marks outside the figure. The portrait of Lucian Freud from 1960 conveys a sense of both men dropping the guards they used in public; swift, multi-directional lines encircle this inward-looking, amazingly energetic subject, his face in shadow. The several drawings of Julia Wolstenholme, also from 1960, were as heavily worked in charcoal;

however, their simplicity suggests her beauty and wary self-effacement, her eyes downcast, the space around light and rather empty. Two self-portraits of 1958–59 and the heads of E.O.W. of the same date set the subject off-centre, and a kind of chiaroscuro made by rubbing away charcoal illuminates their foreheads, with penumbral passages beyond. The situation conveyed in the 1959 nudes in oil and charcoal of Stella lying on her back in the evening darkness of the house in Earl's Court perpetuates the air of exigency, the room sequestered so that such daring work might crystallize. In comparison, the pictures from the same period of a new model, J.Y.M., also in black and white, and identified at this point only by the pose rather than her name, present a spirited nude figure in the studio, luminous in contrast to the darker bed, stove and room. When Auerbach works in oil on paper he introduces strong black contour lines, hinting at something sculptural, as if wet, malleable pigment might be underpinned by aggressively rendered marks.

Julia Yardley Briggs Mills, called J.Y.M. (as in 'Jim') by her friends, began posing for Auerbach in 1957. They met the year he was teaching at Sidcup School of Art. During a class, quite unexpectedly, he heard her address him: 'If you'd ever like me to pose for you privately, I'd be glad to.' She posed twice a week for forty years, and as Frank remembers, 'she was able to sit for an infinite time, sometimes five hours without any break, quite extraordinary, and didn't seem to mind it.' Early on, 'she looked a very harmonious, pale figure ... There was something about the way she posed that was like those models that you get in nineteenth-century French photographs, but finally it is a sidelight. I wouldn't have been influenced by that association when I was painting, and of course, it is an organic human person and she's not playing a part and it's not made up, so what one is painting is one's reaction to this human animal.'

What Auerbach required of his model was certainly experimental and arduous. J.Y.M. resisted admitting she was suffering. Sometimes lying flat on her stomach was difficult, whereas putting her hands up while seated 'just came naturally'. The studio near Mornington Crescent was 'a very bare box, which was taken up 85 per cent by painting paraphernalia, 15 per cent by living conveniences', so many of the pictures have her sitting in front of the paraffin stove, which was the only way of heating the damp and crumbling space, and as Frank explains, when the large chair that served him for many,

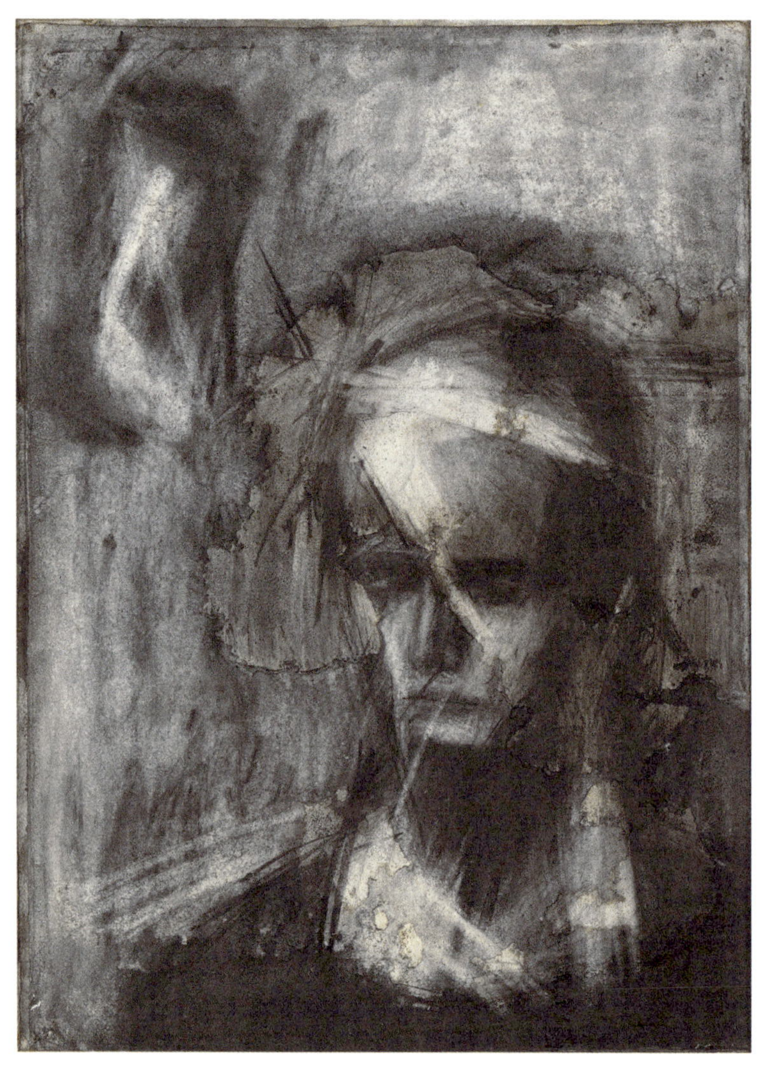

Head of Julia, 1960

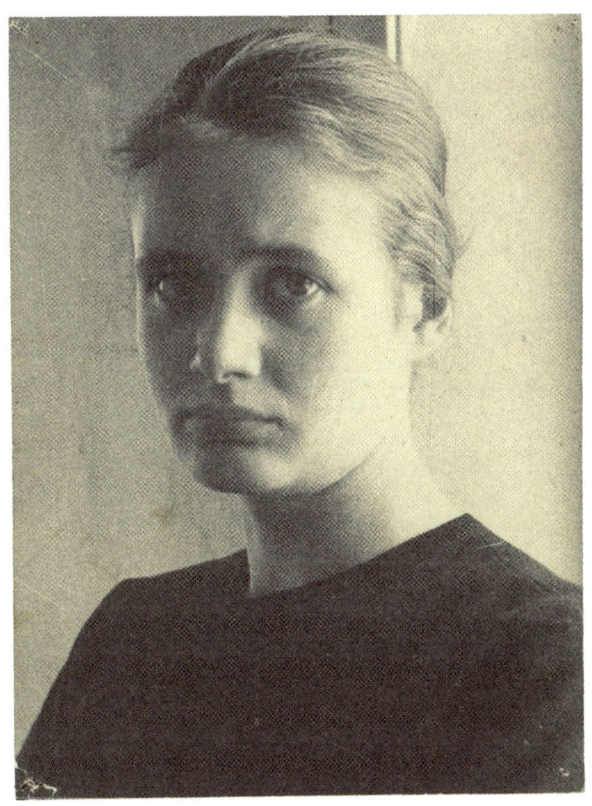

DAVID CRIPPS, Julia Auerbach, *c*. 1960

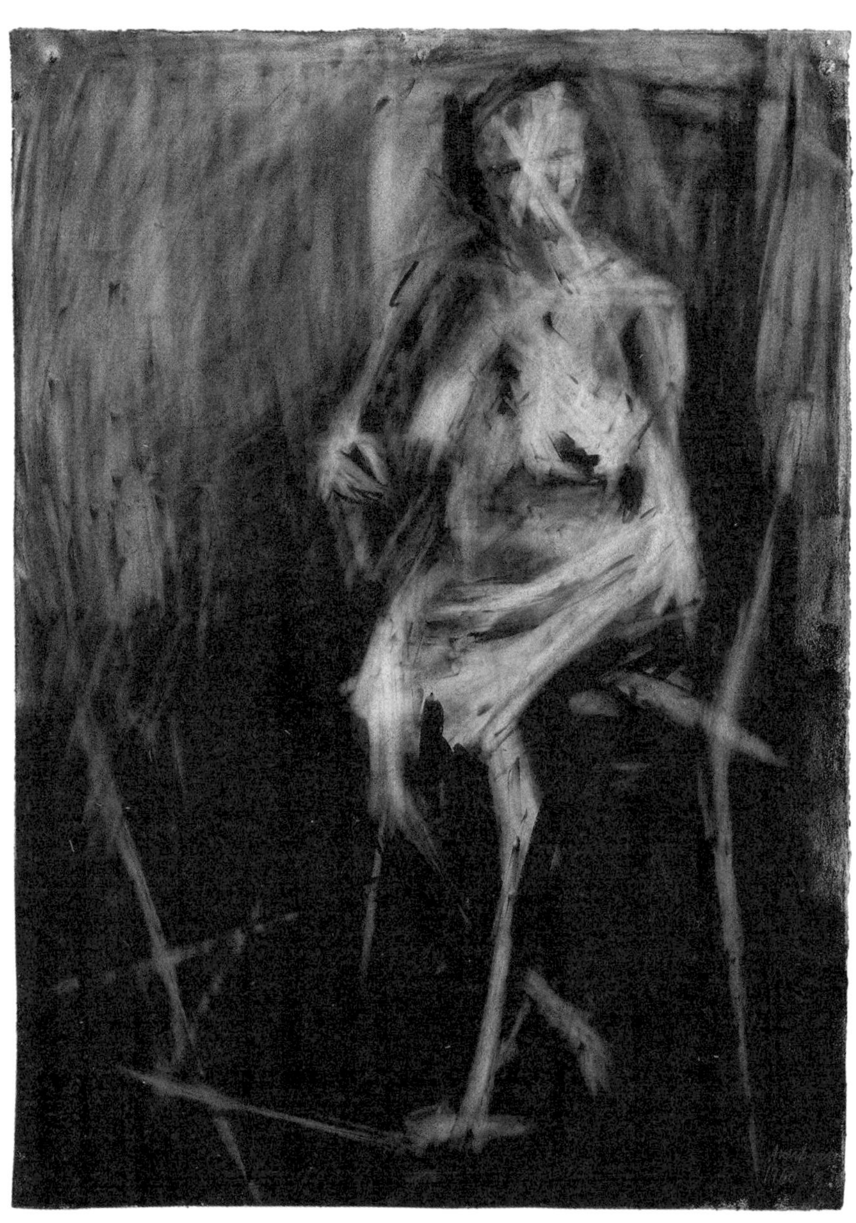

Seated Nude, 1960

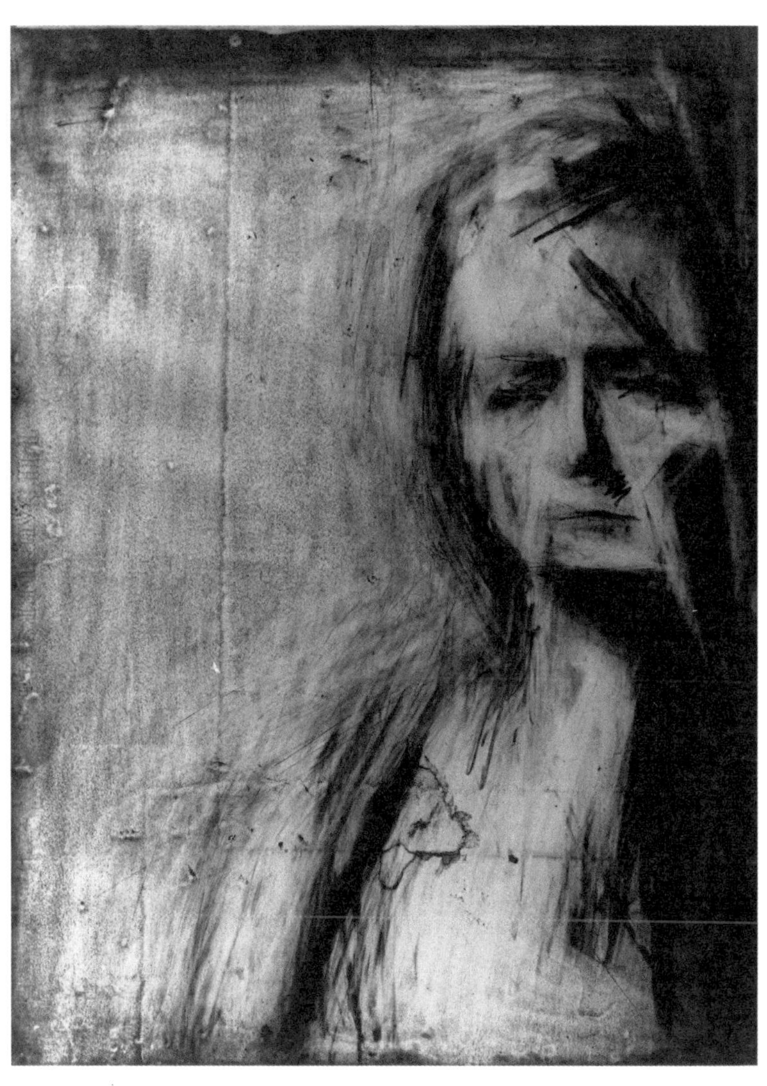

Head of E.O.W. III, 1960

many years, finally gave up the ghost, it was replicated by another, identical one (the rungs just as unforgiving). Comfort and propriety were more or less irrelevant; this was the case not just with Auerbach but also artists such as Freud, Kossoff and Uglow.[4] 'It was normal for us to sit in a small room with no means. We wanted to say something profound and precise, something sharp about truth ... an artist like Giacometti offered hope, to continue and to give everything for a truthful art without any compromises ... The image of Giacometti who created a rich *oeuvre,* inventive and refined, with modest means in a small room, was very attractive. It made a life in art seem possible; it suggested that courage and dedication were as important as luck.'[5]

In the late 1920s, Alberto Giacometti had fashioned reduced, concentrated forms to represent men and women, some virtually two-dimensional plaques – made in clay and plaster – followed by beautiful spikey, more surrealist sculptures, of which the best known are *The Palace at 4 a.m.* (1932) and *Woman with her Throat Cut* (1932). Auerbach finds such works very well conveyed in reproductions and he often looks at them. The 1946 special issue of *Cahiers d'Art* and the catalogue of a Giacometti exhibition in the spring of 1948 in New York circulated in London; they introduced a new development, the portrait busts and standing figures with elongated bodies, their profiles, surfaces and distortions realized through revision by the sculptor using his fingers as much as modelling tools. The results often seemed as if still in flux, as Auerbach's paintings began to become in the early 1960s, for each working day Giacometti was making profound changes, not just altering the outward appearance; as Sylvester reported, 'he needs to do it each time from the inside out, reliving the full process of its growth'.[6]

Working from life in bare surroundings also has an analogy to the plays by Samuel Beckett, who was just becoming known, especially for *Waiting for Godot,* first performed in London in 1955. The suggestion of rather manic, solemn characters, survivors, resonated with Auerbach and accorded not only with the life that he and many of his contemporaries lived, but also, as his sitters experience, his habit of shouting, and reciting verse and denouncing his own efforts. In contrast, those among the theatre audiences who led relatively sheltered middle-class lives were shocked by the Irish playwright and ascribed the absence of props and stage-set and the monosyllabic dialogue to a deliberately avant-garde style.

Painting parallels and new models

Another artist who made an enduring impression on Auerbach was Willem de Kooning: 'I saw black-and-white reproductions of de Kooning long before I saw them for real. When there was finally a chance to see three paintings in [the] 1956 show, it wasn't a case of revelation, I knew the paintings and only went to see how they were made, what colours they were and what size they were.' De Kooning's work appeared in the exhibition 'Modern Art in the United States' at the Tate in 1956 and again in another exhibition brought to London three years later under the auspices of the Arts Council and the Museum of Modern Art, New York. Alfred H. Barr, Jr., the director of MoMA, wrote the introduction to the catalogue of this second Tate show of contemporary paintings from America, beginning by noting the variety and asking what united the paintings. He began with size. 'They envelop the eye, they seem immanent,' and went on to remark that they displayed a flatness that was 'a consequence of the artist's concern with the actual painting process ... a concern which also tends to eliminate imitative suggestion of the forms, textures, colours and spaces of the real world', in ways that are 'never formalistic or non-objective in spirit' or solely concerned with the aesthetics or 'plastic values' of painting. 'Despite the high degree of abstraction, the painters insist that they are deeply involved with subject matter or content.' Barr traced the impetus back to American artists of the 1940s, such as Edward Hopper and Stuart Davis, and stressed that if existentialist echoes could be detected in the artists' words, it was not because they were 'politically engaged'; indeed Surrealism and Automatism were of more relevance to their art.[7] This analysis differed from the accepted idea, then and now, that American Abstract Expressionists insisted upon a 'tabula rasa' approach to the past, eliminating the need for reference to the European old and modern masters.

Abstract Expressionist paintings continued to appear in group and solo exhibitions at the ICA, Whitechapel and various private galleries and are said to have helped shift the focus of the art world from Paris to New York, but an analysis of the politics and critical impact often exaggerates the one-way influence. Auerbach's reactions accorded somewhat with Barr's. Looking back, he suggests that what artists experienced in the 1950s can be viewed from a less ordained, less nationalistic perspective: 'There's always *something* in the air, good painting always captures in a way what is around, and these Americans had gripped large and made splendid an impulse that, partly as a reaction against what had been going on – the mannered formalized painting that had preceded them – made these particular images. They did it large and they did it with conviction and they did it so that anybody could see. But, having worked in Bomberg's class, having an emphasis on being, as it were, inside the painting and that what one did was one's gesture that arose out of one's sensations, then a Kline or a Pollock, although admirable, was in no sense news.'[8]

Auerbach found he was not susceptible to the work of the slightly younger gestural painters working in New York, some of whom were his own contemporaries.[9] Moreover, American art as such was not to be emulated; the painting and drawing by Europeans outside a 'movement' (like Abstract Expressionism or the New York School), pictures by loners such as Antonin Artaud, Nicolas de Staël and Chaïm Soutine, were equally compelling. Indeed, the words de Kooning used to praise the lushness of the tangled trees and hills in Soutine's Céret landscapes sound like Auerbach speaking: 'He [Soutine] builds up a surface that looks like a material, like a substance. There's a kind of transfiguration, a certain fleshiness, in his work.'[10]

De Kooning, a Dutch immigrant to America, speaking about the now iconic work *Woman I* (1950–52) to the critic Harold Rosenberg, explained that the creature who came into existence on the canvas, with her large breasts and prominent teeth, reminded him of something from his childhood in Holland: 'It's just like she is sitting on one of those canals there in the open countryside.'[11] Elements in individual paintings and drawings from this period, although inventive and ostensibly primitive and improvised, also borrow from the art of the past: Baroque, Byzantine, Cubist. The critic Thomas Hess picked up the insouciance and hybrid nature of the 'Woman' paintings, describing one as 'a Michelangelo Sibyl who has read Moon Mullins [the comic]'.[12]

De Kooning's *Police Gazette* (1955), as the art historian John Elderfield explains, is 'a painting of a woman reading that is even more difficult to unriddle, except for a book or magazine depicted clearly at the bottom'; the clue appears when the composition is rotated 180 degrees and we can see that it began with a seated woman reading.[13] What Auerbach admired

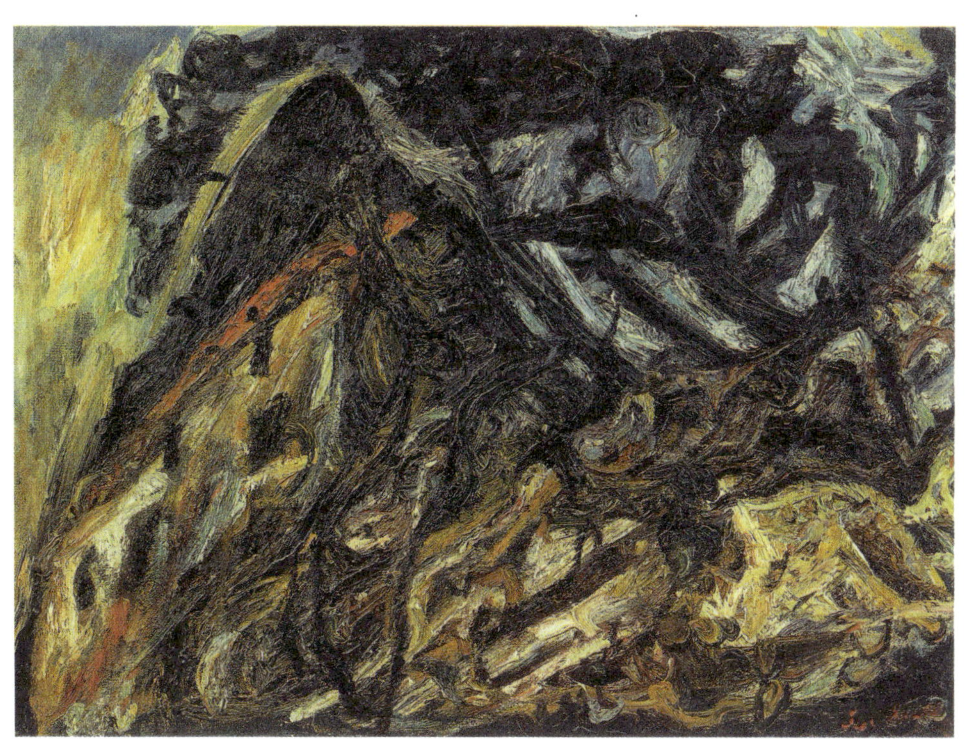

CHAÏM SOUTINE, *Landscape at Céret, c.* 1920–21

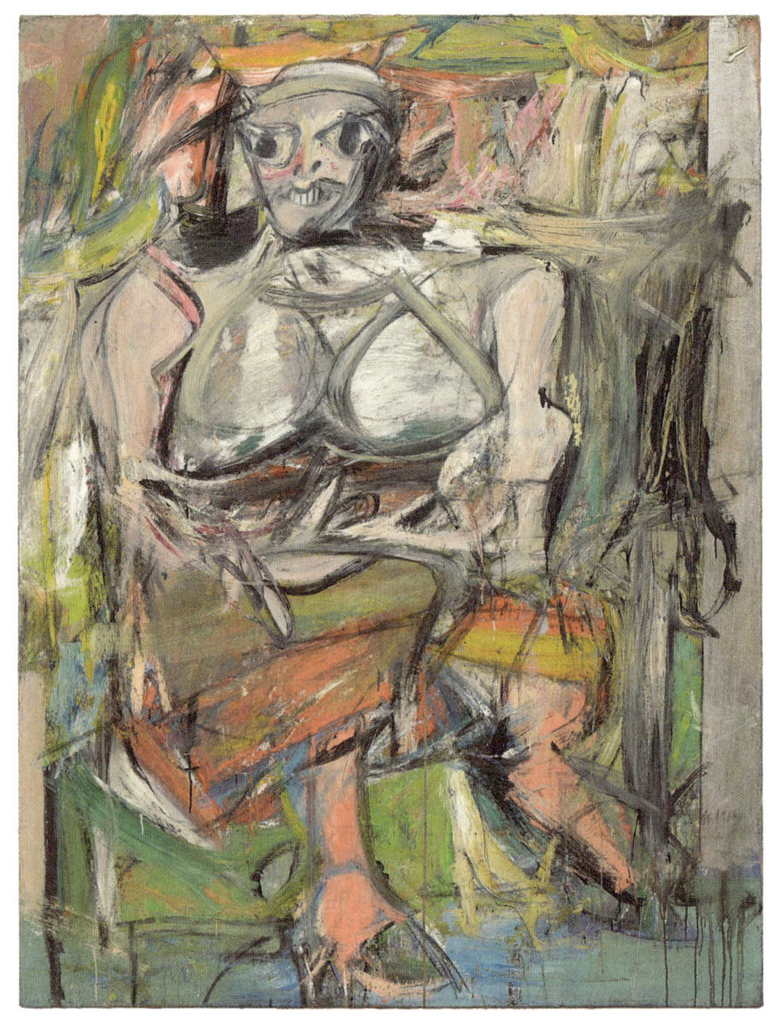

WILLEM DE KOONING, *Woman 1*, 1950–52

in de Kooning was the way each picture was a fresh undertaking; 'the point of reality is that it always contradicts one's preconceptions', thus the whole painting is like someone or some place, not one part. Both artists then and later use lively, inflected strokes that enter the interior of the body rather than simply outline contours, and leave blurry passages where they have pressed newspaper to the surface to absorb the oil. The paintings of J.Y.M. in Mornington Crescent, 1963–65, reveal in the narrow, upright nudes a voluptuous full-length figure balancing on a chair; in the landscape format, her body is an odd lump or extruded ribbon of paint laid on a plank-like bed, with additional strokes carrying anatomical facts hard to locate, and bands of colour above and below. Sometimes the shifts were led by a reaction against expectations. Auerbach had begun to feel that he might be typecast as a painter with a predictable palette. 'I simply felt that the paintings that I had done up till then in earth colours were of a particular sort that might be said to be more haptic, less linear ... I didn't want to spend the rest of my life painting as though I'd been cast in a play, for a particular role, so I wanted to stir the thing up. There is a painting in that series [*J.Y.M. in the Studio IV* (1964)] where there is a sense of this direction, the painting extending beyond the edge of the canvas and entering the room, something that somehow began to feel a bit more electric and alive and speedy than the paintings I had done up to that point, which whatever else you say about them don't look particularly speedy.'

In *Studio with Figure on Bed I* (1966) J.Y.M. lies face down. The more distant vantage point in the vertical version, *Studio with Figure on Bed II* (1966), where the figure is depicted in red paint straight from the tube, accommodates an intended inventory of the corner of the studio, with the variety of images (by Kossoff and others) above the picture rail fixed to the Masonite backboard. Auerbach does not expect viewers to discern details, but then and now, because each picture begins as a record of a genuine experience, he hopes 'that the proportions and intervals are not as banal as they would be if I had simply done something arbitrary'. A few years later, J.Y.M.'s figure is transmogrified, the soft amorphous shapes made with even more malleable paint and bright colours, followed by several puzzle-like interiors with the zigzag indication of a figure who moves from the horizon to the foreground.

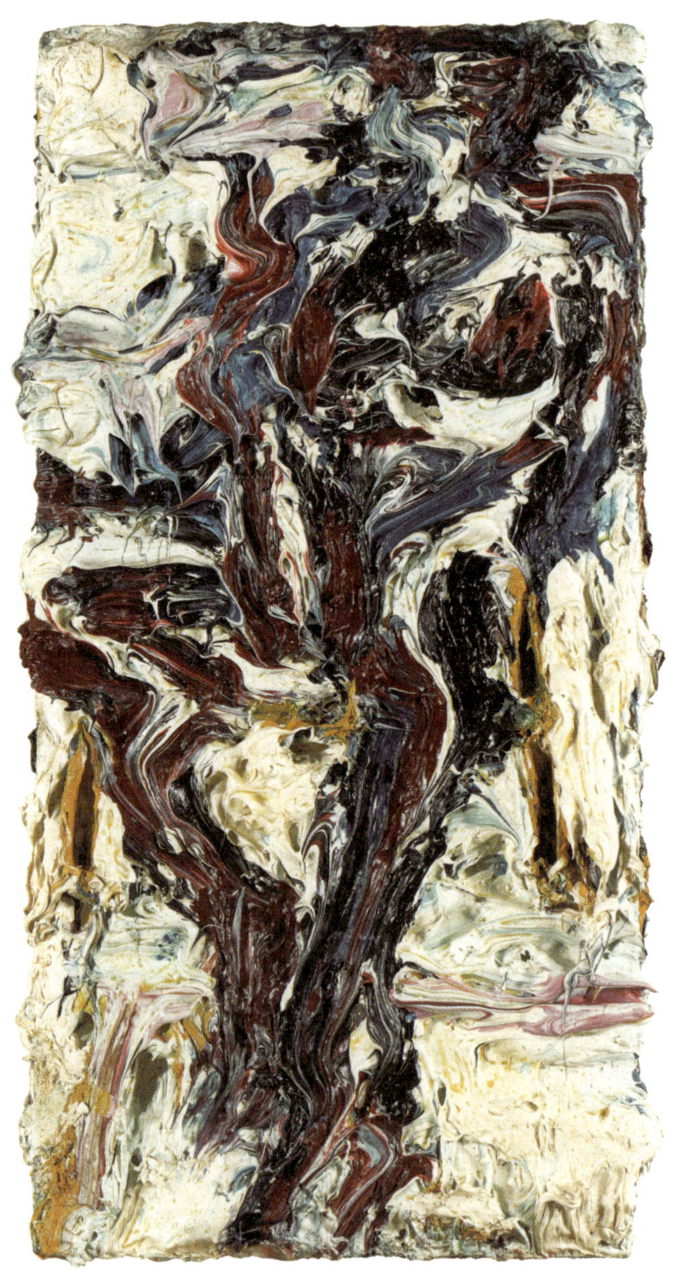

J.Y.M. in the Studio IV, 1964

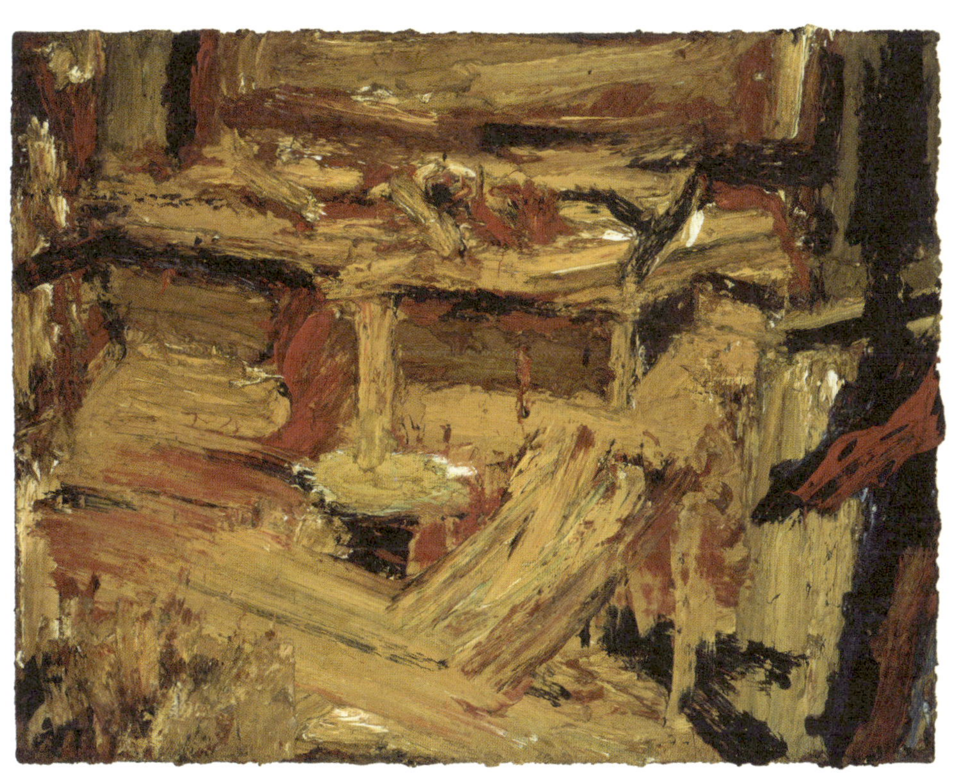

Studio with Figure on Bed I, 1966

Other new sitters encouraged this experimentation and latent pictorial violence (akin to that de Kooning indulged in). A friend of E.O.W.'s, Helen Gillespie, offered to pose for Auerbach. So far the subjects had been extremely close to the artist's life. 'In a way that I can't put my finger on, except that it may have had to do with J.Y.M.'s dedication and partly because she was a model, I felt that she was part of my intimate life. Whereas, with Helen Gillespie I began to try to paint people in the world a bit more than I had before, although as I went on for so long, the act of painting produces, at least in my mind, a sort of intimacy with the forms.' In 1961, Auerbach also asked his cousin Gerda Boehm to sit, which she did very devotedly until 1981. 'It can't have been in her character particularly and I had this head start of having seen her over the years.' Agreeing with my comment that perhaps a certain bleakness enters the works as she gets older, he explained that things 'creep' into the paintings, 'that is part of the magic of painting, in the same way that if I painted a Primrose Hill painting and it was sunny outside, or stormy outside, or misty outside, I never for a moment thought I'd paint stormy or misty but it creeps into the painting ... I think Gerda would have liked to be more useful but somehow was too timid to get into a situation with people that she wasn't related to.'

One of his favourite 'professional' models was Paula Eyles, who came to the studio for four years, beginning in 1968. 'She had children and a partner and posed for a living, and was a very nice warm woman whose life was a bit of a struggle ... looking at it [*Head of Paula Eyles* (1972)] now I think her independence has got into the painting, it looks a little bit Frans Hals-y as though she is going to go off and do something, which she often did. I remember I asked her once after she had been away for a fortnight what she had been doing and she said she'd been "snuggling with her boyfriend Dougie in a caravan".'[14]

In general, the heads of these four female sitters fill the frame, with thick lines underpinning masses of hair and the shape of the skull, and the faces introspective to the point of grimace. Robert Hughes described the heads from 1968–69 as 'grotesque, even caricatural', their graphic brusqueness and jagged black outlines unforgettable: 'These are like latter-day reflections on the sombre, grotesque heads in the human pyramid that surges up in the foreground of Goya's *Pilgrimage to San Isidro*.'[15]

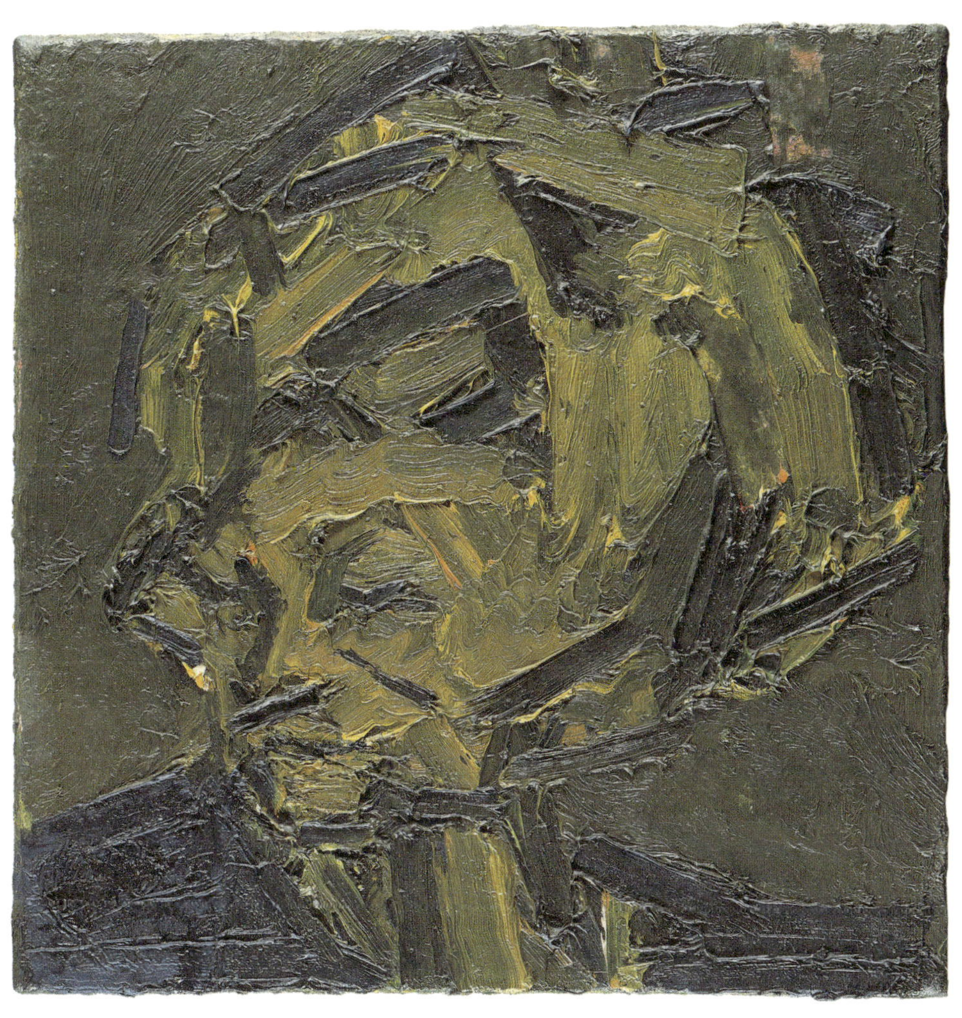

Head of Gerda Boehm, 1967

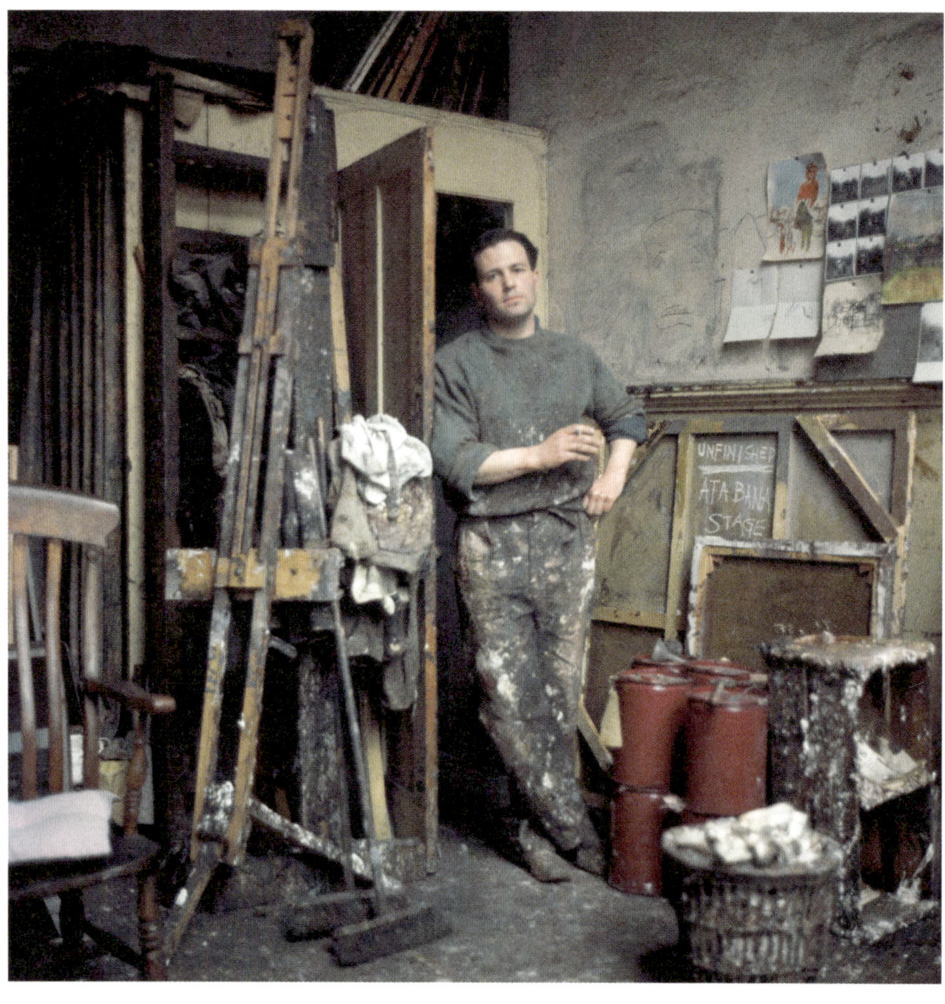

SNOWDON, Frank in the studio with canvas to the wall,
'at a banal stage', 1963

'Fragments from a conversation', 1959

As it happens there is a record of what was going through Auerbach's mind in 1959, his thoughts verbalized in just as dramatic and at times desperate bursts as those in the comparison of his heads to Goya's late work. It came in the form of four pages of conversation with the writer Elizabeth Smart, interspersed by four full-page reproductions of new work, one a sketch of *E.O.W. Nude* (1959) – the actual work (although not reproduced in colour) is radiant and intimate, allover yellow-green. The piece was commissioned by the poets David Wright and Patrick Swift, editors of the magazine *X*, for the first issue, which came out in November 1959. The line-up of contributors was impressive – writers such as George Barker, Anthony Cronin, Hugh MacDiarmid, Samuel Beckett, Patrick Kavanagh and Stevie Smith. Giacometti's evocative text, 'The Dream, the Sphinx, and the Death of T' was translated and illustrated.[16] Auerbach knew and admired Elizabeth Smart, mother of four of Barker's children, and 'Fragments from a conversation' is both a testament and a confession; by the end the reader understands that he will choose the adventure and discipline of painting over anything involving external obligations. The text began: 'Painting is a practical day-to-day thing I think. One might say something clever, one might say something big, but one does something limited. It is a serious thing – like religion – like love – one does the persistent thing, and then the really remarkable happens when something's there that wasn't there before.'

He referred to working from E.O.W. 'I've painted the same person thirty times (one's got to use small words) ... with someone one knows one's got to destroy the momentary things. At the end comes a certain improvisation. I get the courage to do the improvisation only at the end – a gaiety ... a serious word ... Miro is a gay painter.' In the following paragraphs he began to describe the tension and exaltation experienced in the studio: 'In painting one destroys everything, in life one can't do it – the day-to-day crudities destroy all the things one's used to ... known already. It's a sort of rage ... I always finish pictures in anger ... it's exacerbated conscience. One never has power over anything, can never do anything clearly or purely.'

If a picture doesn't relate to one's intimate life, then the artist will be lacking a necessary moral dimension and a sense of obligation to be faithful to what he calls 'the relevances', to a moment that cannot be repeated.

'That's why one paints the things one loves because one is aware of all the relevances maybe, it's the only way to get power over the things one loves ... that's why in the Jewish religion it's forbidden to make images ... because one worships *them* not the things they are images of. One gets suspicious of love, of religion, of everything. In the end it's impossible. In painting one can destroy it [what is on the canvas].' The implication is that formal problems are bound up with a question of conscience and of being true to oneself. He continued with a comparison to Van Gogh, and to Degas at the end of his life: 'their feelings about clouds above cornfields, aloneness, blindness ... it's all contained within their paintmarks. One can feel how it's been done if one is at all alive to anything – the moral quality's always there.'

Since everybody has only a certain amount of energy, it is essential to direct it at what really matters to each individual. 'Fragments' was published the year after Jake was born, and it is clear that being an involved parent conflicts with the single-mindedness art requires. 'Sometimes I think it weakness, madness, a disease, but it's [painting] the only creative thing anyone does except the thing women do ... it's a question of getting up in the morning ... [but] before one can say anything one's got to learn the language.' The way Auerbach recounted finishing *Summer Building Site* (1952), the painting that emerged the day he entered the Royal College of Art and regretted becoming a student again, sounded here like an epiphany. 'I could tell you the date at which I reached it, finding the image – strange and new to me. In the morning I'd been working, very, very conscientiously, painting a building site ... suddenly I was conscious of something underneath it ... this building site, I'd done it again and again, I knew it intimately ... and then there suddenly was the image underneath it ... I'd destroyed all the reminders (that is, of painting) to get a unique thing ... it began to operate by its own laws ... but it's senseless and irrelevant unless it's tied, anchored, to truth. It's a question of freeing the possibilities of improvisation which contain the mysteries.'[17]

This description relates to how he decides when a work is finished. 'It takes a great deal of courage to do a picture because every element in it has to be a response to every other element. If there's a tiny corner that isn't part of this stream of feeling, then the whole thing is gimcrack. And in order to do that one's got to be prepared to destroy everything that's nice about it.'[18]

With Auerbach's progressively destructive and revisionary way of working, the possibilities escalate and hope arises when he is 'painting quickly again and again and again', the success or failure resting on a 'hair's breadth' gesture or the sudden introduction of an atypical idea that might come after a long time trying to make a likeness and unity. By implication the artist needs to conserve energy and ambition for what happens in the studio, but this is continuously affected by external events. 'Fragments' continues: 'Then of course one always has physical needs – food – love – peace. Painting is a form of action, moral action – the bad is intolerable. I often feel it's a disease, a form of weakness that makes me turn to painting … to do something unnatural in order to … but it's also entertaining. One has energy that needs to act.' Auerbach then discusses the different idioms artists use, from 'the pernickety' of Michael Andrews and Delacroix's inclusiveness to the 'gaiety of Tintoretto, the conscientiousness of Rembrandt'. In the National Gallery he drew from their paintings and then drew from his own sketches as if they had been made by these masters. Working becomes an obsession and Frank concludes with the necessity to be single-minded: 'Painters if not committed to painting might spend their energy on other things. Painting is my form of action.'[19]

Stella West in Brentford and Wandsworth, 1961–73

In 2012, the critic Jackie Wullschlager asked Frank to focus on the 'early paintings' about to go on display at the Offer Waterman gallery and his show of new work at the Marlborough in London, and at times his comments echoed those of 1959. 'I was always aware of death because of my background. And in some curious way the practice of art and the awareness of the imminence of death are connected. Otherwise we would not find it necessary to do the work art finally does – to pin down something and take it out of time. If you take a photograph, it becomes historic five seconds later. But if you do a painting: Frans Hals's portrait of a woman – he's yanked her out of the seventeenth century and brought her here and in a small way he has defeated death.'[20] When I showed Frank reproductions of the paintings of E.O.W. on her blue eiderdown in the bedroom of her new home in Brentford, they took him back to the feelings and the circumstances: 'Again, for me, like time travel, these things unlock memories, sometimes more, sometimes less; it certainly takes me back to a time which even though it is forty-five, fifty years ago, it does that thing that painting is supposed to do, that is drag the past into the present and re-animate it. It is very intimate and it is all true, the same eiderdown that was thrown across the bed, the same Stella.'

Stella described the ten years she lived in a small villa on Somerset Road in Brentford, west London, as the best in her life. Frank explained that his procedure was like that in Earl's Court. 'I didn't have quite the freedom to muck up the rest of the house in those days. But again I would kneel, have lots of paint around me, and after we finished store the painting on the top of a cupboard or in a drawer and take it out next time I came.' These paintings where Stella's white flesh seems to float on an icy blue river of paint, the rhythms of the body gradually discernible, suggest the ambience was actually cosy. 'I have to say looking at a reproduction of the painting brings the whole situation back to me very vividly indeed. Neither of us was in any sense neat or tidy so everything was slightly improvised, in fact the bed gradually became a sort of pit that most people wouldn't have tolerated until I finally got a new one ... it seemed an imposition to put an easel in the room, and also there was a basin in the corner to wash in the morning, there was a cupboard for clothes, there was a chest of drawers, and a tiny floor space, and it just seemed the only practical way to work in there. I never found it irksome to work in a crowded small room, to paint or be on my knees unable to get too far away from it, because finally, I think, all that thing of unity is in one's head as much as it is by looking.'

At first Auerbach was resistant to the long journey to the outskirts of London. 'I'm not coming to that bloody little rabbit-warren,' he protested. However, he adjusted, arrived the same evenings each week, and the intense, frequently painful, but creatively productive relationship continued. Although the children had started attending Christ's Hospital (a charity boarding school accepting pupils of all backgrounds) a few years before, they returned home for holidays. Four unusual large compositions made soon after the move describe the house, garden and three of its occupants. Two are of Stella and her daughters standing in their rather abandoned garden, Julia holding a cat and Sarah a guinea pig. A preparatory watercolour, with Stella wearing a red sweater, eight photographs of the garden and what

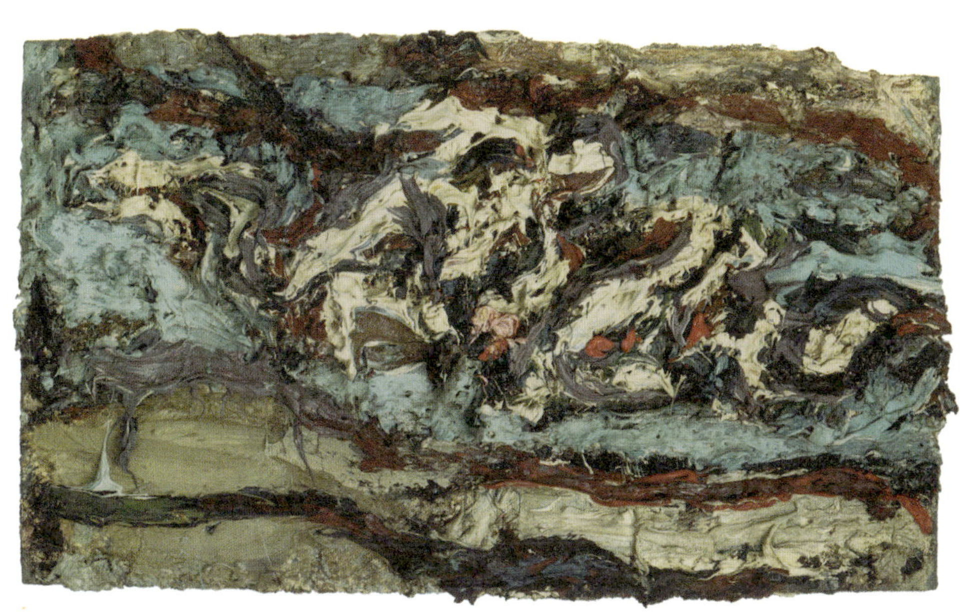

E.O.W. on her Blue Eiderdown, 1962–64

appears to be a Poloroid (Frank owned this camera) are pinned to the wall in one of Snowdon's carefully composed photographs of the Mornington Crescent studio taken in 1963 (see p. 102). Several pencil and pen sketches reference the greenhouse and trellis standing at the back, features reasonably easy to decipher in the first painting (see p. 111), but transformed into straight edges set against organic curves in the second. The *Spectator* critic, Nevile Wallis, a great champion of Courbet and of realist painting, was somewhat surprised by seeing a painting of figures in a garden (the first version was hung in the artist's exhibition at the Beaux Arts in 1963). He wrote of 'Auerbach's incursion into Michael Andrews's territory with a brooding group in a garden, oppressed with a sense of some obscure menace. A unity of vision pervades all these manifestations', nevertheless, the inflection suggesting he caught the difference between this and Andrews's more descriptive *The Family in the Garden I* (1960–62).[21]

The other unusual subject was set indoors, Stella's sitting room. Drawings were begun at Christmas 1963; mistletoe is hanging (see p. 112). Again, the first of two paintings, *The Sitting Room* (1964), now in the Tate, is more readable. Stella appears in profile to the left, leaning forward in her chair, her 'red' hair swept back, while across the room, in the other chair, sits Julia. On the mantelpiece above Stella's head is a sculpted plaster head made by an amateur artist and on the wall a painting in a square frame, one of Auerbach's portraits of E.O.W. To the right is a black-and-white photograph of Dr West. The square format is divided by a tall standard lamp with a scalloped shade, and evening light comes through the doorway leading to the conservatory. When this painting was shown at the Marlborough in 1965 the Tate lecturer Lawrence H. Bradshaw understood how the material facts had been digested: 'the forms are experienced rather than exhaustively explained. There is a depth and atmosphere. The room, as D. H. Lawrence would say, has a soul.'[22]

In *The Sitting Room* (1964–65), the viewpoint shifts to the other side of the room, Stella's daughter Sarah occupies the low chair where her mother was in the earlier picture and Stella stands. It is possible to discern a bookcase, an open book on the arm of the chair, a radio to the right of the fireplace and a three-tiered table. Fifty years later Stella's two daughters identify marks that might be pottery objects in the room, a foot made by a friend and Sarah's black glazed horse. The white outlines of the chairs, lamp and two figures project forward against a harmony of brown planes.

Frank protests that locating and naming features is not the point.[23] 'It was deeply autobiographical. I knew that sitting room very well – the lampshade, and the Christmas cards are up and the picture above the mantelpiece. Those pictures of the sitting room and of three people in a garden were records of a house in Brentford now no longer inhabited by those people. But the only thing is that to make that a true record, it has in some way to be digested and be turned into the artist's gesture ... *The Sitting Room* was a record, a record in the way that certain late Vuillards are, but clumsier. He seems to me to be vastly underrated. I admire his sort of morbid inventory-taking; it seems to me to be a very particular and special quality seen in certain late pictures like that of the dentist [Louis Viau].'[24]

In the same 1978 conversation where Vuillard is cited, Auerbach made a comparison to another interior scene. 'About four or five months ago, I was drawing Picasso's *Three Dancers* in the Tate Gallery, and I was surprised to find how much actual information about the railings on the balcony outside the window, about the window-frames, about hands, there was in that painting, and Picasso's one of the most inventive artists and yet it's full of fact, of information. He's said many things brilliantly; he said "we painters make our pictures in the way that princes made their children – with dairy-maids." He meant these facts, with these facts that we knock against, that when we wake up in the morning, whatever we feel like, and whatever we hope for and whatever we're dreaming of and whatever fancy ideas we have about the curvature of time, these facts, the solid floor beneath our feet and then, these things on the table – that's the stuff of painters. This recalcitrant, inescapable thereness of what I call everyday objects, which to people with an imagination seem about the most amazing thing.'[25]

The longer one looks at pictures of E.O.W. made in the years 1963–65, the stronger the sense of her magnetism and her essence. In several paintings her head is laced with garlands of red paint, dark blue and black marks defining actual recesses for eyes, nostrils and mouth. All were done by electric light, in the evening, and Auerbach acknowledges that this affected the slightly harsh clash between these primary colours and white. 'You've got a head in front of you ... it seems if you made the right marks, you could put

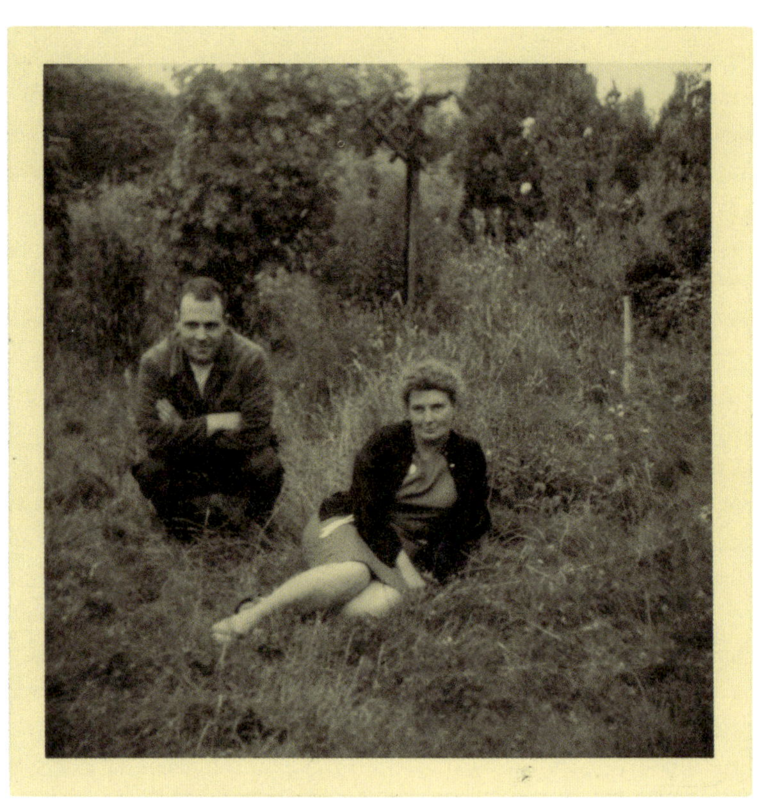

Frank and Stella in the garden of 33 Somerset Road, Brentford, *c.* 1962

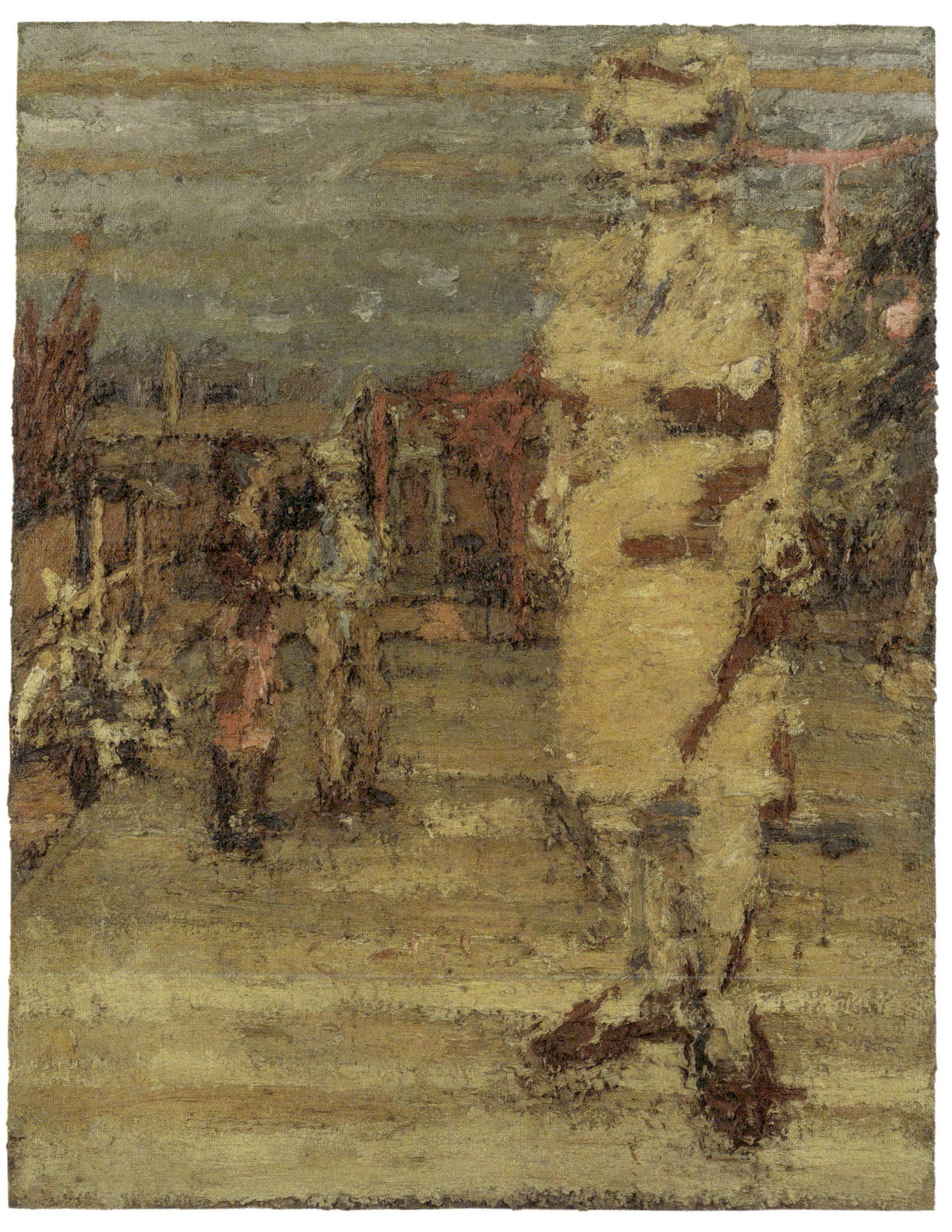

E.O.W., S.A.W. and J.J.W. in the Garden I, 1963

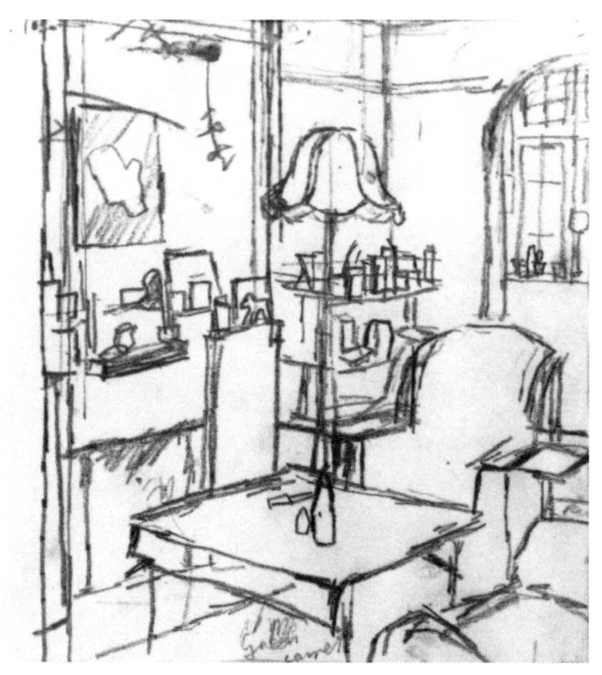

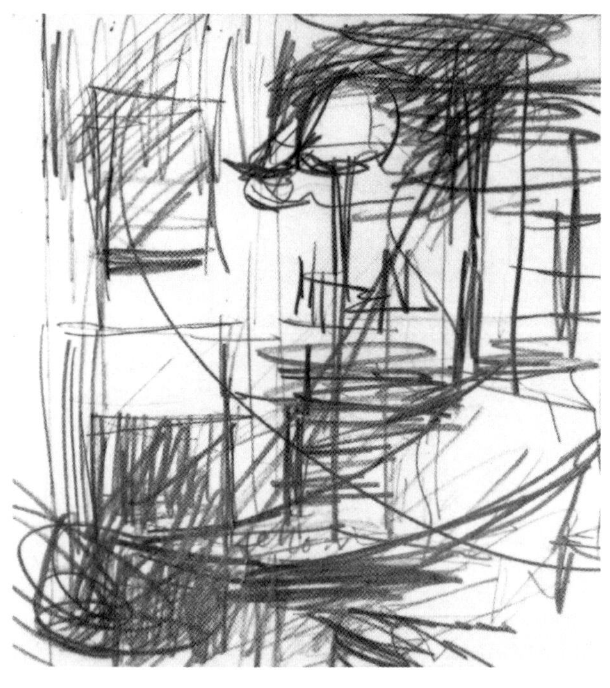

Two studies for *The Sitting Room*, 1964

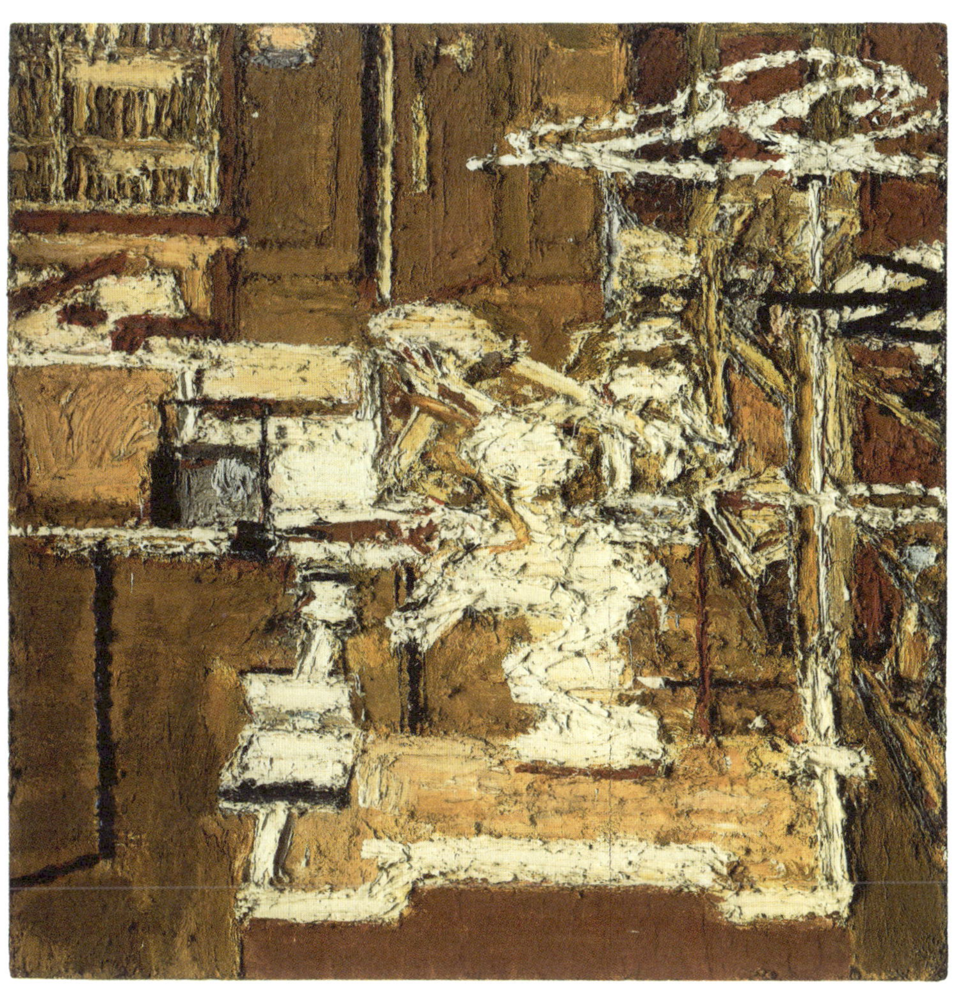

The Sitting Room, 1964–65

it down in twenty minutes, but you try for, you know, two hundred hours, a hundred sittings and it doesn't come right. Now I think I would scrape it off, 300 or 400 times. Then I was less sure of what my methods were; I left some bits on because they seemed to me to be quite good ... I added something and the picture somehow accrued to that sort of thickness. It wasn't that I hoped that my pictures would bear a particular aspect of the world, but that the look of them was the result of the conditions of their creation. And I wouldn't reject anything that seemed shocking or extreme, but on the contrary, I would value it, but I wouldn't do it for its own sake.'[26] On the single day Auerbach took his annual 'holiday', he and Stella amused themselves on the pier at Brighton. She was not someone to go to galleries although she liked to visit the Tate to see the painting by Stanley Spencer of people getting out of the grave. Very occasionally, Frank's friend Lucian Freud would come out to Brentford on Saturday for Stella's roast beef or steak and kidney pie. As for the couple's relationship, she was sanguine. Frank was adored, but as she observed later, as she approached fifty the age gap seemed larger: 'I knew in my bones that it had to end sometime.' Their obsession is not something that can be recounted or probed; Auerbach says this much: 'The truth is that some successful relationships are posited on the fact that both people behave as badly as they are capable of and it deepens the relationship.' He was determined and as Stella admitted, 'I was very theatrical'.[27]

Around 1971 Stella moved closer to central London, settling into another tall house, this time on Elsynge Road in Wandsworth, where her daughters, now adults, could have flats and she the top floor. It was again her bedroom where she posed, the picture balanced on a kitchen chair, and as expected, 'everything got covered in paint, stalactites coming down, the fireplace looked like nothing on earth because he'd flick the paint into it'.[28]

Seven paintings of *E.O.W.* made in the period 1971–72 are primarily blue, white and black (the last head dated 1973 is red and yellow). I asked Frank about one of the nearly monochrome pictures, a small head in profile, where the nose and the back of the head push against the edges of the board. 'Perhaps in some way I wanted a more austere language. I'm just not self-analytical at all, but it may be that in order to concentrate, looking at the paintings, it seems to me that one could say so, although if I were a curator

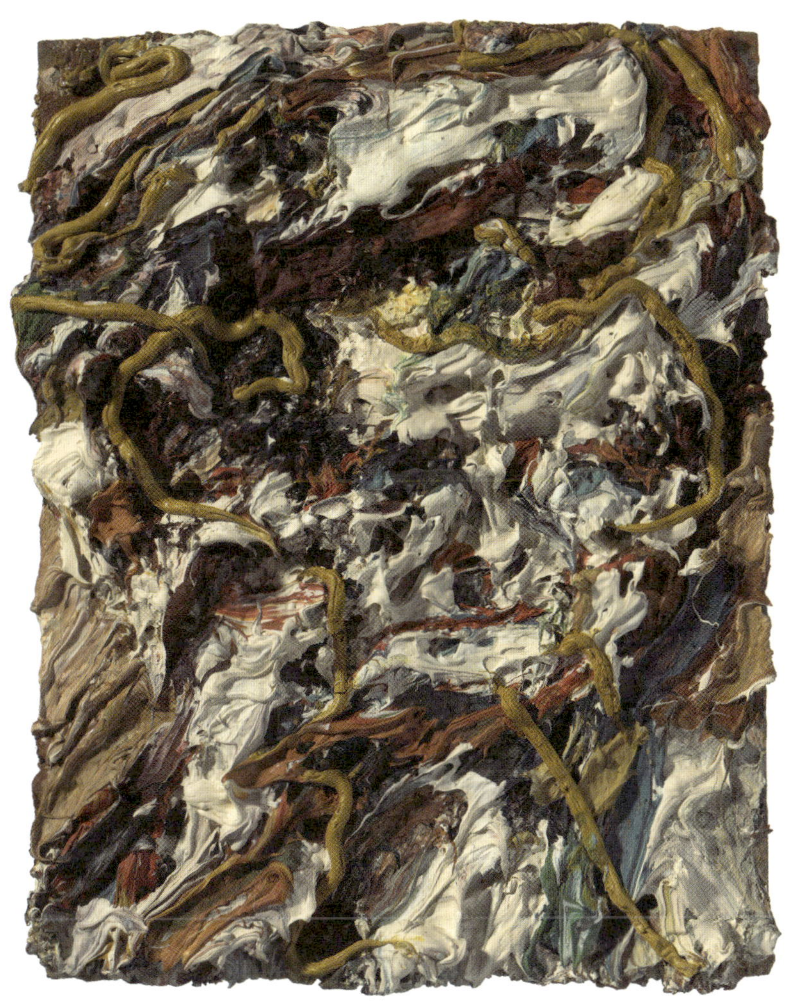

Head of E.O.W. II, 1964

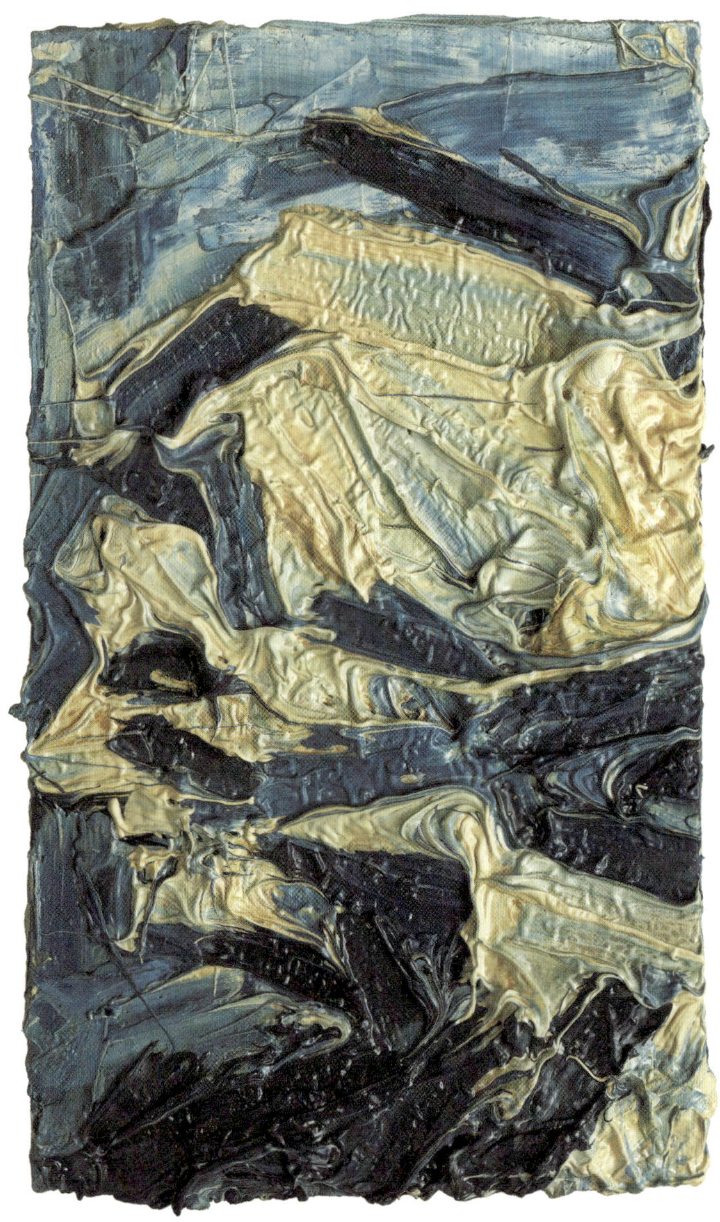

Head of E.O.W., 1972

or art historian I wouldn't have the cheek: "but a more dynamic way of drawing was searched for by Mr Auerbach and therefore he used a more restricted palette so he could concentrate on that."'

In March 1973, Stella bought a ticket to Milan to accompany Auerbach to the opening of his show at the Galleria Bergamini. Then, owing to delays in customs, the exhibition was postponed to October. During July their relationship broke down. Auerbach had met someone else so joining him in Milan was off. Reacting with anger (throwing a vodka bottle), Stella insisted that they cease talking and she posing, feeling the 'heartbreak'. After quite a while, they met as friends, began to speak every week on the telephone, and Frank has kept up with her children.[29] Years later, Stella met a man wearing earrings and chains at a local photography show who recognized her as the artist's celebrated muse. He exclaimed, 'Ah, you are the beautiful E.O.W.' But the vanity of posing for a famous artist, the immortality, was never a motivation for Stella's sacrifices, it was just part of being with the person she loved: 'Nothing stood in his way.'[30]

In her 1986 conversation with Robert Hughes, Stella remembered that Frank talked about his mother and father once or twice, as he got older. 'His mother was Lithuanian, of course, and she was I gather not a warm mother, rather distant. His father was a lot warmer; he used to give Frank strawberries and cream, things like that. But I've seen photographs of her, and she looks rather beautiful. A sort of image comes to me – they used to go to the Baltic for holidays, and he described to me how, as a boy playing in the sand, he would see his mother a long way off, sitting on the rocks; and men were looking at her.' Stella visualized 'the image of a little boy whose mother wasn't cuddly at all'. Hughes observed, 'He was lucky to find you.' To which Stella responded, 'Well, no one could say I wasn't cuddly. Too much so.'

Hughes continued, 'You rarely see such a combination of surface modesty and extreme internal pride.' Stella, 'Yes, you've hit the nail on the head there. Frank's got the pride of Satan. Most people think he's very unassuming and modest, and humble. They are completely wrong. But he can be tremendously kind to some people who really don't matter to him at all.' Hughes speculated, 'But he doesn't suffer from jealousy over his career?' Stella replied, 'No, I don't think so though he can be fairly waspish – though usually about writers rather than other painters.'[31]

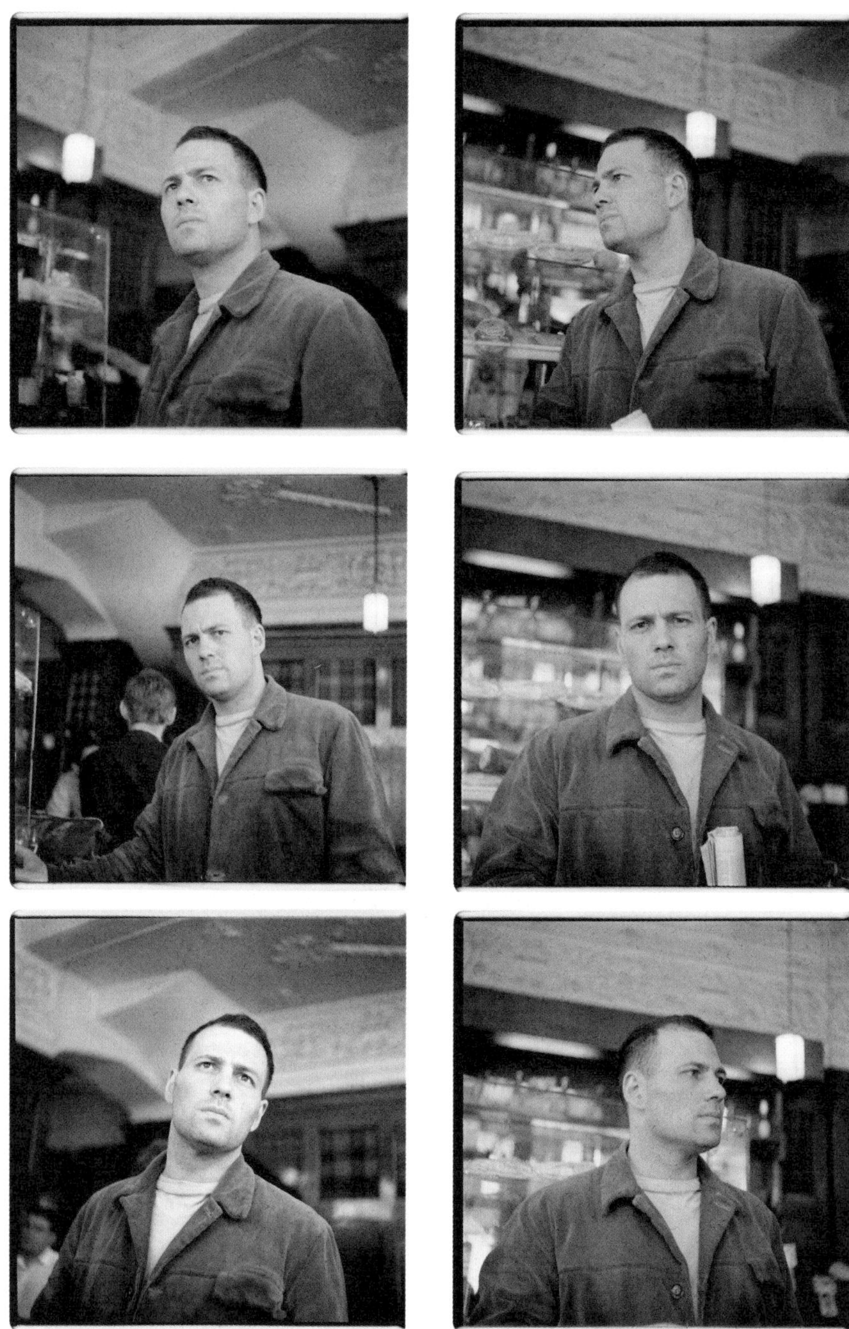

JOHN DEAKIN, Frank in the Golden Lion pub, Dean Street, London, *c.* 1962

The Best Game

'Quick-witted companions', 1956–86

In the early 1960s in the Golden Lion in Soho, John Deakin, the man who became famous for his photographs made at Francis Bacon's behest, asked Auerbach to point the camera at him, and presumably the same day shot some pictures of Frank. A more famous Deakin portrait from a few years earlier has the painter standing in front of a wall, a cigarette in his mouth. Handsome certainly, but on both occasions Auerbach hardly seems relaxed. This was not a golden age of bohemian life; the artists and writers were on edge, artistically, materially and in their private lives. 'It occasionally comes to haunt me, the bad behaviour of my youth. I think, how the bloody hell could I possibly have behaved like that? ... But if one didn't behave badly then perhaps one wouldn't behave at all.'[1]

Apart from the Golden Lion there were various drinking places that are now legendary: 'We drank at the Pillars of Hercules when I was at St Martin's, which was just around the corner on Greek Street. That was the base of Ian Hamilton, a very interesting poet, a stringent editor, but I never spoke to him. And at the Royal College when we went out drinking, Soho came into it. The Mandrake Club, the Caves de France, the Colony Room, the French pub [the York Minster], it became part of one's life.'

'The thing is that the studio was very uncomfortable so I was only there when I was working. One had more energy in those days and I didn't have as many models as I do now. I went for what people go to pubs for, distraction and uninvolving company. One had absolutely no money, so one bought a drink, and sometimes one was able to buy somebody else a drink. Francis [Bacon], with extreme generosity, bought me masses of meals over the years, usually drowned in so much alcohol that one couldn't appreciate the food.' In these places the intense necessity to paint was forgotten, and as Auerbach explained, you could remember what happened before and after, but not during. He came across poets, among them Louis MacNeice, Dylan Thomas and George Barker. Their reputations go up and down, of course, and years later Auerbach is cheered when others appreciate those he values: 'I was rather pleased to find that Harold Pinter admired George Barker; I think Barker is an underrated poet, I knew him a bit. I admired him. I saw and exchanged words with Patrick Campbell and John Heath Stubbs. Stephen Spender, who rarely went to pubs, liked my work and was the first stranger who bought a painting, one of Stella. He was a very gregarious, handsome man; half a dozen of his early poems are, for me, very memorable. Poets go out more than painters, they depend on less paraphernalia and can write in corners of cafes, very few paintings can be done in the corners of cafes, poets like hearing words used violently. George was quite aggressive and irritating and he quite enjoyed chatting and carrying on.'

These places were frequented by artists such as Gerald Wilde, John Minton, Robert Colquhoun and Robert MacBryde, as well as Bacon, Freud and Andrews: 'So there was a time, now almost gone, when I had that curious sense which one has if one's lucky of having quick-witted, intelligent companions with whom I could talk excited drivel for hours and occasionally stumble on a nugget of sense. I suppose I actually spoke about painting more with Francis Bacon than to anyone else, partly because he liked making statements, formulating dogma, laying down rules. Of course they changed all the time.'[2]

Francis Bacon's support and example

On 5 February 1956, at Bacon's instigation, Helen Lessore brought Frank to the National Film Theatre to see Lorenza Mazzetti's semi-documentary film, *Together*. In the art world it is legendary as much as anything for the two main actors, Mazzetti's fellow students at the Slade, Michael Andrews and Eduardo Paolozzi, who play deaf-mute dockworkers in London's bomb-damaged East End. Physically and in their manner the pair appear, as

Auerbach says, to be like Laurel and Hardy.[3] After the screening Bacon took Lessore and Auerbach to dinner at Wheeler's, the fish restaurant in Soho. Seeing Frank's pleasure in consuming his first lobster, Francis urged him to order another.

A month after the opening of his first one-person exhibition in January 1956, Auerbach was regarded as an up-and-coming artist and Bacon let it be known that he had been brought into his own circle. He boasted to Freud, 'I go and talk to this very good-looking painter in the French pub.' Their friendship developed over the years and in the 1960s, when Auerbach was taking a painting from Stella's house in Brentford to the framer Robert Savage, whose workshop was on the Old Brompton Road, he might first have breakfast with Francis in nearby Reece Mews. 'I sometimes saw things he had done. He once asked me for an opinion, which I gave him. I wouldn't have done so unasked. And, he was pretty touchy. I made, in the most tentative way, a comment about what I felt about the painting, which was a triptych, and I said: "Do you want them to look like three cones?" Because for me there was something uncomfortable about the way all the figures tapered towards the top. And he was pretty miffed. But he did change the painting, making the heads bigger, and the whole thing better.'[4] As he had done with the Dutch painter Karel Appel and others, Bacon suggested that he and Auerbach might work on the same canvas. Auerbach declined, protesting that his ways of working, his methods, were too laborious, and they existed for his own purposes.

The first time Giacometti visited London in 1955, David Sylvester took him to see Coldstream at the Slade and to the Hanover Gallery to view their stock of Bacon's work. Returning in the summer of 1964 to look at the spaces in the Tate where he would be showing the following year, Giacometti met and socialized with Bacon; the two artists praised each other's work in very qualified terms.[5] Bacon told Frank that after eating together, he insisted on going on to the club run by the female impersonator Danny La Rue, only to be refused entry since Giacometti was not wearing a tie and the bouncer was unimpressed that he was a famous French artist (as Bacon described Giacometti, who was Swiss). A year later, in July 1965, Auerbach was invited to join Giacometti, his wife, Annette, Bacon and his lover George Dyer for dinner at L'Escargot. The conversation was conducted rather awkwardly in English, French and Swiss-German. Auerbach recalled that Annette was jokey about the skinny figures Alberto made and Bacon, fairly drunk, tried to argue with Giacometti.

Bacon cultivated special ways of fending off unwanted attention. Auerbach once saw him berated by someone in a pub who said, 'I hate your paintings.' Pulling his own collar as if to suggest he felt detached from his painting persona, Bacon replied, 'I don't much like them myself'. This flippant attitude could be unjust. When Frank's former tutor John Minton took an overdose of pills in 1957, his suicide following increasingly desperate behaviour, Bacon commented dismissively, 'he was not an artist'. Auerbach remembers Francis trying to curb Dyer's excessive drinking, on one occasion saying, 'I'm not one to talk but you might drink a little more slowly.' The photographer and later biographer of Bacon, Daniel Farson, had bought Auerbach's *Head of E.O.W. VI* (1961) with Bacon's encouragement, 'and when he needed money he sold it to Francis who gave it to George Dyer, in an effort to provide him with capital – of course, George soon sold it in order to have money to spend'.[6]

Several of the tragedies in Bacon's life are associated with the opening of major exhibitions of his work. Years later they remain disturbing in a special way for the few who were his close friends. The day Bacon's first retrospective opened at the Tate Gallery in 1962, he learned by telegram of the death of his former lover Peter Lacy in Tangier. George Dyer's overdose on the eve of Bacon's opening at the Grand Palais in Paris in 1971 is well known. Auerbach found that Bacon's character changed and he fell out with everybody, including Lucian. 'In what now seems to me to be a priggish way – I was totally mistaken – I thought that Francis felt that one should be sorry for him rather than for this person in whose death he was to some extent implicated. He picked him up, brought him to another life and then, for prolonged periods, ignored him. George was a very warm and simple person.'[7] Bacon made highly original, almost operatic, paintings about his friend's final moments and they are generally regarded as an act of exorcism. Frank insists they are what will last.

Bacon's double portrait of Freud and Auerbach appears an oddly static diptych of two men with strong physiques wearing white T-shirts and apparently nothing else. It is based partly on a photo of French troops in Algeria

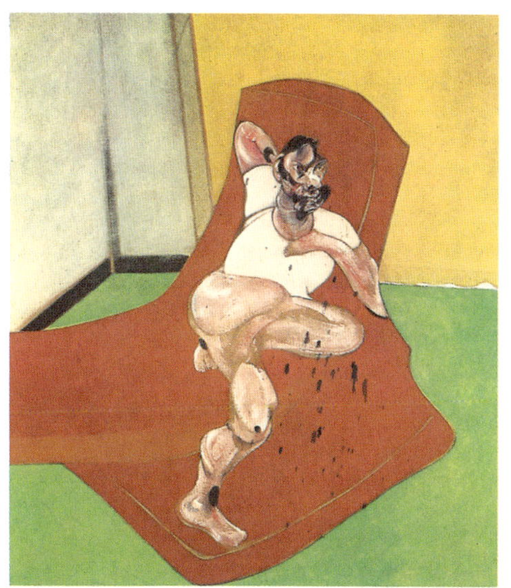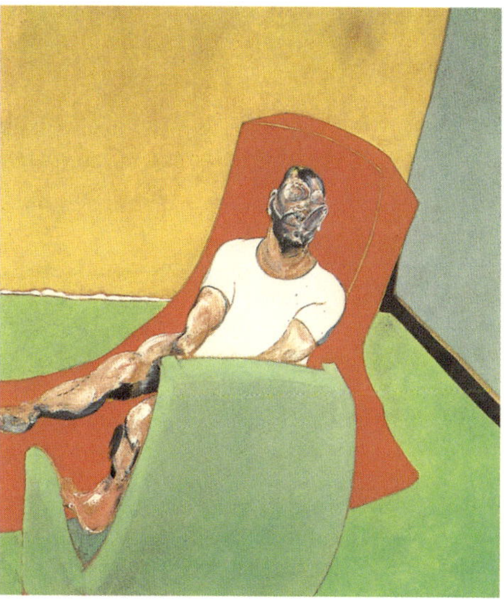

FRANCIS BACON, *Double Portrait of Lucian Freud
and Frank Auerbach*, 1964

from *Paris Match*. The subjects are lounging on red 'thrones' (or mattresses) set in a claustrophobic green-floored and -walled interior. If one thinks of Bacon as the silent – invisible – participant in this 1964 drama, this triangle of painters is, for me, potent in the manner of dream: illogical, uneasy but strangely companionable. It differs from Bacon's triptych *Three Studies of Lucian Freud* (1969), the yellow-ground picture sold by Christie's New York in 2013, which achieves a startling likeness of the super-alert Freud, with something extra-visual about the contorted pose confined within Bacon's familiar oblique-angled space frames. Looking at details in the lavish auction publication, Auerbach observed, 'A feature that is a chin or a nose looks quite different when looked at in isolation than it does when part of the ensemble of the face. Somehow the two have to be reconciled in vivid portraiture. As Degas said, "Art is telling the truth by means of the false".'

Although Bacon famously boasted about the role of 'accident' in his work, the description seems to Auerbach relative and exaggerated since all painters use accident. Bacon's process was more like his own way of assimilating knowledge: 'recognizing the useful accident is a decision (maybe an instinctive decision) not an accident.' As the artist works, 'there is a sort of rehearsal, there is a sort of build-up, there's a sort of accruing of possibilities of how to behave,' until in Auerbach's own experience he tends to contradict what's gone before, rather than synthesize it, and something unexpected, nominally 'accidental', happens. For both artists, with a loaded brush and a swift gesture, the fluid paint nearly subsiding, there is a fine balance between chance and manipulation; and if lucky, in Bacon's words, the image becomes more real and begins to conjure up appearance 'with a vividness that no accepted way of doing it would have brought about'.[8]

From what Auerbach observed, Bacon was much more organized than is obvious from pictures of the studio in Reece Mews (reconstructed in Dublin); despite the heaps of material, he knew where everything was (as does Frank). Bacon took from tabloid photographs, as well as limited edition specialist publications. However, as the writer and Bacon-specialist Martin Harrison has said, 'his recontextualizations completely altered their original meaning'. Curiously, there was a precedent in British art in Sickert's late work: the pictures that began with press photographs from the *Daily Express* or *Daily Sketch* of brides, weddings and news events, such as Amelia Earhart arriving at an aerodrome outside London following her solo transatlantic flight. As Harrison and art historian Martin Hammer have documented, these paintings 'presaged the morphology of Bacon's 1960s portraits'.[9]

Sickert's late paintings were shown at the Hayward Gallery in 1981–82. Auerbach had suggested the exhibition; long an admirer, he wrote a short foreword for the catalogue, making his usual distinction between idiom and the final painting. 'If one were to ascribe a development to him, one might say that Sickert became less interested in composition, that is in selection, arrangement and presentation, devoted himself, more and more, to a direct transformation of whatever came accidentally to hand and engaged his interest, and accepted the haphazard variety of his unprocessed subject matter ... He made obvious his frequent reliance on snapshots and press photographs, he copied, used and took over the work of other, dead, artists and made extensive use also of the services of his assistants who played a large and increasing part in the production of his work. But these interesting ways of producing paintings would have been, of course, of no interest if the resulting images had not conjured up grand, living and quirky forms.'[10]

The single painting by Auerbach that seems to make reference to lens-based imagery, *Gaumont Cinema, Camden Town* (1963), was then and is now somewhat of an anomaly in his work. Although the perspective is downwards to the scattered spectators partially filling the theatre, with the dense lower area rendered in warm reds and yellows, our attention is arrested by a large head and arm of a man smoking on a blue screen in the upper left of this horizontal canvas. Years later Richard Cork wondered whether this subject matter constituted a latent 'Pop' aspect. Auerbach discounted the implication of anything second-hand, in a reply to Cork's questions delivered in the third person via the Marlborough: 'The image on the screen represents a cigarette advert. Paying four shillings to enter, there was half an hour to draw before the film started and another ten minutes in the dark before he left to resume the painting. This went on for over one year; he said it cost him a lot of money! He cannot remember the films that were showing at the time – he wasn't interested in them, but he remembers there was one with Vincent Price', which he watched to the end.[11]

Given the date of *Gaumont Cinema* – 1963 – Cork may have associated the painting with those by the newest group of Royal College graduates,

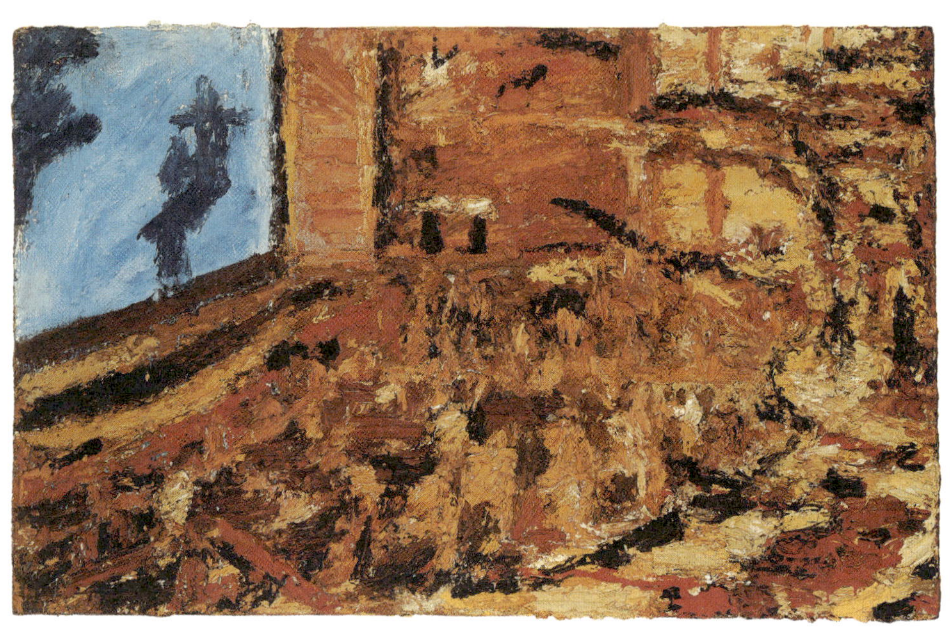

Gaumont Cinema, Camden Town, 1963

who were inventing and borrowing styles with less emphasis on formal qualities and more on joining disparate sources in lively and self-exposing ways, such as David Hockney's *Man in a Museum (or You're in the Wrong Movie)* (1962). Auerbach served for several years on the juries of the 'Young Contemporaries', the annual show of work by British students initiated in 1949, the period when Lawrence Alloway was the Chair, and artists such as Bernard Cohen and Andrew Forge were on the jury. In January 1961, Auerbach insisted that the pictures submitted by David Hockney, a second-year student at the college, should be included, commending their urgency, conveyed in inscriptions like raw graffiti and in their content. One painting selected, *Adhesiveness* (1960), depicted two figures in a '69' position (the title was taken from Walt Whitman, who used the term to denote 'manly love').

Although artists such as Hockney, Derek Boshier, R. B. Kitaj and Patrick Caulfield were born only a few years later than Auerbach, in the Whitechapel Gallery exhibition of 1964 Bryan Robertson hailed them as a 'new generation'. More tellingly, Auerbach realized attitudes had changed. Whereas in the 1950s painting figurative pictures was 'a sort of Robinson Crusoe activity where you have to construct your own way of doing things' – and he preferred to work away quietly with some success, bolstered by a few sales and the early reviews – in retrospect he became aware that there had been no 'mantle of glory cast over one, and it took me some time to realize that it hadn't happened and that success in a dealer's gallery in London is confined to a tiny circle'. In contrast, these artists were more extrovert and they 'had the feeling that the world could actually be conquered … instead of believing that you have to be this kind of Ishmael'.[12]

Exhibiting at the Marlborough from 1965

In the spring of 1964, Auerbach was approached by Harry Fischer from the Marlborough, an ambitious gallery with considerable international standing and business acumen, suggesting that they organize a retrospective of Auerbach's work. Fischer, together with Frank Lloyd, who was also a Viennese émigré, had founded Marlborough Fine Art in 1946, and a third partner, David Somerset, joined in 1948. For many years they had staged historic exhibitions from Van Gogh to Egon Schiele and Kurt Schwitters. In 1964, they opened a branch in New York and soon after began to represent the Estate of Jackson Pollock and prominent American artists such as David Smith and Mark Rothko. Fischer proposed a retrospective entitled 'Ten Years of Painting by Frank Auerbach', which would be accompanied by a catalogue containing a three-way interview with the London gallery's star painter, Francis Bacon (who had urged them to sign up Auerbach and expressed an interest to participate), and David Sylvester.[13]

Before closing the Beaux Arts Gallery, Helen Lessore had planned a final show for the spring of 1965 devoted to Auerbach's work, so the new arrangement depended on her being willing to lend eleven paintings from her stock of works made between June 1963 and April 1964 (and giving the Marlborough a commission on the sale of these), and the new gallery bending to the artist's desire that two recently completed large figure compositions be included. These, as Frank explained in a letter to the gallery, he regarded as 'absolutely essential to make the exhibition as I want it to be. Even on the most short-term commercial considerations, I should have thought we stood a better chance of selling pictures from an exhibition which makes some sort of impact.'[14] Fischer's original idea had been to pair work by Lucian Freud and Auerbach, but 'as it happened, when I went to see Lucian, I could not find anything suitable for exhibition and there was so little that I was really at a loss to know what to do.' He prudently accepted that this first exhibition would be a 'forerunner to the big show' of Frank's work a couple of years hence.[15]

Auerbach wanted his inaugural exhibition to stay open for a full four weeks – the month of February 1965. He regretted the inadequate space at 39 Old Bond Street and a catalogue of the most modest dimensions, while saving his voice for something he would continue to demand ever after, the freedom to 'select the pictures to be hung solely on the basis of quality'.[16] Most of these were recent: the tall, naked figures of *J.Y.M. in the Studio I–VIII* and another one of her seated, four pictures of E.O.W., three heads of Helen Gillespie and one of Gerda Boehm. The single 'essential' figure composition *E.O.W., S.A.W. and J.J.W. in the Garden* (1963) shown in the end, which was over six feet high, was almost too large to be carried up the gallery stairs (see p. 111).

After he joined the gallery, Auerbach's direct contacts at Marlborough were with John Synge, James Kirkman, until he left in 1972, and with Valerie Beston, who was with the gallery from its first year and also handled Bacon.

Auerbach advised Miss Beston and Kirkman as soon as he was ready to send a newly finished painting to the gallery, often adding the warning that the picture would require two people to bring it from the framer's van into the gallery. The sense of event and the artist's apprehension about whether the pictures were required are evident. In a letter written on a Sunday evening (*c.* 1966), he describes the newest landscape as 'considerably better (more of my daemon in it)' but certain to take a month to dry, and in April 1966 he reports that 'what may be the best, and certainly the heaviest, of the street scenes' is finished.[17]

When there were sales such as that of the *Head of Helen Gillespie III* (1963) to the Art Gallery of South Australia in Adelaide, Auerbach would send notes like: 'Things seem to be going almost too well. I am going on Safari to Southampton on Saturday' [he was accompanying Stella to see her daughter Julia off to Australia]. An exchange of letters in the summer of 1966 indicates that Auerbach was broke, and thus deeply relieved when he signed a better contract with the Marlborough, explaining to Fischer that with the upgraded prices and advance, 'It really does give me every opportunity to do something worthwhile in the next five years.'[18] As he admitted privately to Kirkman, after apologizing for not sounding more cheerful at the good news, his anxiety was chronic, 'my sense of Hubris is so strong that when something good happens I expect a thunderbolt'.[19]

A fairly perilous financial position continued, with the Marlborough meeting bills for paint and framing, which they set against sales. In 1972, Auerbach queried his accounts with the gallery, taking note of another rise in prices written into the 1971 agreement, and Miss Beston was happy to report that 'the picture is much brighter' and the Marlborough actually owed him money: £438.34.[20]

Friendly letters indicate shared preoccupations and opinions. For example, Auerbach commented in a note to Kirkman on 10 January 1967: 'I still think that the [Henry] Moore looks a bit like wholemeal bread.' Miss Beston wrote in April 1966 about a feud between Truman Capote and the theatre critic Kenneth Tynan that began in the *Observer* over the author's bestselling 'non-fiction' novel, *In Cold Blood*, which had been serialized in *The New Yorker* in 1965 and published in hardback by Random House that month. Capote had arrived after the murder of the Clutter family on their farm in 1959, a New Yorker entering a small Kansas community to write a book about what happened; he inveigled himself into the lives of the townspeople and his book focused on the gruesome details. Tynan's review implied that the author rather willed the execution of the killers so his book would have an effective ending. Auerbach took sides: 'I am for Capote – against Tynan, after all Capote involved himself with these people and laid himself open to charges by people such as drama critics, one might prefer a saint to Capote – but I identify myself with writers rather than with saints.'[21]

One of Auerbach's new cityscapes, the wide format *Behind Camden Town Station – Autumn Evening* (1965) was chosen for the cover of his next Marlborough catalogue. The exhibition opened in January 1967; among the twenty-five paintings, drawings and screenprints were two of Mornington Crescent Underground station that take in the traffic island with the statue of Sickert's father-in-law (Richard Cobden) added to the title.[22] In an exceptional one, *Mornington Crescent with the Statue of Sickert's Father-in-Law III, Summer Morning* (1966) there is a shift to brighter colours, light blue against butter yellow. The obstructive, linear marks relate to what the artist saw on a particular day, but they are not always decipherable by viewers: the striding stick figure under the lantern-like street lamp in the upper right corner might be Cobden or it might be a passer-by. To either side of the bulwark of Mornington Crescent station there are the open channels of the roads running south. Information about the location is curiously specific without being linked to perspective or measured scale. In an undated letter to Miss Beston, Auerbach provided a diagram of one of the Mornington Crescent paintings with annotations like 'hole', 'man with wheelbarrow', 'distant houses', and 'I can't remember if that is a man or a cement mixer'.

The art critics continued to comment on the thickness of the paint; one had reservations about the 'blinding chromatic variations' and several characterized his work as expressionist. John Russell, writing in the *Sunday Times*, praised Auerbach's new 'streetscapes', regarding them as 'a prime example of the way in which he can adapt the metal sinews of city life to his purpose', and then addressed the pictures of people with more caution. 'Where the human body, and more especially the human head, are in question the problems are quite different: the image in such cases tends to settle

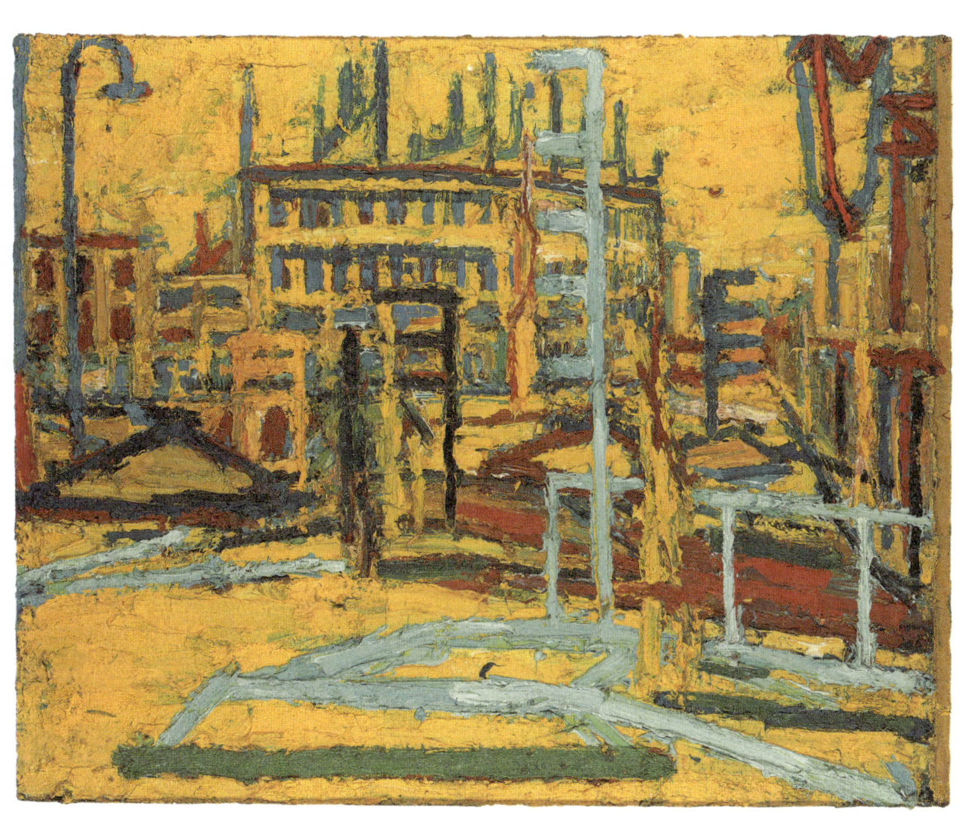

Mornington Crescent with the Statue of Sickert's Father-in-Law III,
Summer Morning, 1966

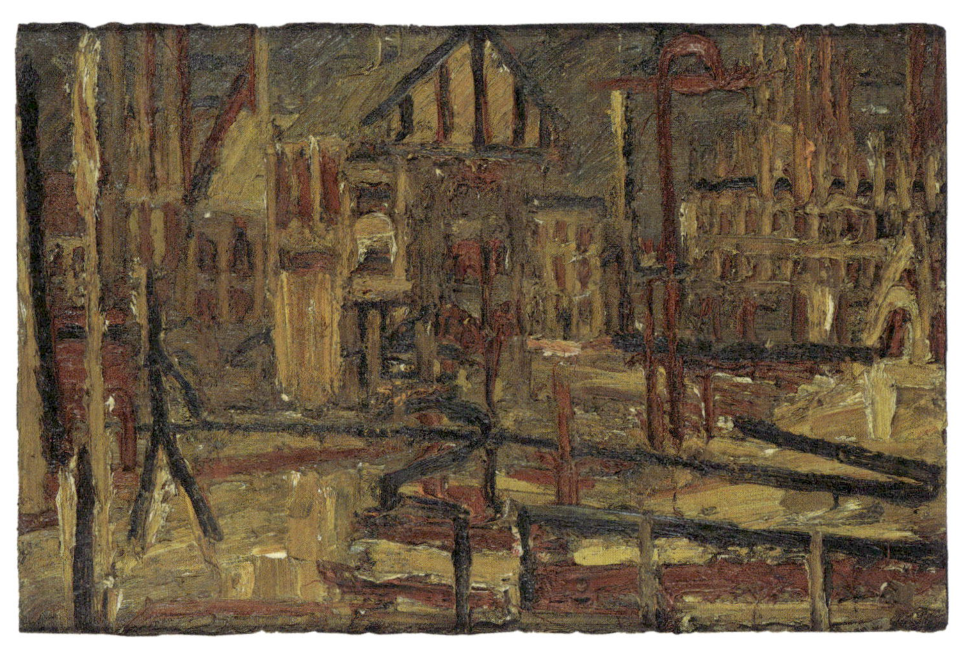

Behind Camden Town Station, Autumn Evening, 1965

slowly towards one corner of the picture, like a collapsing parachute, and the fascination of the work resides in the pull back and forth between the image (the head, as something intimately known) and what looks to be the chaos and savoury confusion of the paint.' He concluded that Auerbach was renewing the notion of figure painting with works where 'ideally the end result would be a maximum of informed tenderness in the vision presented and a maximum of original eloquence in the paint'.[23]

Lucian and Frank: A lasting bond

Critics reacted to Lucian Freud's exhibitions at the Marlborough in 1958, 1963 and 1968 with considerable alarm and often hostility – Lawrence Alloway in 1958 going so far as to say 'the new portraits reveal a disastrous interest in painterly values ... the richer pigment he uses is subjected to the same obsessional fussing as his line, so that it takes on a weird surface animation'; other critics, such as Nevile Wallis, disagreed, appreciating the 'unquiet spirit' and predicting Freud was destined 'to outlive most contemporary reputations'.[24] Slightly against his will, while still a student, Auerbach had found himself impressed by the intensity of Freud's paintings and drawings of the 1950s, although 'when one is young one tends to think there is a particular virtue in one's own idiom. But as time has gone by one realizes that quality matters more than style.'[25] Even with this new looser mode Freud worked in an incremental way, his scrutiny of people exhaustive, painting close-up 'naked portraits' that disturbed most viewers with their detail, whereas by this period Auerbach's paintings had become almost entirely the result of the last bout of work. He would lie awake wondering how he could afford the massive quantity of materials his particular way of working required so as to be able to scrape off, carry on with what was on the easel and still pay the rent. Money makes him anxious and he is mystified 'how other people are so insouciant about it'. Frank remembers subsisting on rice, lentils and tahini until he was 50.

In contrast, Freud slept only a few hours, sought out parties and danger and simply spent money; the betting and debts resulted in threats to his life and the necessity to pawn possessions. His obsession with horse and dog racing, for example, was different from that of Bacon who ran (and frequented) gambling clubs – although in Freud's view, he seemed to stake

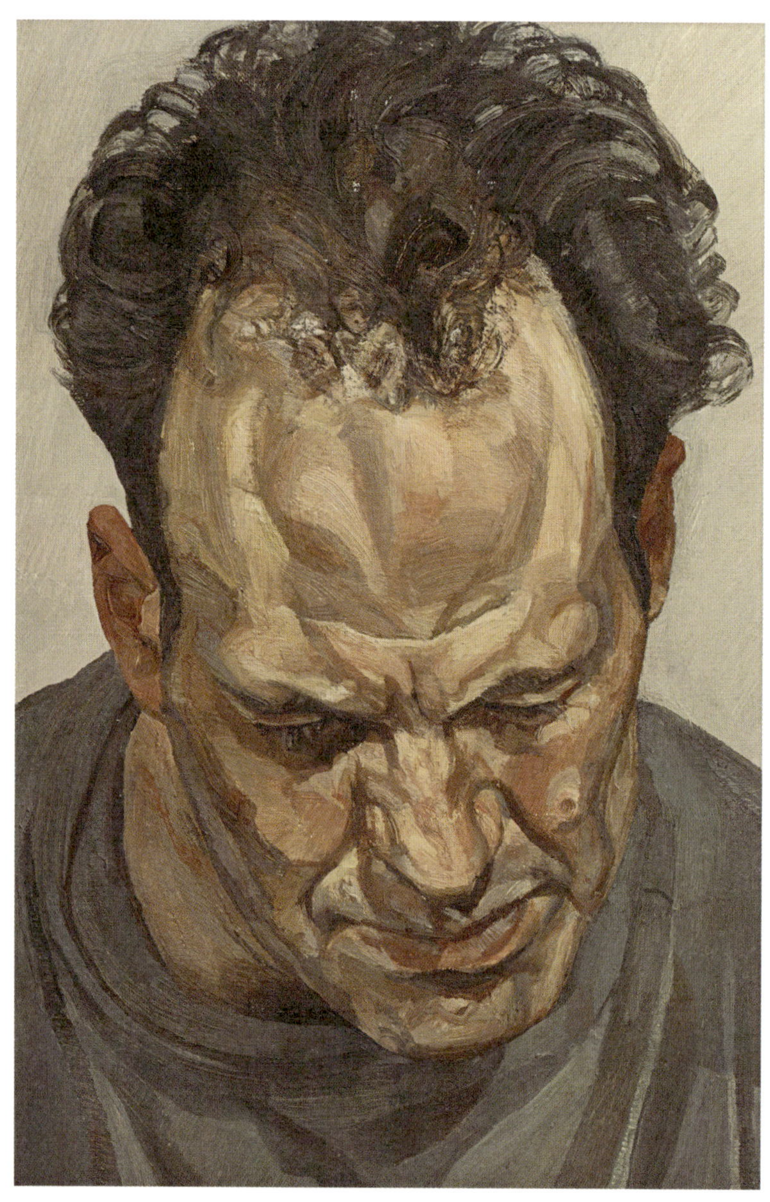

LUCIAN FREUD, *Frank Auerbach*, 1975–76

what he could afford to lose. Auerbach accompanied Lucian to one or two 'travelling chemmy games' in various Kensington flats before they were quite legal, but never developed a taste for this time-consuming Chemin de Fer card game popular in the 1960s. However, he has admitted that 'I did have a fruit-machine addiction for some years.'

In 1975, Freud asked Auerbach to sit for him. 'I was a good but reluctant sitter, always conscious that time and energy were leaking away. I was leading a more mobile life ... and Lucian caught me at a good moment – for me a more flexible moment. I would sit in his very austere Paddington room, always considerately warmed, for about three hours or so. I found the process strenuous, but was convinced it was worthwhile in the sense that something was being made. I don't think that I would have sat for anybody else by then. I cannot imagine working with – for – a more interesting person.'[26] Once in winter the pipes froze in this flat on Thorngate Road and Lucian scooped snow from the roof to make the coffee – the result for Auerbach the most delicious in his memory. The first portrait was abandoned; the second is a masterpiece, a close-cropped view of his head from above, a painting about intelligence and self-awareness that is much more resonant set back in its dark frame than imposed on a white page in reproduction.

Auerbach's drawings were as authoritative as the oil paintings, and for both artists success was marked by a quality that Freud identified as distinguishing a painted from a photographed portrait: 'the degree to which feelings can enter into the transaction from both sides'.[27] In the mid-1970s Auerbach had embarked upon bold charcoal, chalk and oil drawings of various sitters, the results striking in the way they convey personality, with rapidly made lines executed over weeks of attempts. In a drawing from 1975, Bruce Bernard looks much younger than his age: 47. The optimism of Bernard it reveals connects with his appearance when a model for Freud in the 1990s. Bernard wrote about Auerbach when the Hayward exhibition opened in 1978, describing a friend who works 'in a concentrated turmoil of aspiration and invocation', predicting that viewers would see 'the transformation of some of the abstract painter's vocabulary for his own far-from-abstract ends, and the originality of his ambition, as true innovation'.[28]

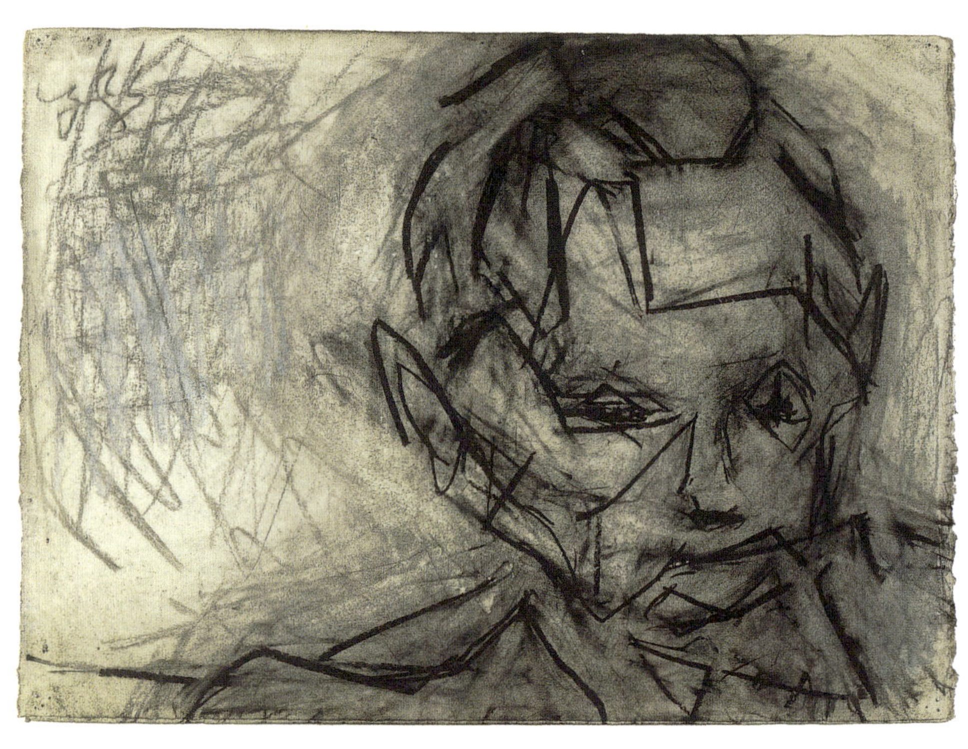

Head of Bruce Bernard, 1975

In subsequent years, Lucian was in the habit of telephoning to ask Frank to look at one of his paintings nearing completion. To accommodate Auerbach's exacting timetable they would meet very early and Freud would cook a lavish breakfast. Auerbach recalls: 'He didn't, to put it mildly, always do what I suggested, but he'd incorporate it in his own process. Bill Coldstream used to get Euan [Uglow] to come over and look at his pictures, but I think their work is more cerebral or something ... my idiom is so different, I repaint the whole picture so if someone said why don't you, whatever ... [such] advice would be of little use to me.' On rare occasions Frank found comments from others welcome, 'perhaps, once or twice', and he sometimes asks the sitter, '"do you think it's finished" and if they say "no" (often coming from Julia) that's useful and if "yes", they might be right', but as I know from my own experience it would not matter if he himself had any doubt.

Freud envied Auerbach his ability to work from the outdoors and the way that Frank's pictures were 'decisive'. One senses this perspective in his choice of paintings when he began buying Auerbach's work in the 1980s. He lived, for example, with works that were masterpieces of landscape painting: *Primrose Hill – Winter* (1981–82), *Mornington Place* (1973) and *The Chimney, Mornington Crescent* (1987–88).[29] When Auerbach was invited to exhibit paintings and quick sketches related to the old masters at the National Gallery in 1995, Freud supplied a short catalogue introduction. 'It is the architecture that gives his paintings such authority. They dominate their given space: the space always the size of the idea, while the composition is as right as walking down the street ... The weather changes, so does the light. The times of day and night are recorded, the mood is one of high-spirited drama. In fact his work is brimming with information conveyed with an underlying delicacy and humour that puts me in mind of the last days of Socrates.'[30]

The bond between the two artists was special; it possessed something of the relationship of two friends in a novel: both charismatic and driven, both born in Berlin (the Freuds living in the more upmarket neighbourhood of Charlottenburg, near the edge of the Tiergarten). As children they read some of the same German books, their English was spoken with precision and with, as the journalist Andrew Billen observed, 'a dash of German dissonance', and, as the same interviewer said of Frank's stories, 'executed with deliciously cutting turns of phrase'.[31] Frank described Lucian as 'inherently

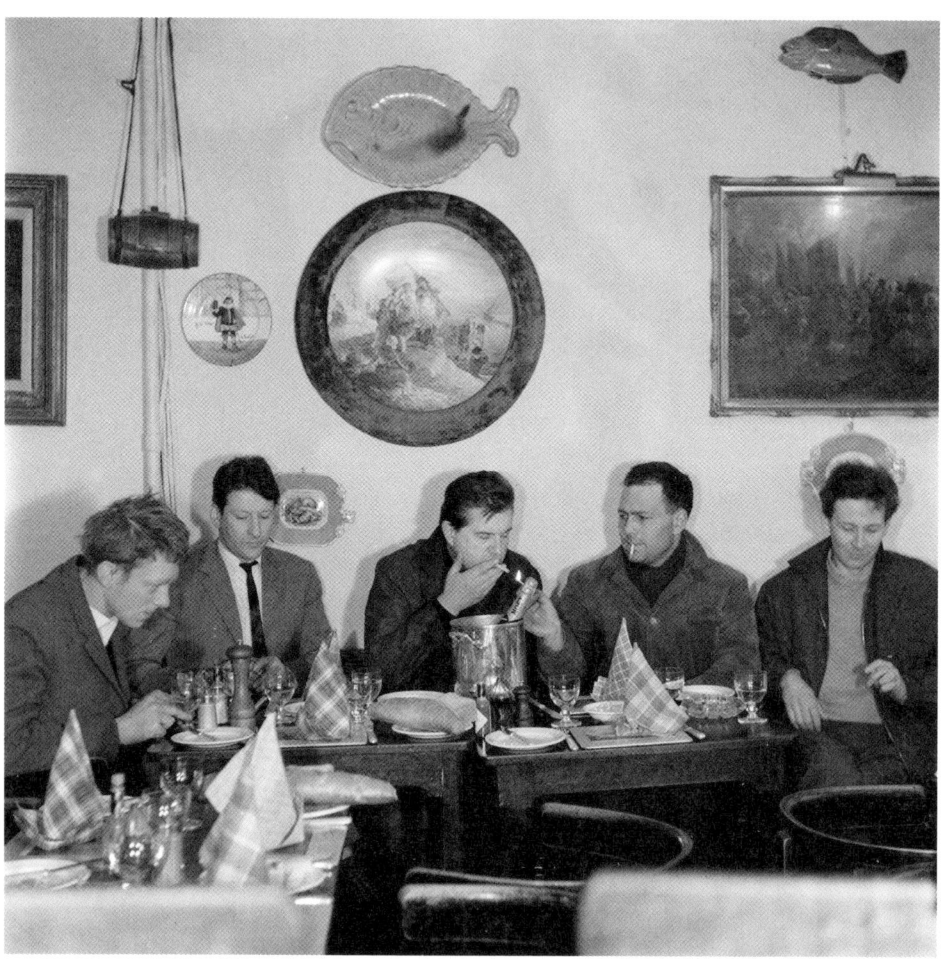

JOHN DEAKIN, Wheeler's, Old Compton Street, Soho, 1963. From left, Timothy Behrens, Lucian Freud, Francis Bacon, Frank Auerbach and Michael Andrews

glamorous, first because of his heredity and then because he was extra-ordinarily attractive, quick-witted, energetic and daring, with his own morality'.[32] At the end of Freud's life, Auerbach wondered over and over, as his friend became distracted and weaker, whether a particular painting already begun would be finished, and was relieved when the nude of Perienne was taken away in April 2011, three months before Freud died. As the last picture, *Portrait of the Hound* (2011), progressed, taking several years, the heavily painted right hand of Freud's assistant David Dawson almost lifted off the surface, and light coming through the window facing the garden was reflected on the white sheet covering the mattress on which the man and dog rested. It seems to me to indicate that Freud hoped to bring the out-doors inside, the painting's terrain suggesting a snowy landscape with just an isolated man and his dog left, and in David's intensely alert expression a note of farewell.

The 'School' that was invented

In 1961, the *London Magazine* asked a number of artists, including Auerbach, 'What is the most important development in British painting since the war? ... Assuming such a thing as an international style exists, how do you see your work in relation to it?' Frank replied: 'I cannot answer these questions because they seem impertinent to my situation. I think of painting as something that happens to a man working in a room, alone with his actions, his ideas, and perhaps his model. He is affected by his circumstances, and by the standards and events of his time, but he seems to me to be the sole coherent unit. I cannot think of British painting as an entity, I do not understand the phrase "international style". These concepts seem to me irrelevant to an activity which postulates the persistence of a unique and individual experience.'[33] A decade later, conceptual art was gaining favour and Auerbach observed that young artists 'started doing demonstrations and typing little notices to put on the wall'. Thus 'the only people who painted figurative pictures were the people who really had to. It stopped being the common current mode.' From his point of view the situation was actually better, 'because it meant that only those people who really wanted to paint did so and this became an eccentric activity ... you just did it in a way as an outcast, which was very, very healthy.'[34]

Auerbach continued to regard art as the reinvention of the physical world, and the challenge for him was how to pin down one's reaction to the fact that we are moving in space and encountering matter and volume. Art from all periods, if it succeeds, attacks fact from an unfamiliar point of view and in his words an image that looks genuine and fresh is often one that as it is made seems 'actively repellent, disturbing and itchy and not right'. In my 1978 conversation with Frank he reiterated that view: 'I wouldn't reject anything that seemed shocking or extreme, but on the contrary, I would value it, but I wouldn't do it for its own sake. I mean to do it for its own sake then becomes part of the world of advertisement and fashion.'[35]

At the time, the 'School of London', a term initially coined in the 1950s as a label like New York School and Ecole de Paris, was re-introduced. R. B. Kitaj used the expression in his introduction to the catalogue of 'The Human Clay', the 1976 exhibition that resulted from the Arts Council's invitation to him to purchase drawings for their collection. Kitaj sought with almost religious reverence images of 'the single human form as if they could be breathed on, whereupon they would glow like beacons of where art has been and like agents of a newer art life to come'.[36] Among the 103 works included (a number of the paintings and drawings were loans), some were by artists from an older generation such as William Roberts (b. 1895), and a few were by those normally considered abstract artists, such as John Golding and Anthony Caro.[37] Kitaj described London as his 'adopted city', a place of 'artistic personalities', and 'speaking for my own life in art' he singled out those whose work meant the most to him: Bacon, Hockney and Auerbach.

The photograph taken by Deakin in Wheeler's restaurant back in 1963 became a trope; this staged photo, a commission by Francis Wyndham for *Queen* magazine, interpreted as if it were a club meeting heralding the 'School of London'. Freud, Bacon, Auerbach and Andrews gesture to each other, Timothy Behrens, a younger painter, looks on. Enthusiasm for defining a group with these four, plus Kossoff and Kitaj, spread from curators and critics, and shows organized by the British Council in the 1980s, to the commercial art world and private collectors. But the 'School of London' lacked any of the expected criteria – a manifesto or shared idiom, the rebellious spirit of a single generation, or even social compatibility – and Auerbach thought the concept 'rubbish'.

Kitaj also claimed that the majority of the artists he identified with were in some way émigrés, describing his choice as 'also very "diasporist"', citing those born outside London.[38] That contention is just as debatable. Although he was born in Ireland, Bacon's parents were of English descent and he spent much of his youth in England; Kossoff was born in London of Russian Jewish immigrants; Freud and Auerbach identified with being English and Andrews came from Norwich. Only Kitaj felt foreign. Conveniently their 'foreignness' and 'Jewishness' were associated with the subjects looking so anxious. If Auerbach had any voice in his work being thus marginalized, he rejected the premise. He described Kitaj as an 'impressive, inspired visionary', whom he saw two or three times a year. In 2008, Auerbach wrote in reply to questions by a student called Katia: 'I don't feel I belong to a Jewish school, I don't think there is such a thing – I feel myself to be Jewish in the sense of being a person, in all other respects exactly like everybody else, who has been made to feel uneasy.'[39] On various occasions he has explained that he would not disavow his Judaism as long as anti-Semitism exists, 'but religion and ritual mean nothing to me'.

Katia went on to ask whether because of his origins was her teacher's assumption that there might be a link between Auerbach and twentieth-century German and Viennese painters like Ludwig Meidner correct. Others have wished to connect Auerbach's work to Oskar Kokoschka's early paintings or perhaps to Ernst Ludwig Kirchner or another German Expressionist. Auerbach rejected this line of thought: 'I am not an expressionist and I do not like expressionism – precisely because it intends to provoke a reaction', suggesting to me this would be like the strategy of a demagogue. Earlier in this exchange Katia was told, 'I *never* think that my painting should induce a specific emotion – somehow that seems to have something to do with effect, and suggests that the painter invests less than he hopes to evoke. I do think it very important that the subject (Abstraction is of course also a *subject* – a view of life, it is not "a way of painting") should be felt to be momentous; the "emotion" is the result of the qualities the painter invests, transmuted and united by some sort of miracle where the painting becomes independent.'[40] The subject might connect to anything, including recent events and political indignation. Auerbach admires, for example, Richard Hamilton's paintings about 'the Troubles' in Northern

Ireland and work by Otto Dix reacting to the violence of war and society during the Weimar years.

A more meaningful group exhibition of artists working from life was the one devised by Andrew Forge and presented in New Haven and Santa Barbara, in 1981, with the rather unexciting title, 'Eight Figurative Painters'. It was structured around the impact of three older artists (Bomberg, Bacon and Coldstream) and extended to Patrick George and Euan Uglow. As Lawrence Gowing was preparing the catalogue introduction, he asked Auerbach to come to the Slade, where he was professor, and quoted his observations throughout. At the end of Gowing's text Frank explains that what these artists have in common is the tension that produces the pictures. Their ways of behaving in the studio are simply manoeuvres to get each to 'the point where the will is surrendered ... One finds oneself subservient to what the model is doing. Without knowing why one is doing these things, one is simply inhabiting it [the scene]. Two painters' ways are simply two separate manoeuvres to get to that point.'[41]

Painting Titian and other artists

Whereas Bomberg and Kossoff 'were a formative influence', and Lucian and Francis 'good and valued friends', Auerbach insists that 'My main influence is – of course – great art; the artists I have never met who are always communicating through the work and memory of their work.' When pressed for names and art that he likes, Auerbach often proposes less well-known works, for example, Edouard Vuillard's *La Causette* (1893), and Fernand Léger's study for *Les Constructeurs* (1950) with its fusion of metallic architecture, clouds and men; as well as art without named creators, such as Aztec and Egyptian sculpture. Whenever Auerbach speaks of the old masters, he adds another caveat: 'I could cover three pages with names and I would not exhaust the list. They have all affected me deeply. But although we may be stimulated by works of art we make our pictures from living sensations. The aim of painting is this: TO CAPTURE A RAW EXPERIENCE FOR ART.'[42]

Writing a somewhat formal letter to *The Times*, printed on 3 March 1971, when the question of a campaign to save Titian's *Death of Actaeon* for the nation began, Auerbach makes a similar point by emphasizing the value of 'source material':

Sir, Your correspondents tend to write of paintings as objects
of financial value or of passive beauty. For painters they are source
material; they teach and they set standards. In this respect,
reproductions are good but are no substitute for paintings, good
paintings are no substitute for extraordinary ones.

I know that painters have used Titian's *The Death of Actaeon*
to help them in their work. I too have found it exceptionally useful;
in as far as painting can, sometimes, be thought of as a profession,
it is an irreplaceable professional facility.
Yours faithfully,
Frank Auerbach,
Care of Marlborough Fine Art (London) Limited,
39 Old Bond Street, W.1.

A year later, speaking about the same painting in a radio interview, Bacon voiced his intense identification with Titian's tragic late work. Seizing on the moment when the hares attack Actaeon, who has been transformed into a stag, he highlights the wild, erotic fantasy, 'the tearing of the human image to bits'.[43] Six years earlier Auerbach had uncharacteristically accepted a commission to paint from the rape scene by Titian after the story of Tarquin and Lucretia. *Study after Titian I* and *II* (1965) were the first of eight pictures made at the request of David Wilkie, a very reticent English collector who worked in an insurance office.[44] Wilkie's attachment to art had been fostered in the army when he was posted to Rome at the end of the war and went to see the Vatican collection. Then, in 1949, sight of Titian's *Tarquin and Lucretia* (1515) in the 'Art Treasures from Vienna' exhibition at the Tate produced a memorable effect: 'for a fraction of a second I had the impression that the room was on fire.'[45] Wilkie initially asked Auerbach to interpret the Vienna version of Titian's *Tarquin and Lucretia* rather than the more elaborate painting in Cambridge of the same subject.

The two paintings were done entirely in the presence of J.Y.M., who posed for Lucretia. The canvas was turned on its side so she could recline while approximating a woman resisting rape, her arms warding off Tarquin: 'I think it could have gone flat if I had simply copied a reproduction of the Titian ... It is somehow assumed that because these were mythical and biblical themes that these were done, possibly from a few engravings, a few drawings or paintings by others, but more or less out of his head, and I always felt the people in Titian's paintings were as likely as not to be portraits. In the recent biography by Sheila Hale she suggests that he actually took models along with him when he was going somewhere to fulfil a commission. There is a Venetian type of woman, who would be present in Veronese and Tintoretto and Titian, and to a certain extent in Bassano, and we know what she's like, quite plumpish and she has a particular classical head, she's a woman of Venice.'

The Wilkie commissions were shown at the University of Essex in 1973 at the initiative of Michael Podro, professor of art history and theory. In a review of the exhibition, the British philosopher and writer on aesthetics Richard Wollheim wrote at length about the complex relationship between Auerbach's paintings and Titian's original. 'Consider, for instance, the two versions of *Tarquin and Lucrece* [the title used on this occasion]. These differ quite radically, and the most obvious differences lie in the weight, the handling and the colour of the pigment. To these differences it is surely right to assign different ways in which the central incident – a sexual assault – is interpreted. One painting (No. 1), the thicker of the two, represents the assault as a physical event, occurring in the realm of activity. The other (No. 2) represents it as a wish fulfilled in a daydream. Indeed, I would say of this second painting that it conveys with tremendous power the sweet, languorous equivocations of onanism, in which violence typically sugars itself over with a kind of objectless sexuality.'

Wollheim argued that our initial response stems from our perception of the surface: 'For instance, if we look at the second Auerbach painting, we observe towards the top left-hand corner that the painting miraculously swells out into a great double bloom of luscious pink and grey and white pigment. This occurs at a point on the canvas which corresponds to, in Titian's painting, the stump or hilt of Tarquin's dagger. Regarded simply as a contribution to sexual imagery, this blossoming of the paint has an obvious rationale. But to grasp its full significance we have to go back to Titian's painting, and see what he made of this passage: or, perhaps better, we have to go back to our perception of Titian's painting, and see what we can make of what he made.'[46]

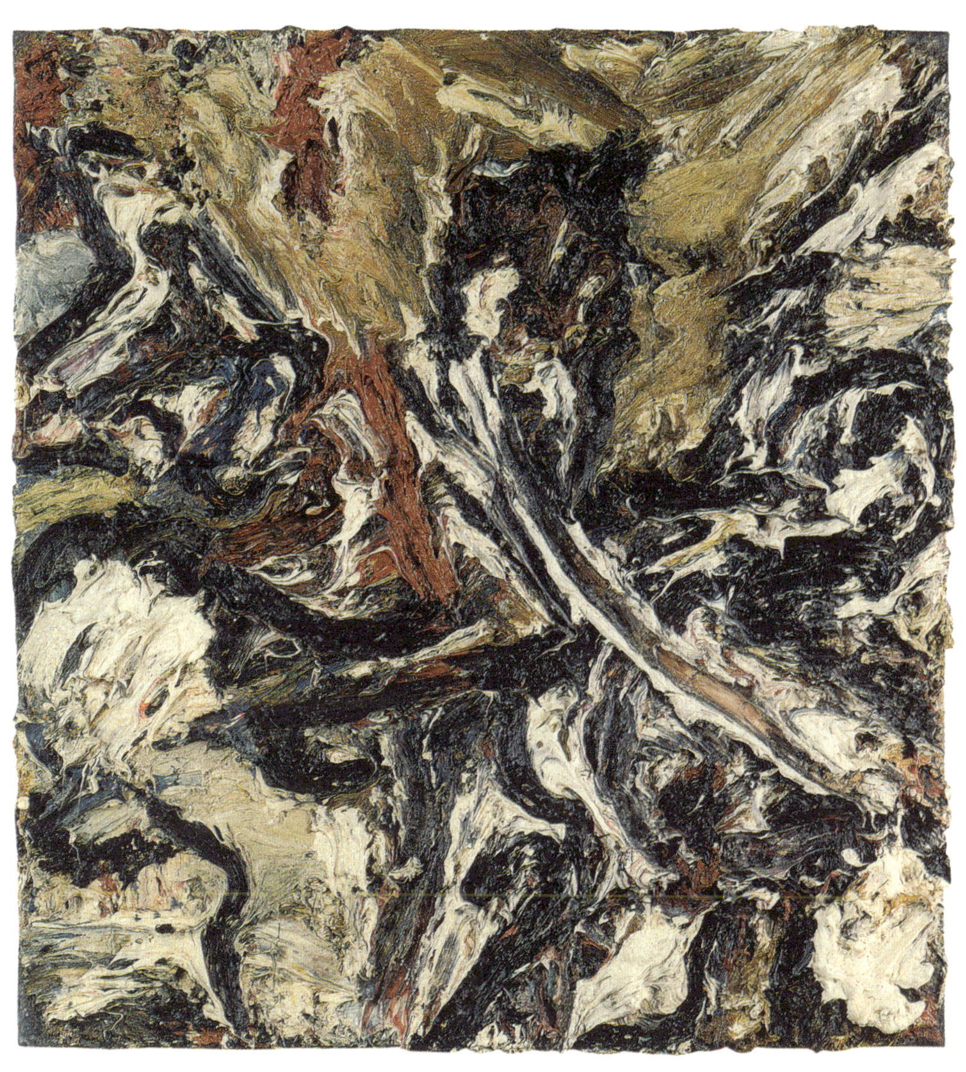

Study after Titian II, 1965

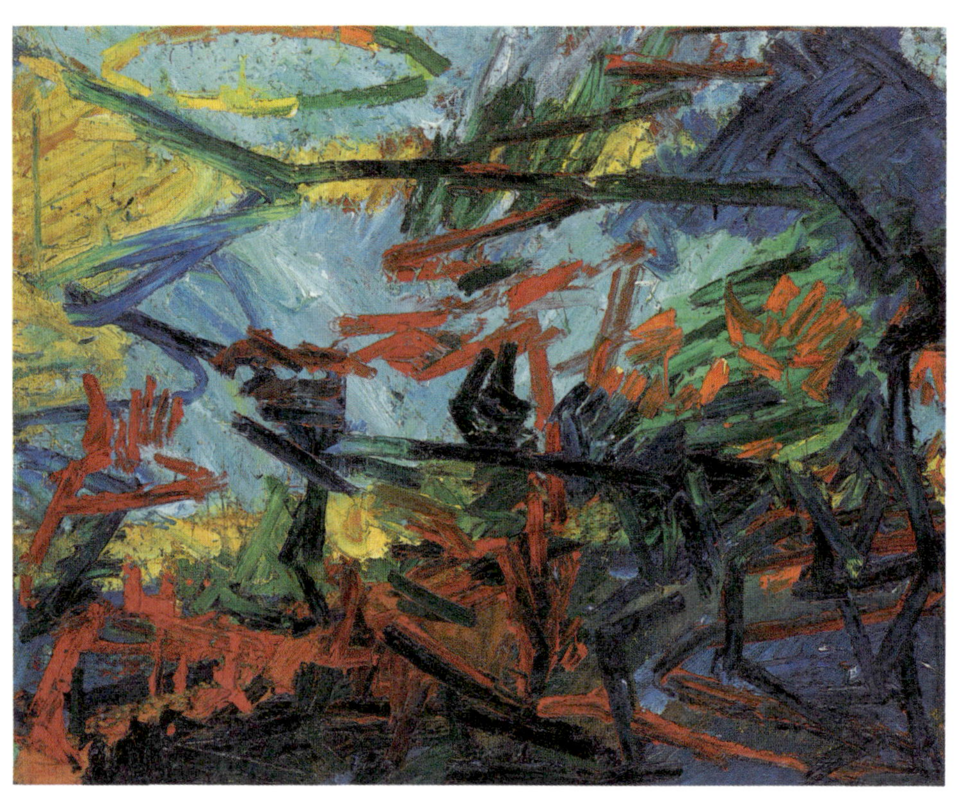

Bacchus and Ariadne, 1971

As Wollheim pushed his analysis into the area of critical theory about contemporary painting, he considered the 'trenchant' essays written by Clement Greenberg and Michael Fried, who defined a 'canonical succession' from Manet through to the present, including as their contemporary examples American artists such as Morris Louis and Frank Stella. Wollheim's quarrel with their thesis was not the application but the premise, 'For what illumination is generated by appealing to the nature of an art whose nature is said to lie exclusively in self-reference.' Although he recommended comparison to the Titian 'original' to fully appreciate the contemporary 'copy', he appreciated that the facture is very different: 'The assertiveness of Auerbach's handling emerges as a kind of tribute to the ambiguity of Titian's.'[47]

The next Wilkie commission was an interpretation of Titian's *Bacchus and Ariadne* (1520–23) and, as Auerbach recalls, it required dozens of drawings made directly from the painting hanging in the National Gallery, 'often immediately before I rushed home to get on with my "portrait" of it'. The bright primary colours of his *Bacchus and Ariadne* (1971) were associated with the shock of seeing the painting post-restoration and the energy that expands from inside.[48] Michael Podro identified parallels with Bomberg's early *Vision of Ezekiel* (1912) – 'both make use of simple lines or stick-like figures to purge the subject of superfluities' – and compared Auerbach's 'copy' to an earlier landscape, *Primrose Hill* (1967–68). 'There, too, the striations of paint seem to reconstruct the subject without anywhere making the explicit curvature or volume ... The sharp patterning of the zigzag brushmarks resolve themselves into sharply realized spatial clues – an overhanging branch in the foreground, parallel pathways running horizontally across the park, the increasing density of overlapping trees as we look up the incline of the hill.'[49] There is a remote correspondence between the éclat, radiant colour and thrust of the strokes in de Kooning's landscapes, such as his V-shaped *Suburb in Havana* (1958), and later works, and Auerbach's equally gravity-free, beaming, fast-moving Primrose Hill skies and terrain of these years.

This *Primrose Hill* (1967–68) was acquired by the Tate in 1971 and as it was being catalogued, the artist replied to the queries of the curators and the director, Sir Norman Reid, warding off generalizations. He said he avoided a routine method; many drawings were done at the beginning of the day and one at midnight, 'so as to have an impulse, an idea, a new act, a newly discovered structure, to work from – and then to paint with older and newer drawings pinned up.'[50] Auerbach tried to counter Reid's use of the term 'preparatory drawings': 'One looks – tries to understand what one sees as solid matter in space – and then makes a pictorial image, not of the projection on the retina, but of the mind's grasp of the material ... There is no one-to-one relation of mark to object (such as lamppost, branch, puddle, etc.). The painting is a single indivisible image of my grasp of their relationship.'[51]

Inside a painting

Auerbach responds to other dramas of extreme passion, such as Tintoretto's *The Origin of the Milky Way* (1575), which he drew in 1985, as if events from life and the imagination. In 1992–93, he focused on Rubens's *Samson and Delilah* (*c.* 1609–10). In the words of the National Gallery curator Colin Wiggins, its theme is about 'love, betrayal and mutilation, about shadow, sweat and warmth.'[52] For Auerbach, 'if one looks at the hands there is something terribly poignant about the peasant hands of Samson and of Delilah and the sophisticated, tricky, sly Iago hands of the old woman and the barber ... the yellow, the red and the purple drapery, that great knot of purple like a tear which underscores the fleshy drama which is an orchestrated accompaniment of poignancy and waste. It's sort of obvious that she's betrayed him, that he's ruined and that she loves him.'[53]

Frank's comment on Cézanne's *The Painter's Father, Louis-Auguste* (*c.* 1865) is representative of his ability to live vicariously through paintings, even those with 'ordinary' subject matter that on the surface hardly seem charged with emotion: 'it's an audacious, marvellous picture, the object rendered raw and newly perceived ... it comes at you in the most amazing way – that floor and those feet and that chair – who can forget them? But of course Cézanne's inside. He hardly knew he was making chairs or what the things were called. He was inside the painting.'[54]

This tall portrait, oil on house paint on plaster on canvas scrim, was mounted on the wall in the Cézanne family house, the Jas de Bouffan, in Aix-en-Provence for many years. True to his dislike of possessions, Auerbach has not retained works of his own (and is not very inclined to look at earlier pictures when they go on view), but there are some paintings that can be identified as more autobiographical than others. This was the case with the

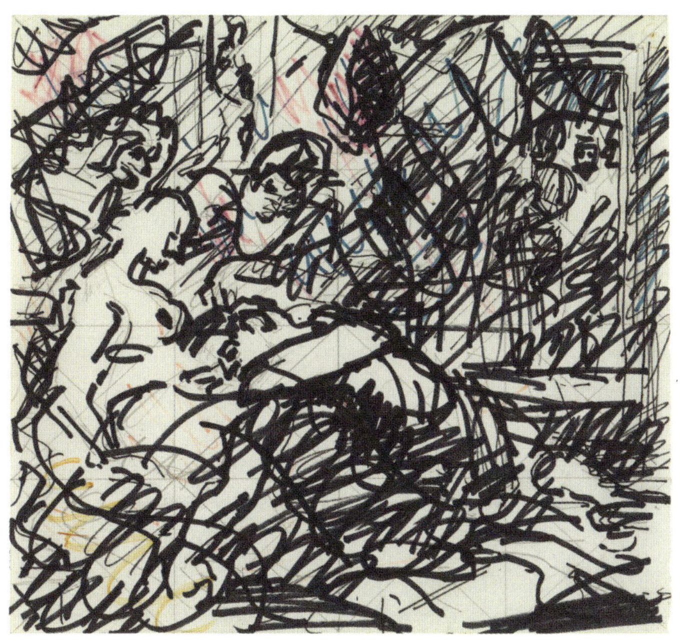

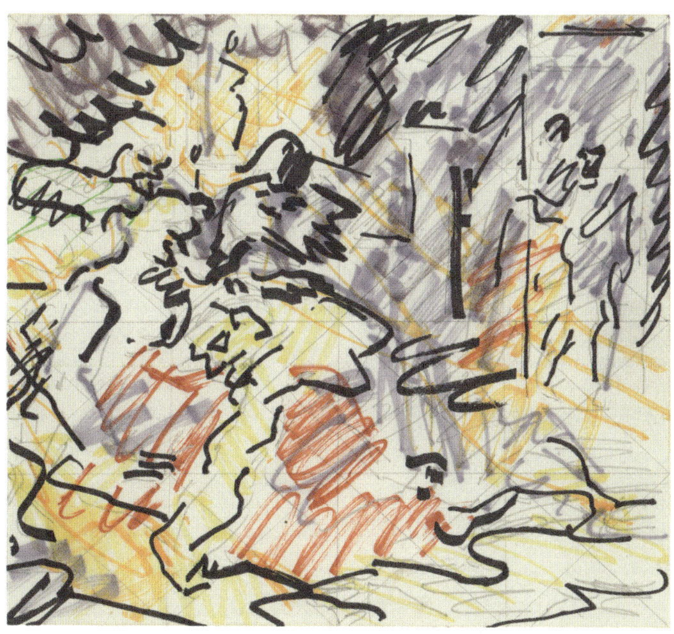

Two drawings after Rubens's *Samson and Delilah*, 1984

next subject set in a domestic interior, which dates from 'a time of considerable change for me when certain people re-entered my life'. The change had happened after Frank acted on an impulse to reconnect with his teenage son in 1975. His invitation to Jake to visit the studio on Thursday afternoons was open and the two formed the habit of eating at a rather edgy Greek restaurant on Royal College Street in Camden. In 1976, equally quietly, Frank got together with Julia while keeping up his practice of sleeping most nights in Mornington Crescent. Jake and Julia became regular sitters. Paintings such as *Head of Jacob* (1978–79), and a three-quarter length seated figure finished in 1980, *Jacob*, indicate his exceptional height, good looks and fortitude. The intimate, close-up *Julia Sleeping* (1978) is the first of many pictures of her lying down, her head viewed from every angle.

Interior Vincent Terrace (1982–84) records Julia's front room in Islington, with the cat and the dresser; she is seated at the table, an ashtray in the middle. In a second version Jake joins her. Frank, Julia and Jake, left to right, are the figures on the steps of St Pancras station (1978–79); Julia and Jake come down Euston station steps in 1980–81. For some 'irrational' reason in one of the *Euston Steps* paintings (1980–81) a vision of Meryl Streep in *The French Lieutenant's Woman* (the film was newly released) crept into the scene. Such transposition recurs fairly often, and should remind the viewer not to over-interpret the contents; throughout the urban landscapes figures might come from 'someone I had some relation with recently and I bung them into the picture and take them out again'.

As time goes on, Frank quite often describes people from his past I have never met. The most depressing prospect, for him, seems to be that of a couple, both artists, moving to the provinces, supporting themselves by teaching, becoming engaged in local cultural activities, their art in quantity and quality diluted by an agreeable married life. He cheers on artists who are taking risks and expresses relief when they enjoy sales and praise. This loyalty and engagement extends to those within his own circle. Jake had a reasonably high-prestige, well-paid job in his early twenties, but, as he recalls, 'I was seriously bored and was considering launching myself into the precarious pursuit of work in films ... I asked Frank for his advice (I now think I was probably looking for his approval). He said "I would prefer you to be drinking yourself silly in a pub in the West of Ireland than to be bored for another minute."'[55]

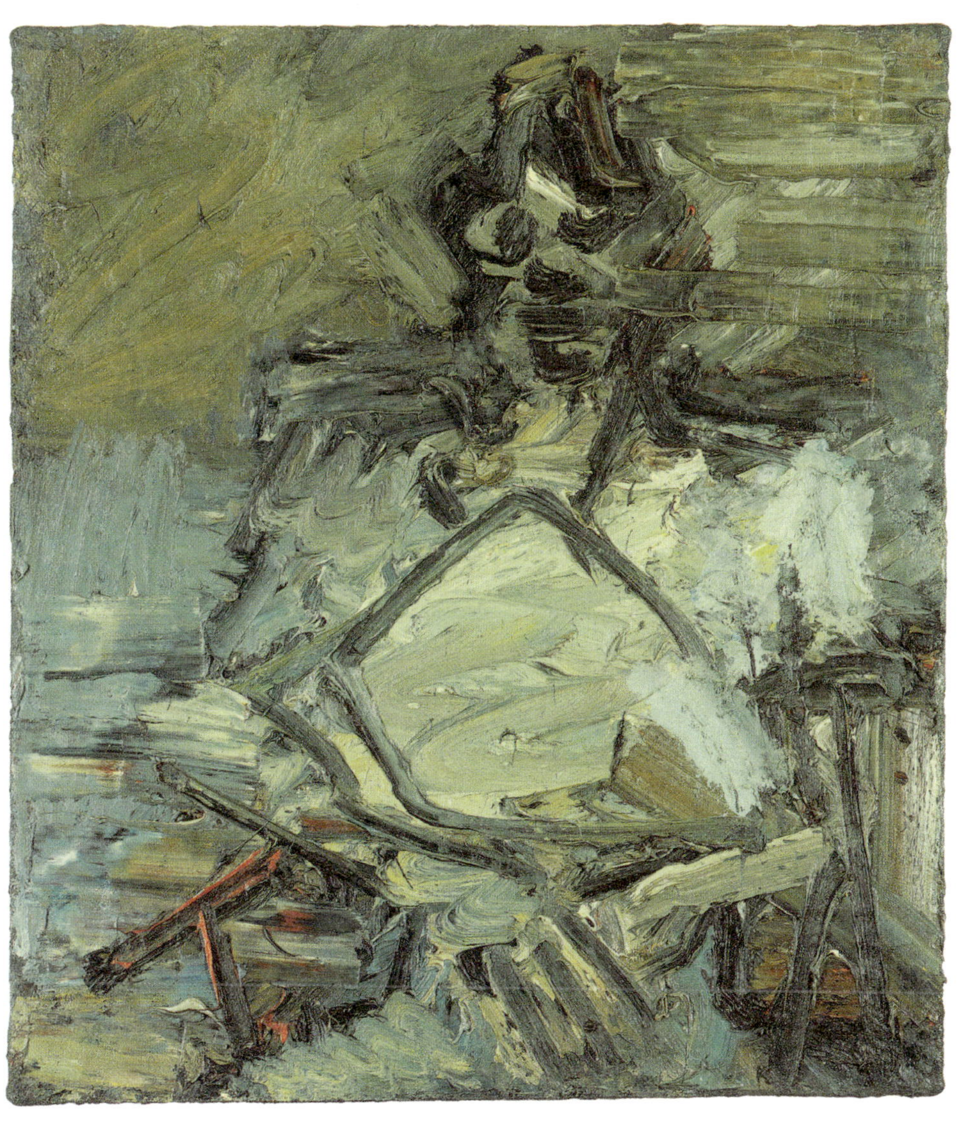

Jacob, 1979–80

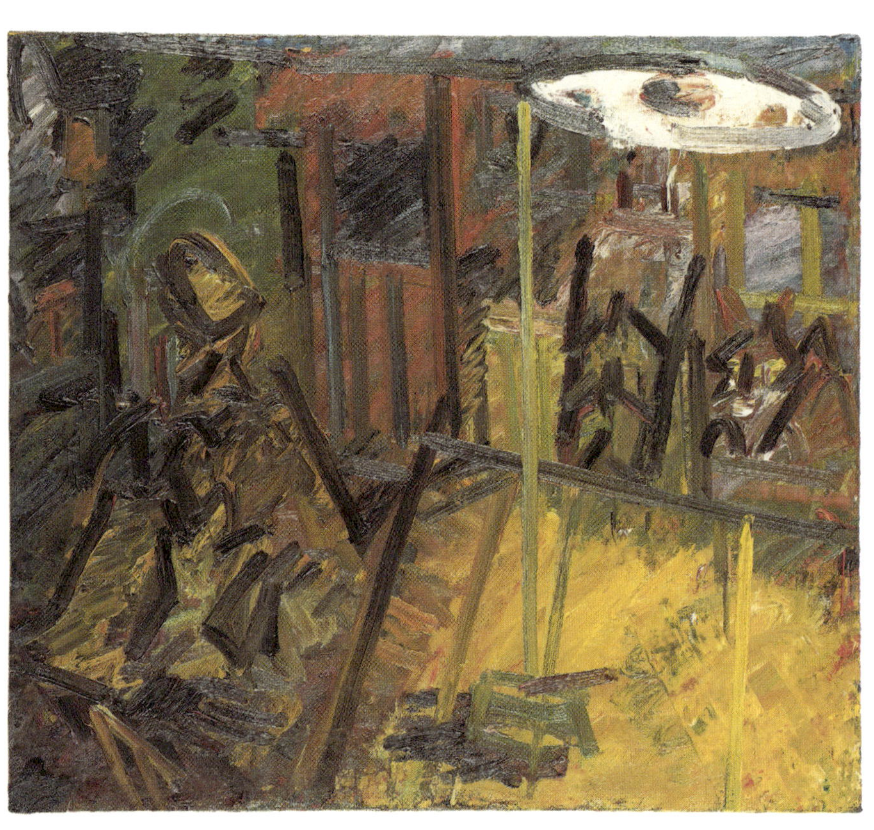

Interior Vincent Terrace, 1982–84

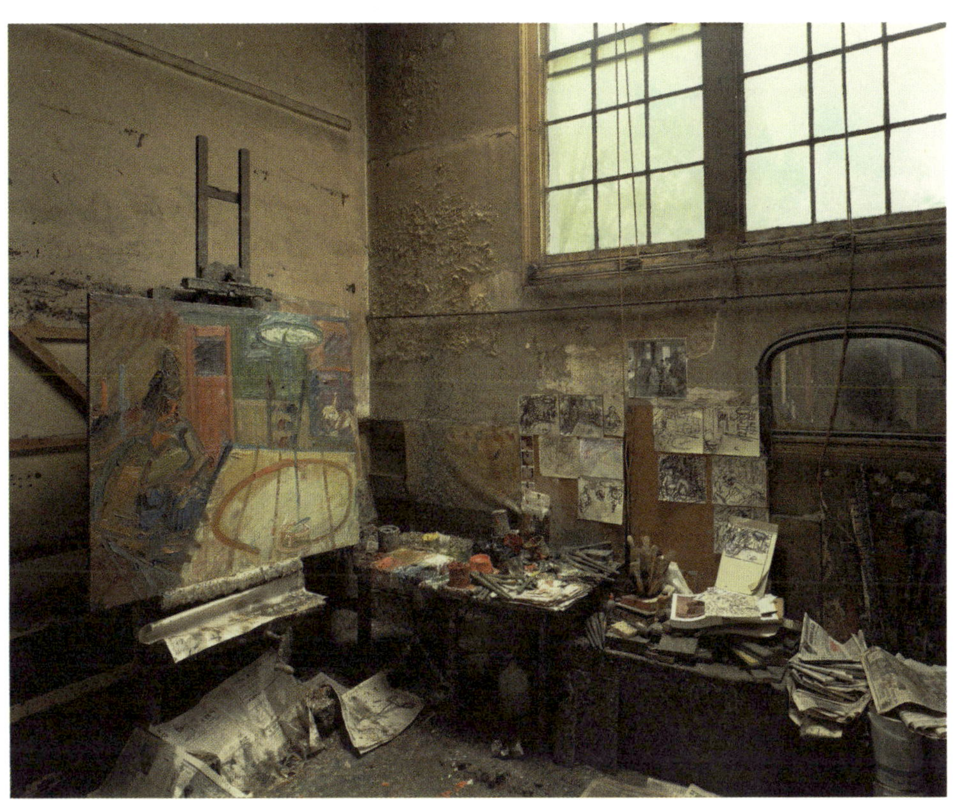

The studio with *Interior Vincent Terrace* (1982–84) in progress, 1984

'A cultural activity': Travelling for exhibitions and art

Nearly all the visits Auerbach has made abroad have been in connection with hanging one of his own exhibitions. He arrived in New York on 16 September 1969 for his first show at the Marlborough-Gerson Gallery in New York. As always, it was his intention to return home as soon as possible, but the city was so exciting he stayed eight days. Michael Roemer met him off the plane and took him to The King of the Sea restaurant on 3rd Avenue, the place that boasted, 'The flounder you eat today swam last night in the Chesapeake Bay'.[56] During a second visit, in 1982, one of the most memorable experiences was going to the night court in the Bowery, a place where the authorities charged those brought in before midnight in order to keep them over. 'They were mostly whores, with their pimps waiting in the seats, who just had to pay a fine. An older, dressing-gowned black man got up. The judge said, in an old-fashioned tone, "Most of us go through our lives without once being accused of murder. Our friend here has the distinction of being accused of murder for the second time in his life". He was charged.' On a postcard he sent to me Frank spoke of other diversions, 'I got up at 6, watched a respectable businessman buy a *Times* and a gay magazine, had three breakfasts, walked down from 58th to Canal Street, got some pencils at Pearl Paints ... In the Marlborough I felt as though I had shrunk crossing the Atlantic' (the 'I' referring to his art).[57]

Roemer drove Frank to Pennsylvania to visit the Philadelphia Museum of Art and the Barnes Collection in the suburban town of Merion, where Cézanne's *The Card Players* (1890–92) made an enduring impression. 'The particular way in which the people are scrutinizing their hands and the way a child is looking over the shoulder of one of them to see the cards, I've never seen anything that's quite as convincingly true. The followers of Cézanne were aware only of his violent breaks with the previous style and latched onto that. *I* think these violent breaks with the previous style were in the interest of fact. Gradually the style falls away and one's left with these card players.'[58]

On one occasion the excursion was simply to see paintings. Leon Kossoff and Auerbach flew to Amsterdam in September 1972. In the Rijksmuseum the 'special' guide who let them in out of hours became impatient as they lingered in front of Rembrandt's *Night Watch*. Travelling by

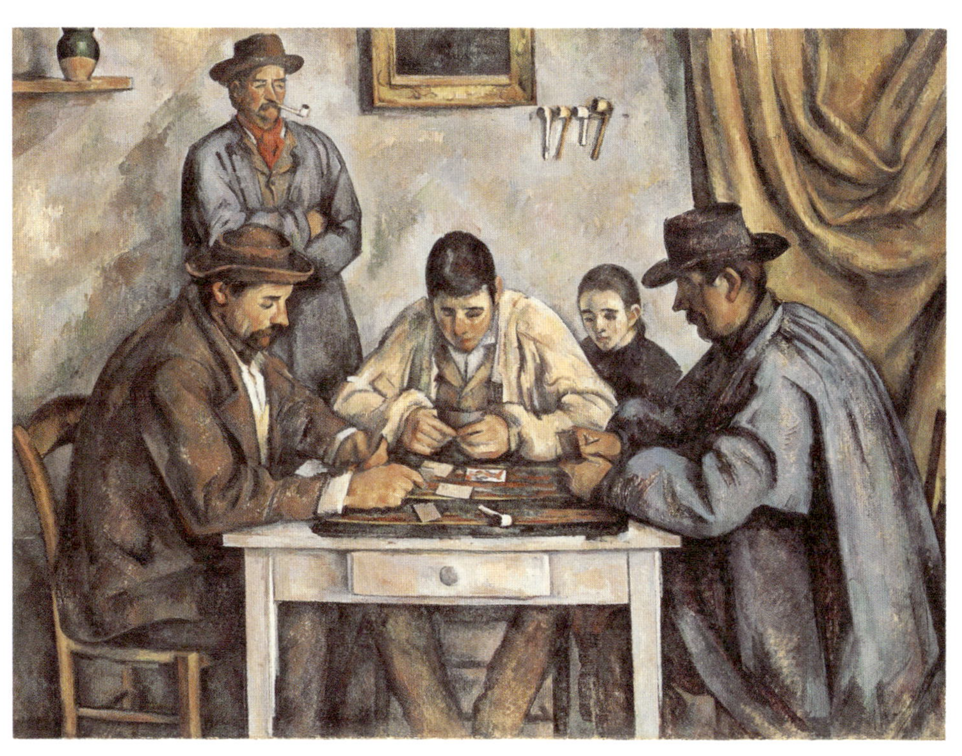

PAUL CÉZANNE, *The Card Players (Les Joueurs de Cartes)*, 1890–92

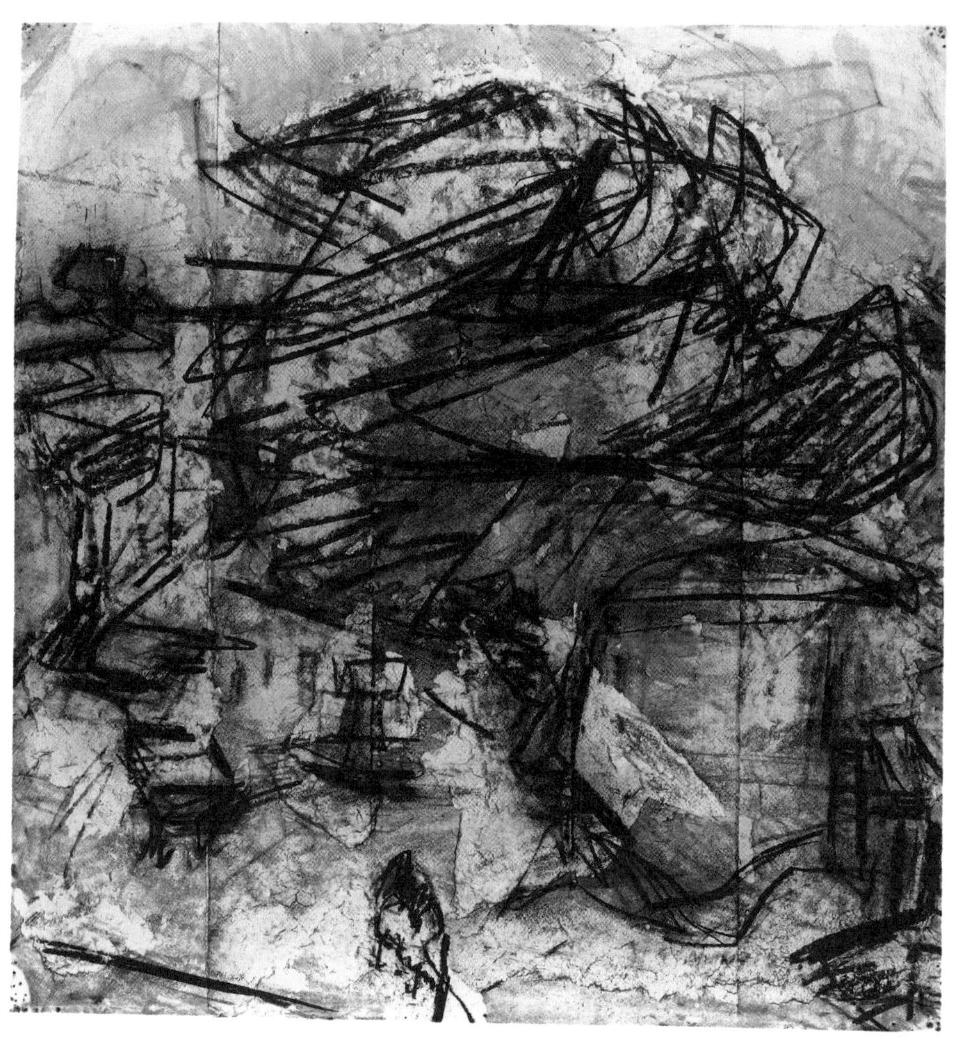

Tree at Tretire, 1975

train, they made rapid visits to the Hals Museum in Haarlem, the Boijmans Van Beuningen in Rotterdam, the Gemeentemuseum in The Hague and the Stedelijk in Amsterdam. Frank was struck by impressive groups of work by Dalí and Malevich.

Auerbach's international reputation was growing in Europe as well as the United States. The show at the Galleria Bergamini on Milan's elegant Corso Venezia in 1973 allowed him to view Leonardo's much restored *Last Supper*, 'which functions, *in situ*, as though it were taking place, dissolved into the wall, behind the other, real table, where the monks ate'. Actual works routinely bring new reactions. 'I thought I had no use for Leonardo da Vinci, he is not the artist I feel warmest towards, but I can't deny that when I saw the *Last Supper* in Milan, and [later] the drawings in the Queen's Collection and so on, they present one with an imagination that once one's met, one can't forget.'[59] 'Whereas the abilities of artists from the past are often lost, living artists must make their own discoveries. 'If one meets a great quality or great fervour or great intelligence one's first impulse is just to rush home and have another go ... it's not an effect of aping it, in fact, because one tries to leave it behind ... the activity of painting is not like spitting, it's a cultured activity.'[60]

Sometimes the foreign trips were entertaining in a social way. In 1974, Dublin's Hugh Lane Municipal Gallery of Modern Art, as it was then called, arranged to show the six outstanding works by Auerbach that Sir Basil Goulding owned.[61] An Irish cricketer and squash player as well as businessman, Goulding and his wife collected art, lived in a very modern house in the suburbs and entertained. The Earl of Rosse, active in the preservation of art and a member of the Arts Council of Ireland, drove Frank around Dublin, impressing him with his knowledge of Gilbert Stuart's paintings, ranging way beyond the portraits of George Washington. He remembered Rosse's very agreeable wife, Anne Messel, Lord Snowdon's mother; she had looks like those of Vivien Leigh.

The scope of another Marlborough 'branch' exhibition at their gallery in Zurich in 1976 was ambitious, virtually a retrospective, with two paintings from the 1950s, sixteen from the 1960s, fifteen from the 1970s plus works on paper, various studies for Primrose Hill landscapes, and a new print of the tree outside Brigid Campbell's Herefordshire house, Tretire.

In the Kunsthaus Zurich, Auerbach saw Giacometti's work arranged by subject. 'Father: paintings, drawings and sculptures; mother: paintings, drawings and sculptures; Diego: paintings, drawings and sculptures, and so on. I can think of one other artist – not Degas, not even Matisse – where the three media are so clearly expressions of one single vision. That artist is Michelangelo.'[62]

In early 1984, Auerbach was invited to represent Britain at the XLII Venice Biennale in 1986. As soon as he was approached, he outlined his ideas to the director of the fine arts department at the British Council, Julian Andrews: thirty works 'if they were discrete and independent images, would probably fill the space without looking wilfully austere and negative'; his preference was for a spare hanging and a wall colour 'grey or perhaps blue-grey'.[63] The light in the British Pavilion during the Biennale brought out the radiance in Auerbach's pictures, and the show was widely acclaimed; he shared the prestigious Golden Lion prize with the German painter Sigmar Polke.

The Marlborough organized a celebration lunch, which took place at Harry's Bar on Friday, 27 June 1986. One of the things that Auerbach relished about his rare travels was the food. The menu was one with local style: *ravioli speciali di pesce, fegato alla veneziana con polenta*. Just off the plane and arriving late, Jake remembers the glamourous atmosphere and this exchange with Robert Hughes, next to whom he was seated:

'Waiter, get this man a Bellini ... [to me] Have you ever had a Bellini?'
'No.'
'Do you know how it got the name?'
'No.'
'The colour is supposedly reminiscent of the great master's angels'
bottoms before the age got to the paint.'

Frank and Julia went for the day to Padua, Auerbach's first experience of Early Italian frescoes *in situ*, and he was struck by the 'radicalism' of what he saw in the Arena Chapel. 'It's very interesting because the light has faded the frescoes at one's own level, at ground level and because light hasn't attacked the frescoes as they go into the darker ceiling, they're pretty fresh up there ... There was a guide going around and saying, here somebody's weeping about something, some biblical scene and you looked and that's what they were doing. He [Giotto] represented the emotion and the drama directly. I think they're done in response to feelings, so that the gesture would not be done with any sort of view of correctness thrust into you but if somebody touches somebody gently or the cherubs are blubbing because of death, it's done out of feeling.' John Tusa, who was interviewing Auerbach for BBC Radio 3, speculated, 'And wonderfully innocent?' 'Yes, but then in a sense there's a sort of element of innocence in great art. There's an element of innocence in what was perhaps the most sophisticated painter who ever lived, that's Velázquez and yet if you see a portrait of Philip IV there he is. You don't think this is Velázquez being clever, it's just he's ingested it.'[64] In a later conversation with me he extended the observation, 'I saw a fragment of a Giotto fresco that had been peeled off the wall, and it was obviously breathing. The outlines had to do, not with silhouetting something, but with understanding it and understanding that it was pulsing with the space next to it.'

The critic Judith Bumpus, interviewing Auerbach for an article published in the run-up to the Biennale, suggested that rather than hardly venturing out, perhaps it might be more daring to travel more often in the future. Frank's reply was direct: 'It would be more daring to be a bull-fighter, or a stunt pilot or an acrobat! The daring that I'm talking about is simple daring in painting ... I'm naturally timid. I'm frightened of heights, I can't swim, I can't drive, I'm afraid of large dogs. It seems to me to be sensible to avoid the seaside, bridges and Alsatians. Painting is a relatively safe way of being courageous.' In the studio the artist has to be prepared to throw away a picture that would be convenient to finish: 'And I think one does a good painting by destroying a rather good one, not by destroying a rotten one. So there's always this moment when one gambles, when one flings away everything in the hope of getting something better ... I think one's got to be prepared to starve to death in order to keep on doing that.'[65] As his financial situation has improved, Auerbach's desire not to repeat himself or release an ordinary work creates just as extreme a mental pressure, one that matches the physical exertion, and not illogically increases with age.

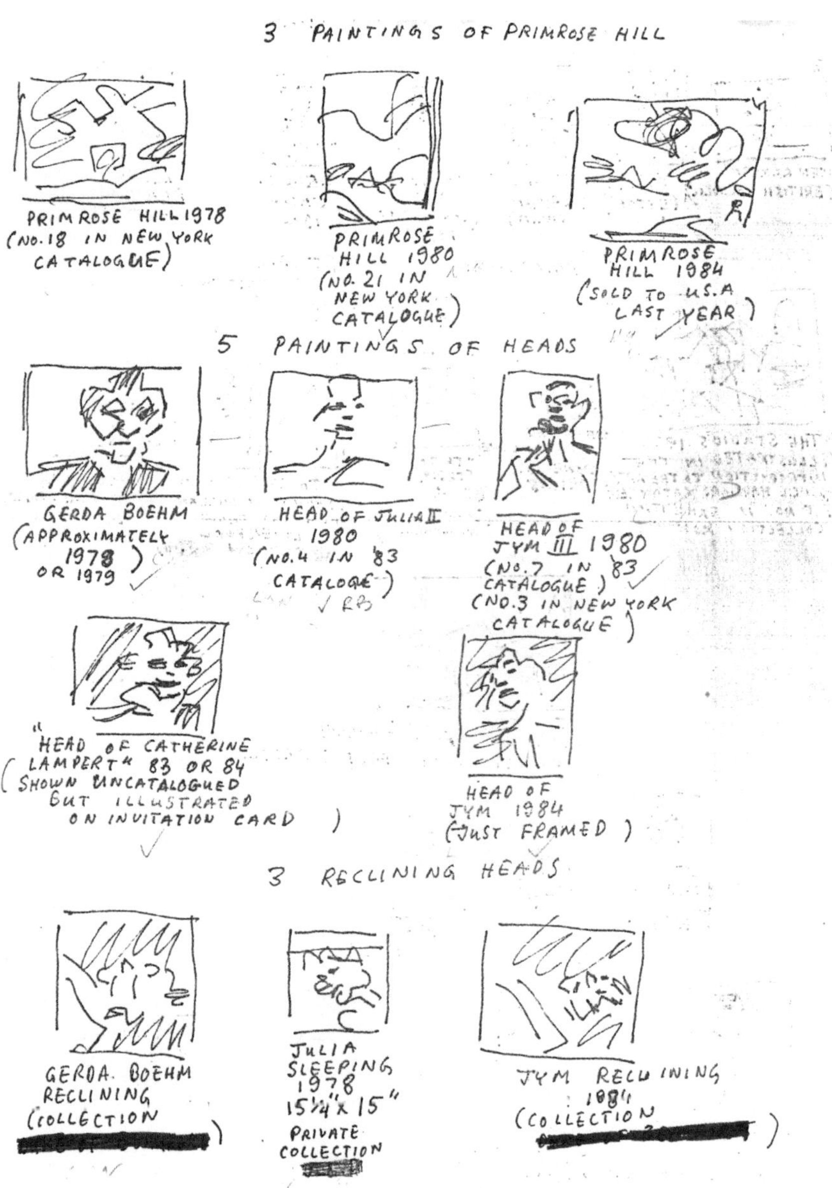

Page from letter to Miss Beston with ideas for Venice Biennale exhibition, 1984

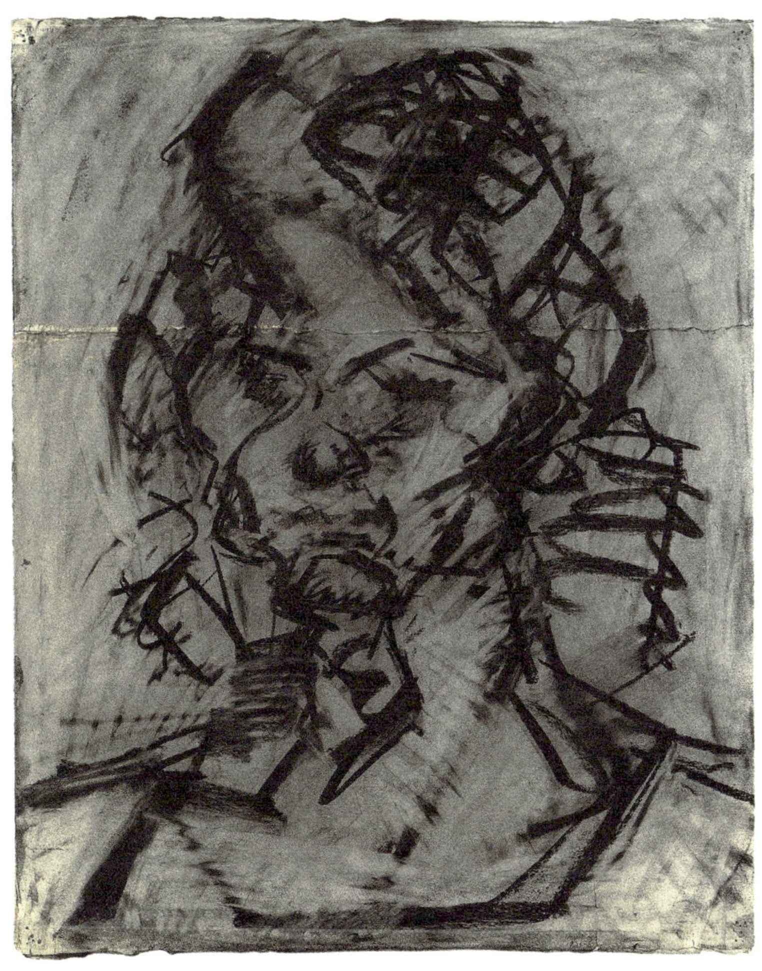

Head of Jacob, 1984–85

A return to Germany, 1986

In order to hang the Venice exhibition in the German tour venues, Auerbach had to make two more trips to Europe, the first to the Kunstverein in Hamburg in October 1986. He was accompanied by Geoffrey Parton, by now his primary contact at the Marlborough, and Kitaj who came along to share the experience of Frank's return to Germany after forty-seven years.[66] The food and to some degree the German language seemed familiar, yet it was in no way a momentous return. In the dead of winter the following January they went to the Folkwang Museum in Essen. As Geoffrey reminisced when we spoke in 2013, knowing that Auerbach ceased to travel twenty years ago, even as far as Dulwich or Cambridge in 1992, 'When he did go away, he really enjoyed himself.'

The critic Doris von Drateln, anticipating a German audience engaging with the work, interviewed Auerbach for *Kunstforum*. She was impressed by his seven-days-a-week routine and rather shocked at the primitive nature of the studio; she suggested such dedication to art implies an almost monk-like self-sacrifice. Pursuing this line of thought she received a disarming reply. 'I would like art to save things that are in danger of disappearing. I must say that I am never bored when I paint. In the first place, the world is very interesting, life is interesting and seems an unearned gift; perhaps one wants to give something back. In addition, painting is a wonderful game. One has little power over the crises in life, or in friends' lives. One cannot control wealth or poverty, happiness or misery. I am only in control when I am in the studio. Then I am close to life.' He added, 'If one is told that the man next door has been poisoned, or that someone has been run over in the street, one tries to behave decently but the real instinct is to get back to the studio and the brushes to make sense of these events.'

Perhaps thinking of twentieth-century painting in her country, from the Neue Sachlichkeit artists to an artist such as Joseph Beuys, he reflected, 'It is possible that German painters address the public more than I do. I can't do that. But if more people concerned themselves with their art they might do less harm. It might be a better world. So, if I cannot save the world, I might save myself.'[67]

And, in another interview, in 1988, with Richard Cork, if readers wondered how the implicitly autobiographical content of Auerbach's art related to the death of his parents and millions of others in the Holocaust, Auerbach was concerned to deflect such thoughts. 'I'm not certain that I became aware of evil any more than any other child who reads a fairy tale about the wicked step-mother in Snow White having her feet put into red-hot slippers, as they do in the German version ... I think that there are very few people who don't have some sort of experience of loss and danger at an early age. If it doesn't take a real form, it takes a fantastic one.'[68]

'I am happiest with a brush in my hand here'

Frank insists that painting every day of the year is a form of indulgence rather than toil. 'I'm just having fun in the studio, I'd rather do that than go to the theatre or sit about ... In the same way that people play games that have an element of intractability, something like chess, games with an infinite set of possibilities and difficulties. Or in the way that people perform a sport that doesn't come naturally to them, or solve complicated puzzles [he is good at crosswords]. In that way, one does this immensely difficult, immensely challenging thing in the studio, with the added bonus that if one should finish something, which is relatively rarely, one surprises oneself. I can't foresee the end of my pictures or my drawings. I keep on working, and trying to do them in the hope of finding this result which to me is surprising, more surprising than finding an Easter egg as a child.'[69]

On the last visit to New York, in 1994, Frank and Julia were put up in a suite at the Lowell Hotel that included a study, kitchen and bathroom (with a cockroach) and lots of telephones. He remembers running around trying to find one that operated when Robert Hughes rang. On Frank's way home lightning struck the wing of the plane. 'I thought then what an absolute total idiot I would feel if that was how I died – in such an irrelevant way. If, on the other hand, I had been standing in front of a canvas on which I was working with terrific fervour and energy and something burst inside me, that would be fine, even appropriate, as there is nothing I really want to do except to paint ... One never knows how much time one has got left ... I've been to New York three times and I found it enormously exciting. On my first trip in 1969 for five days and nights I simply didn't sleep; I just walked around Manhattan literally drunk on the city. But that was then and now I am happiest with a brush in my hand here.'[70]

Auerbach has never liked crowds or appointments, and has always needed time alone, as most artists do. Jake recalls, 'In the days before Frank's reputation for hermithood was a reality rather than a useful semi-fiction, we would occasionally do pub quizzes (which we both love, quizzes are still a pleasure). It isn't surprising that Frank knows a lot about a few subjects ... Painting, theatre, poetry for example ... what was surprising is how much he knows about so many subjects ... Cinema, politics, history and more ... Now, when a tempting opportunity to spend an evening away from the studio might come up ... It might be considered but these days it is almost always rejected.' The phrase of his father's that rings in Jake's ear is: 'Painting is the best game I have ever played, why would I want to do anything else?'[71]

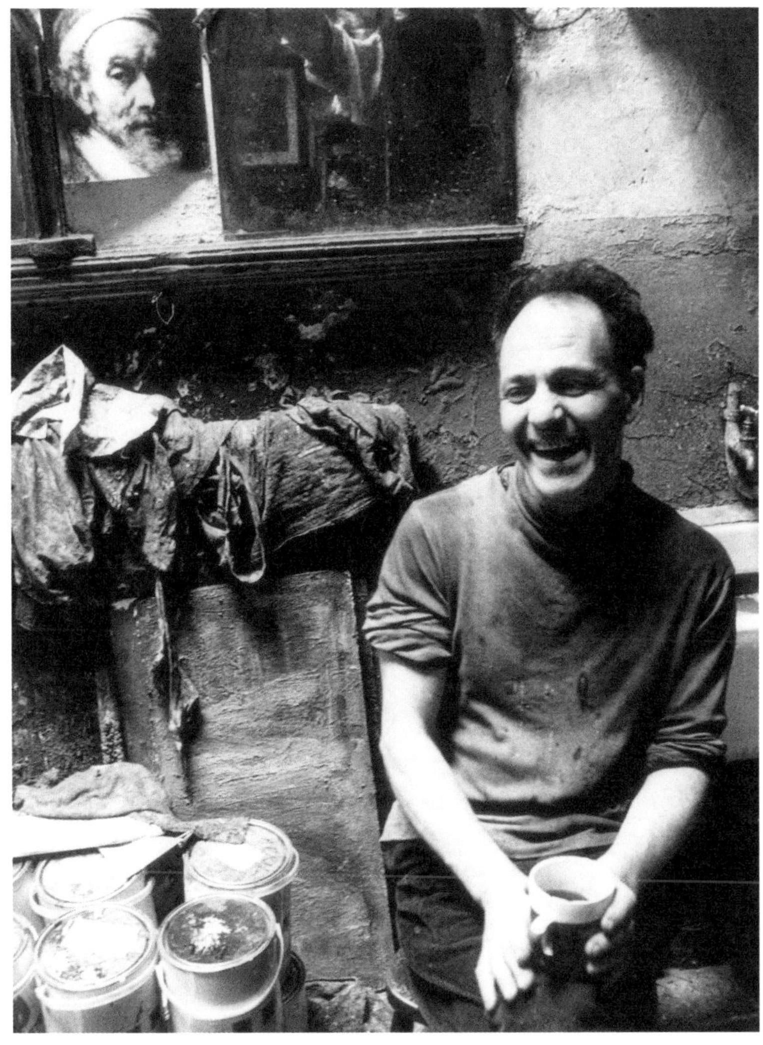

BRUCE BERNARD, Frank in the studio, *c.* 1983

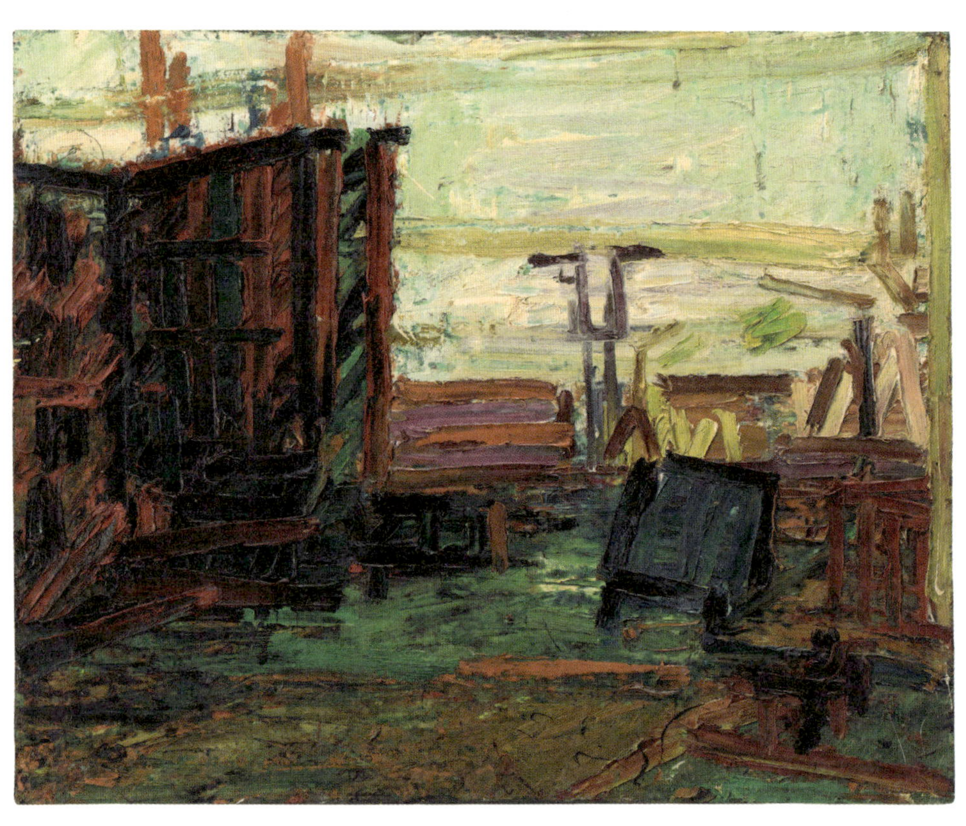

Mornington Place – Morning, 1972

Idiom and Subject

Beginning and finishing

An artist's idiom distinguishes their work from that of another, yet Auerbach believes it is not entirely controlled by will: 'Whatever else I can change I can't, anymore than anyone else, change my handwriting.' Like his penmanship, which is extremely clear, with capital letters for emphasis, his pictorial idiom is characterized by marks that are unusually legible, often made at different speeds. There are hooks, swipes, broken brushstrokes and tiny inflections. Close-up, curvy traces left by the hairs of the brush and furrows formed by his scraper are evident and somehow vital.

Auerbach works across the whole picture, all the time, with the result that the surface remains unusually unified, as if kept at a constant, fresh temperature. Often viewers assume that the picture is merely the sum of all the daily versions, when actually his idiom demands removing the fresh paint before beginning again the following day. Another way in which he identified with de Kooning was that this older painter 'actually had an irrational feeling that the paint would rot unless it was one continuous coat of wet paint'.[1] By the 1970s the impasto was becoming more fluid and adventurous in terms of colour. For example, *Mornington Place - Morning* (1972), exhibited in Milan in 1973 and brought from an Italian collection to Sotheby's London in 2014, where it was cleaned and re-photographed, was described by the auctioneers as having in the foreground 'a scumbled verdant pavement that recedes into the distance of a warm silvery skyline [that] anchors luscious crimson and purple tones intersected by lattice-like scaffolds of thick cadmium and orange pigment'. When face-to-face with the picture, a juicy blue trapezoid conveys velocity and it becomes evident that it is actually a lorry pulling off on the right.

After weeks and months on a picture, the surface might become somewhat corrugated or bumpy and a single stroke crosses boundaries and appears inflected; from varying viewpoints the terrain is quite material. By the 1990s, in order to achieve greater surface freshness and flexibility, Auerbach adopted a very extreme process: 'It became necessary for me to scrape the thing down thoroughly before I started working, so that except when I was ill, I've never had more than a day's break on a big painting, and I scrape it down every day because if I left for two days it would become much harder to scrape down.'

In answer to a question from the American art historian James Elkins, posed in the course of writing his book *What Painting Is* (1999), Auerbach replied: 'As soon as I become aware of what the paint is doing my involvement with the painting is weakened. Paint is at its most eloquent when it is a by-product of some corporeal, spatial, developing imaginative concept, a creative identification with the subject. I could no more fix my mind on the character of paint – than it may be – an alchemist could fix his on mechanical chemistry. I have put this clumsily – but I am certain that you understand.'[2]

Near the entrance to the studio 2.5-litre tins of paint are clustered, bought from Stokes Paints, the Sheffield family firm that manufactures for 'every use', from tools, furniture and agricultural equipment to heavy duty engineering; supplying artists is a sideline. The brand is high in oil content, the white especially heavy and sticky, their particular terre verte, Indian red and yellow ochre not quite like those of any other manufacturer.[3] The artist's thinning solution is paraffin; in the 1950s a man Auerbach met at Bromley College of Art had checked it out and, with a bit of oil added to the solution to make it less volatile, declared it safer than white spirit. Various artists' colours are bought in tubes. In 1987, Auerbach purchased a second studio, a flat in Finsbury Park, as security against something happening to the one he had near Mornington Crescent. There he paints his wife, Julia, using acrylic paint so as not to cause problems with the lease in a residential house. Given the medium and its fast-drying qualities, he admits to being slightly more enterprising in the colours he orders.

The finished paintings continue to be a total surprise to him. He increasingly wants both a command of his material and an inventive way of putting it down, even more so as he has been gradually trying to eliminate 'pictorial scaffolding' and, indeed, anything that could be explained. One of Auerbach's aspirations in the 1980s and beyond was to emulate Matisse and 'to paint by juxtaposing one area of colour against another and hoping that it will make the form.'[4] Frequently the dominant tones and colours change completely the following day: 'I think colour has to do with relationship and one can transpose it into a different key and it can be the same relationship. In fact, if you think of the paintings that have been done … the difference between Venetian colour and Rembrandt's colour … can you say that either of them is false or true … they're both arbitrary.'[5]

Searching for more 'technical' information, I speculated with Frank that when painting people he was more likely to use smaller brushes, to which he responded, 'I don't know what I'm doing. I don't think so. Certainly in some bits of the landscapes I find myself working with the wrong end of the brush or reaching for a matchstick on occasion to do things with. I usually have several sizes of brushes on the go. In a sense to be able to do the most delicate things with a big brush seems the nicest way of painting, but sometimes I need a little brush. There is a very good painting by Piazzetta, *The Sacrifice of Isaac* (after 1735) in the National Gallery (I was told it wasn't very authentic), painted with a big brush. The idiom isn't really the thing. With Veronese you can see the pencil lines underneath and somehow the older I get, the more marvellous I think Veronese is.'

As Auerbach has said on several occasions, artists must hold many things in their head; their thoughts will be travelling along certain paths and trying out certain possibilities and structures, creating certain hopes. He resists anyone tracing developments year on year or dwelling on similarities between pictures done in the same vicinity since he has no sense of essaying or finishing a series. 'I've more or less sleepwalked all my life.'[6] An enduring comparison is to the experience of astronomers and physicists as they make discoveries, a point brought out in two books that fascinated Auerbach: *The Sleepwalkers: A History of Man's Changing Vision of the Universe* (1959) by Arthur Koestler, which he read in the 1960s, and James D. Watson's *The Double Helix: A Personal Account of the Discovery of the Structure of DNA,* published in 1968. Going back to a figure from the seventeenth century, Johannes Kepler, as an example, Auerbach explained: 'Kepler tried to find the orbits of the planets and was absolutely convinced that they were elliptical and went on until the amount of measurement and knowledge that had been accrued began to create a unity of its own, and he did come to the point where he more or less correctly plotted the turning of the planets around the sun. That's a very grandiloquent comparison, of course, but it's a little like that, you keep looking, and you keep measuring, you keep moving it [a form] up and down, you keep trying to make it and its background one, and then you gradually begin to exclude certain things that you've put in by habit and you begin to see it more freshly and with any luck at the end you may find a bold way of stating how what you've learnt has come together.'[7]

The paintings still in progress Auerbach regards as horrible; the situation becomes so extreme that he feels if 'you let yourself off the hook and stop twenty seconds too soon it won't be any good' and the only thing to do is scrape everything off again.[8] The more the picture speaks back to him, the more it animates and challenges, the more likely it might mysteriously 'escape the thicket of prepared positions' and emerge as something surprising that is also a resolved entity. Nothing gets easier. Actually, the older he gets, the more reluctant he has become to let anything out of the studio that does not measure up to a high benchmark or is too like anything done previously. The last session is not necessarily dramatic, at least from what a sitter sees. 'It's a strenuous physical effort but occasionally, if the knowledge is accrued, if one's rehearsed the thing so much, it's surprising how much comparative delicacy and unity and likeness one can get very quickly.'[9] This comment brings to mind the way Marckwald insisted on serious rehearsals, act by act, for the school plays, yet in *Everyman*, Frank's inspired delivery of a speech was unrelated to anything prepared. Even two of his lines, 'I will make my testament Here before you all present', seem prescient.

As soon as the works are finished they are brought to the gallery to rest until dry enough to be photographed and framed, the larger landscapes hanging on the wall in Geoffrey Parton's office at the Marlborough, the smaller ones laid flat in a box. Both framed drawings and paintings are under glass, a practice Auerbach began after Bacon persuaded him of the advantage, which, apart from protection against touching, encourages viewers to step back and see the whole image. 'I'm not really interested in the paint per se, as paint, I couldn't care less, and the glass distances people a bit from the paint.'[10]

Seeing the black-and-white photograph is a bit like when a writer reads his handwritten work typed out. Auerbach has often thought a picture was finished that wasn't. 'I get it back from the framers and scrape it and repaint it. I've got a whole collection of things that have been photographed, framed and then repainted.'[11] Three criteria help him decide: the picture should convey a sense of something specific in the tangible world; it should function like a machine, 'every part of it performing a function'; and it must seem 'an object like nothing on earth'. These ideas, outlined in a letter published in *Cambridge Opinion* in 1964, were reiterated when Frank was interviewed by Jake for *The Last Art Film* (2012). There he used a blackboard and chalk to illustrate the point, adding that it must 'feel exact, having the expression that your idea has', and further emphasizing the importance of a 'tense, surface character' by sketching the recognizable design of the Union Jack.[12] However, there is no simple answer to the question of how he knows a picture is finished, mimicking T. S. Eliot's jaunty declaration: 'in so far as there is some discernible difference in quality between one creative artist and another, that difference lies in the critical faculty.'[13]

Subjects: Landscapes since 1977

'I've never been moved by a real landscape as I have by paintings of landscape. It's because every moment is transmitted by human will that we identify ourselves with it. In a painting you re-experience what the painter experienced, one brushstroke over another, it's like a *perpetuum mobile*.'[14]

Before Auerbach acquired the freehold to the studio in *c.* 1983 he was 'in continual fear of being thrown out or something going wrong, and I may say that before it was re-built I think the Council if they'd seen it would have disapproved of it. I needed this space so I clung to it like a drowning man to a raft.'[15] In a state of anxiety, he began paintings of the entrance to the row of three studios in 1977, focusing on the view between the red-brick Victorian house on the left and a block of 'modern' houses on the right, down the alley, with the backs of terraces in the distance and further still the gleaming white upper floors at the back of Greater London House, a grand Egyptian Revival building, now offices but formerly the Carreras Tobacco Company factory. Around the same time he began painting the looming façade of the Camden Palace theatre, with its 'happy' eyebrow-like arched windows and roof surmounted by a copper-covered dome.

As soon as Auerbach engaged with these built-up street scenes, he yearned for something more organic, telling me in 1978, 'I've done these subjects because I've wanted to do them in both cases, but there is a certain limitation in the angularity of the conjunctions. To turn to a new subject isn't a conscious thing and it isn't even a thing of ambition because I think my ambition would be to paint some large figures, but the circumstances of my life at the moment make me feel that this would be an artificial image. I don't know how, but these things are in some sense symbolic. On the other hand I have become tired of these angular geometries which I've dealt with and tried to supersede, and so recently I've gone to Primrose Hill and I've drawn the clouds and there are certain massy, turning, pillowey, featherbeddy convolutions of earth and sky that have seemed to me a stimulus to try and get an image that extends my repertoire.'[16]

The drawings made each morning are useful for gathering information; one day Auerbach might draw a street, concentrating on all the chimneys, and the next morning focus on the television aerials. 'Often I find myself looking at the one I've done today. The drawing is a mnemonic so one remembers what one saw outside so it is only one step removed from working with a model present. I do sometimes find one drawing is more stimulating or odd.' Questions about what can be identified – the vehicle, the jogger, the expression flickering across a sitter's face, whether these belong to a single occasion – will elicit replies along the following lines from Frank: 'There are all those things, sometimes unrecognizable to other people, but they are certainly recognizable to me. Some things are just brushstrokes and I don't remember what they are. Courbet when questioned replied, "C'est la peinture".'

A hawthorn tree with angled trunk on Primrose Hill became the subject of seven paintings in the years 1985–87, with the branches spanning the upper register of the canvas: 'a tree that shoulders the cloud ceiling'.[17] However, the choice of tree was a sort of accident. 'I don't know how or

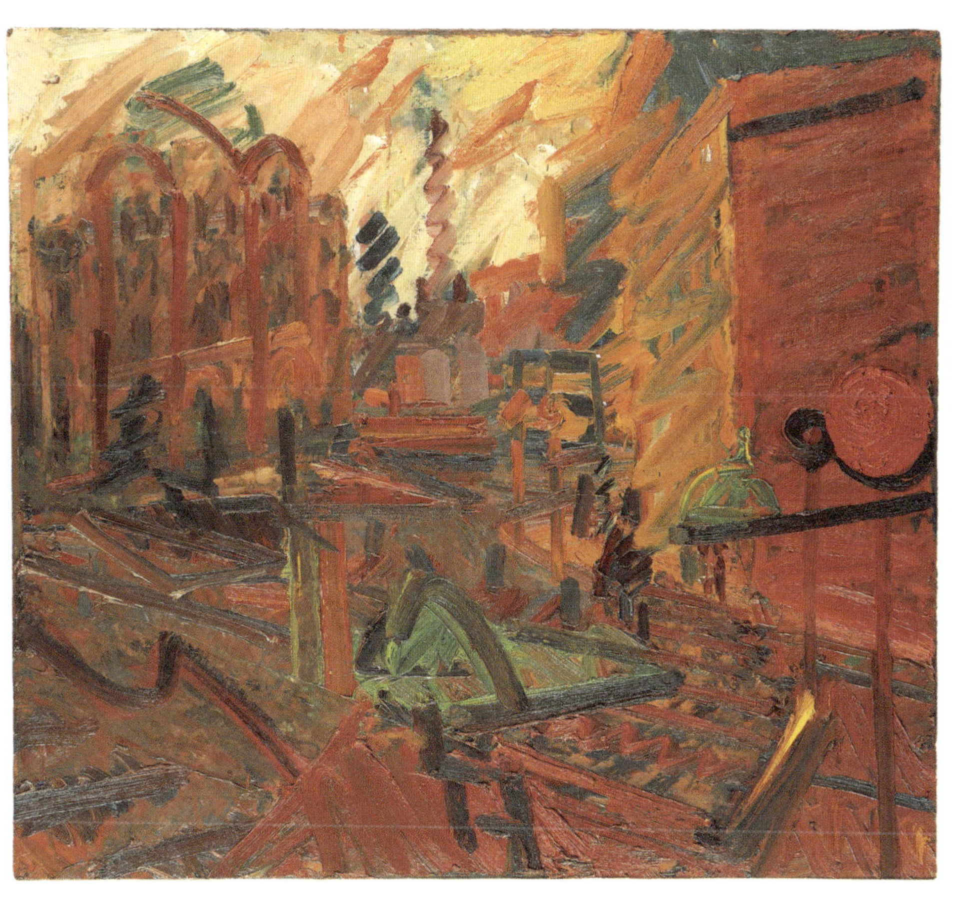

Camden Theatre in the Rain, 1977

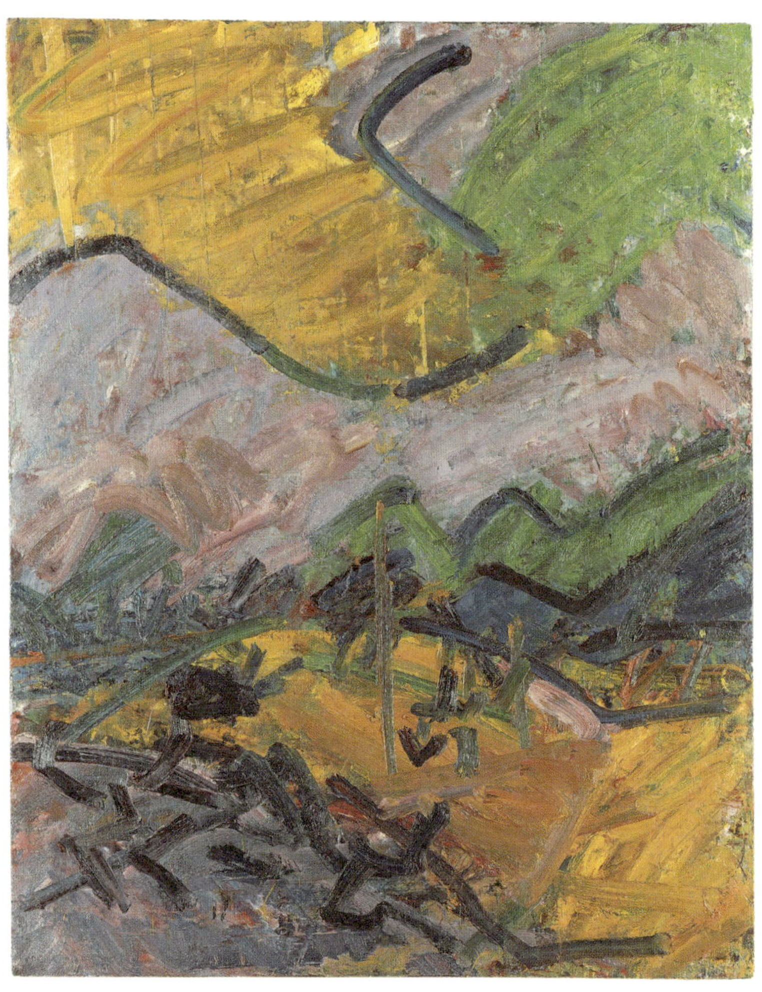

Primrose Hill, 1979–80

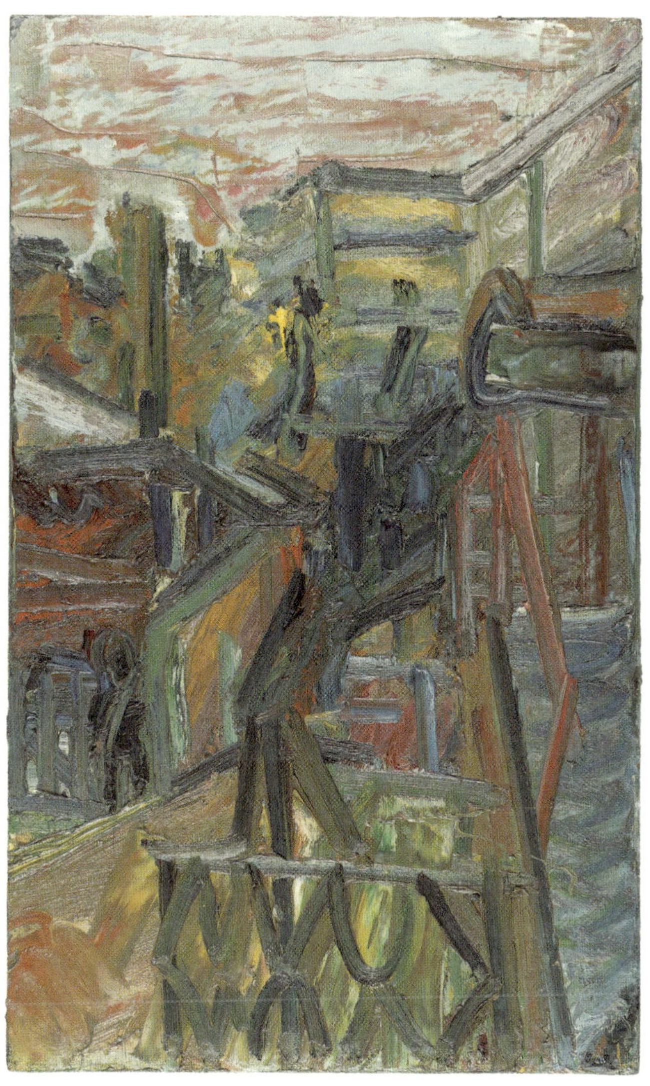

The Studios – Spring Morning, 1980–81

why I was doing that tree, partly for the sake of variety ... sometimes Julia came with me – the white coat is Julia. That's a dog, there are people. That one is striding up the hill, but these facts are not really relevant because it changes. I've got a feeling a man was taking off his jogging bottoms, something fairly complicated. As the painting goes on, people come in, sometimes they disappear.' Auerbach remembers trying to get the feeling of the branch shaking in the wind into the rhythm of the painting.

Going out at dawn to draw provides both information and a kind of compost. 'I never visualize a picture before I start. I have an impulse and I try to find a form for that impulse. The great benefit of manuring the thing with reality is that reality continually belies one's expectations: where one expects the grand sweep it suddenly starts becoming petty, where one expects it to be hard it becomes soft, the proportions – almost every day one goes out there, one has different sensations about them.'[18] Actually this is not so different from painting people; the sitters are sometimes simply some kind of anthropomorphic raw material: 'they're there to feed this new, independent image that one's trying to make, that stalks into the world like a new monster'.[19] A photograph from 1987 shows two sets of drawings pinned to a board, for the *Tree on Primrose Hill* (1987) and *From the Studios* (1987), the latter taking in a large plane tree with an indication of a man in the foreground, the artist. A sketch of *The Vendramin Family* by Titian and his workshop in the National Gallery is partly visible under one of the *From the Studios* drawings, perhaps to help resolve one of the compositions.

When the Mornington Crescent studio was modernized by the architects Long & Kentish in 1990, the inclusion of a small kitchen, a mezzanine level for the bed and an indoor toilet meant he lost space. Auerbach began to find it more convenient to concentrate on one large landscape at a time and to make small versions of the same subject, sometimes beginning one mid-way through working on the large picture. After 2010 this practice has 'crept up on me again, now it's almost always that I have one or two, or three, or in some cases four little ones on the go, which are not replicas and are not studies, they are just to keep one's mind moving, different conceptions of the subject'. I ask him if the smaller landscapes are treated less dramatically, in a different vernacular. 'I don't know what they look like to other people; I just do them. But in both cases it is a question of getting

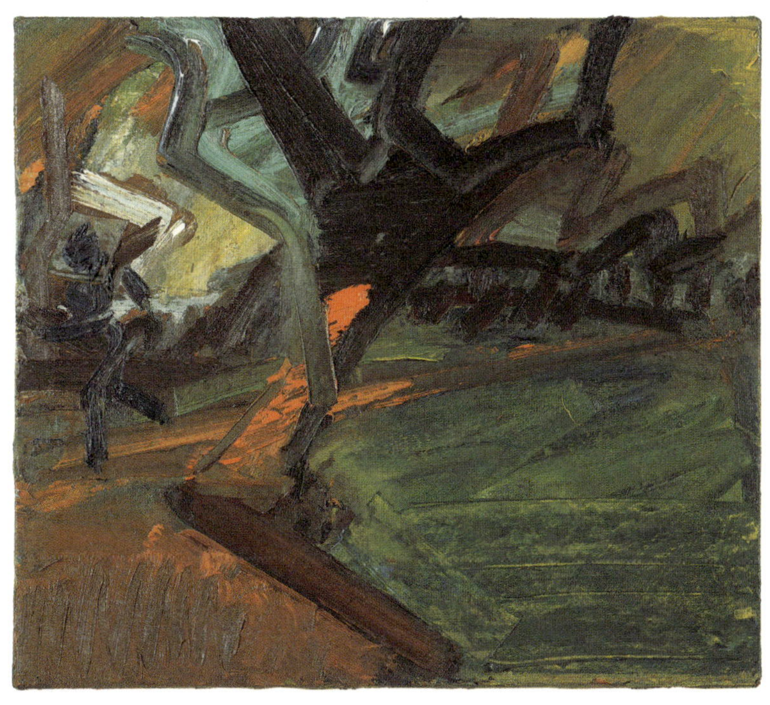

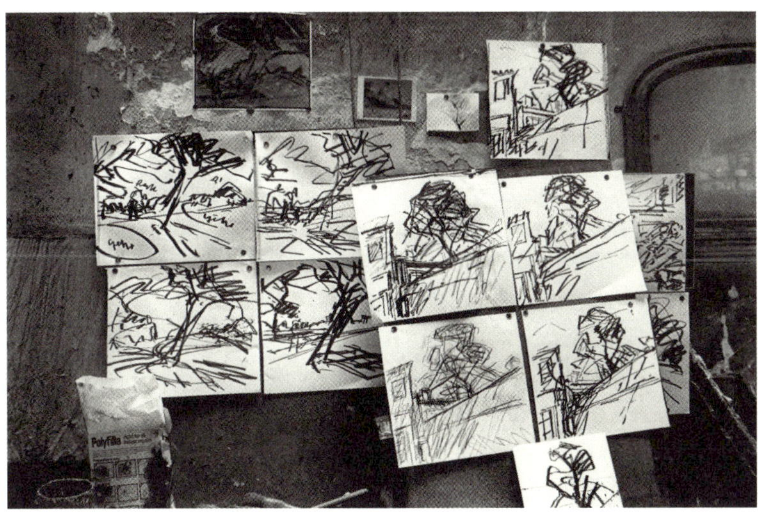

Top: Tree on Primrose Hill, 1987; *Above:* CHRIS STEELE-PERKINS, Drawings for
Tree on Primrose Hill and *From the Studios*, with sketch after Titian, 1987

something that hangs together formally, and the actual idiom, whether it's got harsher lines or softer lines, is almost an accident, because the day before it might have had an entirely different look.'

Over time Auerbach found that when he was working for more than a year on a picture he might have done over two hundred sketches for a painting and was gradually getting even more dependent on his subject. This exhaustive research has parallels to writers' methods. For example, Auerbach describes the books by Philip Roth that feature activities such as fishing and cutting through ice as 'very good novels' because 'he feeds in an immense amount of research, which is like doing drawings every day. Graham Greene was the same.'

The chimney in Mornington Crescent is another local landmark that Auerbach frequently passes. Thinking it rather remarkable, like Cleopatra's Needle, the Egyptian obelisk on the Embankment in London, he first tried to paint it in 1987. To him, the configurations around this towering form seemed like canyons. In the direction of another new view, south down Hampstead Road, the set of three tower blocks with 'different coloured head-bands on them' ended up in one painting.

In a way the pictures of Mornington Crescent and surroundings are not dissimilar from the early building sites: there are always new street barriers, shops, signs and obstacles, and yet the concrete shapes remain unchanged. Auerbach began painting a pub awning near Mornington Crescent station in 2008. 'If one feels one sort of mastered it, it loses its appeal perhaps. I have no memory and it may be that I go out there again and start doing it in drawings. I once had the extraordinary experience of doing two paintings of Primrose Hill from exactly the same site and until I had finished the second one I hadn't even realized it was the same site, because until I had finished with it, all I was thinking about was the identification with the material which I saw in front of me as if for the first time. Age plays a part. There is a sort of jostling and one has to be sort of tough to draw around there... the last few paintings outside have the street that I'm in, or the house that I'm in, so it means less walking about in the morning and one is cosy. It's surprising how many people see what you are doing, and minicab drivers say, "You're the man that draws in the street." Everything feeds into painting if you are receptive. Nothing is planned and

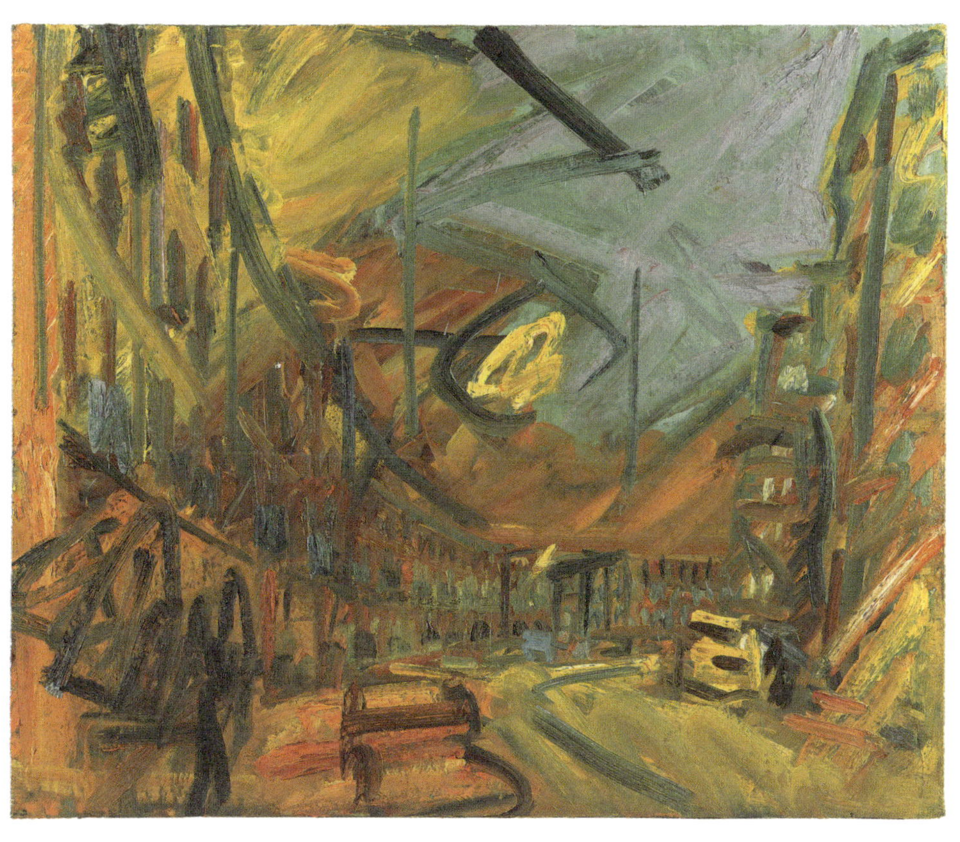

Mornington Crescent – Early Morning, 1992–93

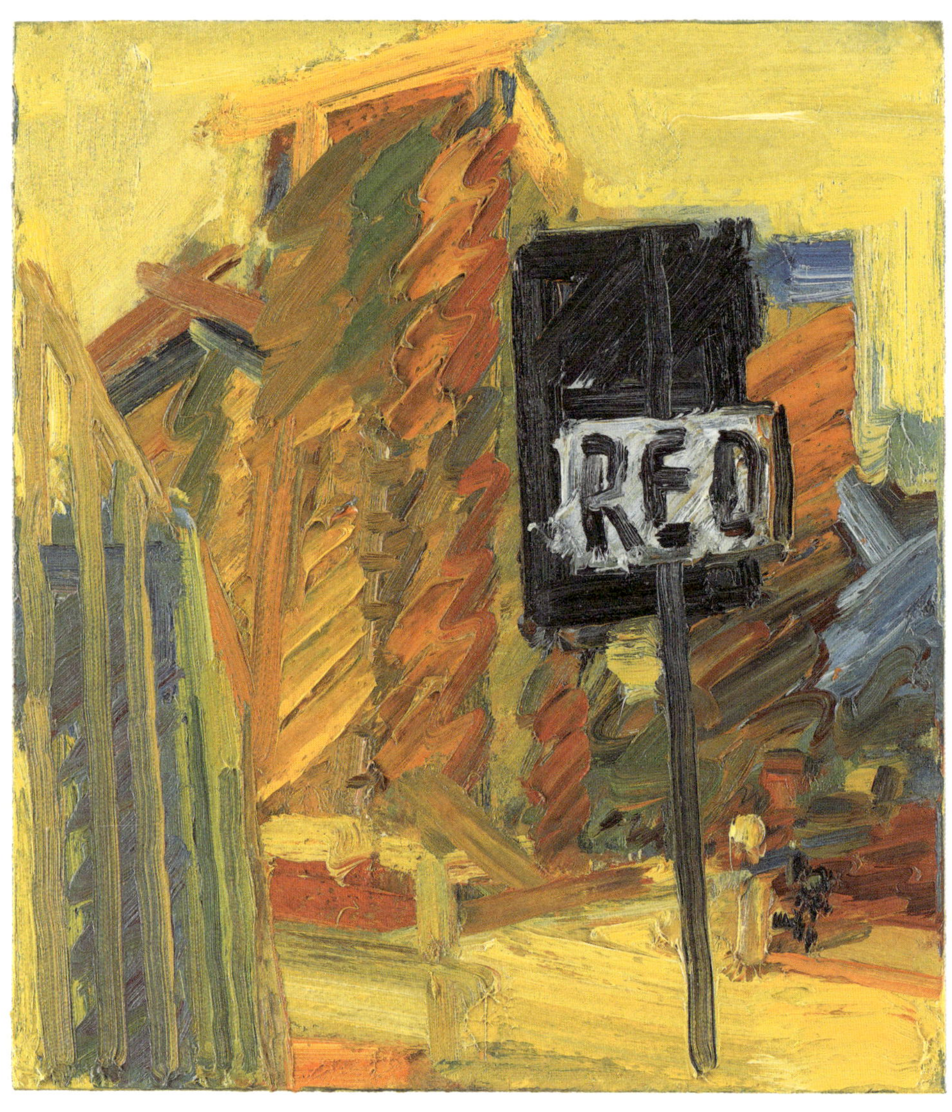

Tower Blocks, Hampstead Road, 2007

nothing needs to be justified. It's got to do with sensation. It's all done on one's nerves.' He remains dependent on the Mornington Crescent studio, sensing that if he lost it he would be 'like a snail without a shell'.

I asked Frank if when responding to what is far away and wishing to connect it to something in proximity it feels metaphorically as if he is gliding through space, then zooming in. 'Yes, that's part of the excitement of painting. There is an eloquent piece of rhetoric by Giacometti where he says, "The distance between one side of a nose and the other is like the Sahara, boundless."' A passage in the painter Rackstraw Downes's little book, *In Relation to the Whole* (2000), begins by discussing the difference in method between Maupassant and Chekhov, then he finds parallels in terms of artists with contrasting approaches, 'for instance, in the way Rubens shows you around his newly acquired country place, the Chateau de Steen, with exhilarated rapidity and an eye for the typical, rushing you off into the distance like the pilot of a tiny plane skimming the hedges in an eager take-off; while Constable, who borrowed a lot from Rubens's compositions, wanders through the landscape of *The Hay Wain* at a more ruminative pace, allowing himself to be diverted by a gentle, affectionate attention to the individual things around him.' Nudged to respond to Constable's *Hay Wain* (1821), Auerbach answers more broadly: 'As a painter you use everything, you use your sketches and you use your imagination. He [Constable] cared enormously about detail but it isn't mimetic realism. You get the same sky in three different paintings.' He went on to compare the two giants of English art: 'When Turner paints a frosty morning it somehow seems like an enchanted vision; whatever Constable paints always seems like lived-through reality ... But there isn't a Turner that doesn't somehow fly and there isn't a Constable that doesn't burrow.'[20]

Frank's imagination operates like Rubens, Turner, Jacob van Ruisdael, Constable and many others in his exploration of a city park and various intersections, which for him are as thrilling to explore as an 'estate'. Does he know what part of Camden Town will be next, though he has said he never thinks in terms of sequences? 'Sometimes when I finish a picture, I just wander around with a sketchbook and ideas and some of them I don't like. Then I find something that seems attractive', he replies. 'It was very different at the beginning. I was looking for compositions, I know I was.

The drawings I did for early paintings seem to me to have a composition, and now, I am thinking of ones of the *Pillar Box* [2010–11] and ... *The Bridge* [2006]; I very much look for things that are not compositions at all, that don't seem like art. I see whether I can try and paint them, something that for some reason or other is not a fitting material for any particular sort of picture but a piece of undigested reality. I try to find a way of making something of it.'

Subjects: Painting women in rooms

Honoré Daumier, one of the artists Auerbach responds to, found it impossible to work directly from life, whether in the streets or in the studio. His pictures depended on memory and empathy and yet they seem not just anatomically convincing, they are also really lively. Auerbach commented that the only work he missed in the Daumier show at the Royal Academy of Arts (2013–14) was one of the 'sweaty' nudes. There are only a few, all intended as paintings that might be accepted by the Salon jury or as subjects for a few ill-fated commissions Daumier began in the post-1848 period; for example, a kneeling, loose-haired woman supposed to be *The Magdalen in the Desert I* (1849–50) and two buxom, swaying *Women Pursued by Satyrs* (1850).[21] The subjects from his neighbourhood on the Ile Saint-Louis – the laundresses, the man on the rope, the clown – solid and believable as they are, are not there to play a role; there is no literary, metaphorical or naturalistic backstory. As with Auerbach's work, there is the same intense and precise atmosphere conveyed by the way the paint is laid on (and removed) that convinces the viewer it is both true and very human. 'If something looks like a painting it does not look like an experience; if something looks like a portrait it doesn't really look like a person.'[22]

Robert Hughes tried to establish a line between Sickert's nudes and Auerbach's, specifically the older artist's 'two-figure interiors of 1903–10', which he saw as deriving from Degas's brothel scenes: 'a man dressed, a woman naked ... In their dense ribbed paint, these Sickerts describe a sexual world of Edwardian England: the curt randiness of a middle-class using the lower class as its brothel.'[23] When he was a student Auerbach distanced himself from the admirers of Sickert's Camden Town interiors, but he has an inborn sympathy with the milieu. 'Helen Lessore wrote somewhere that

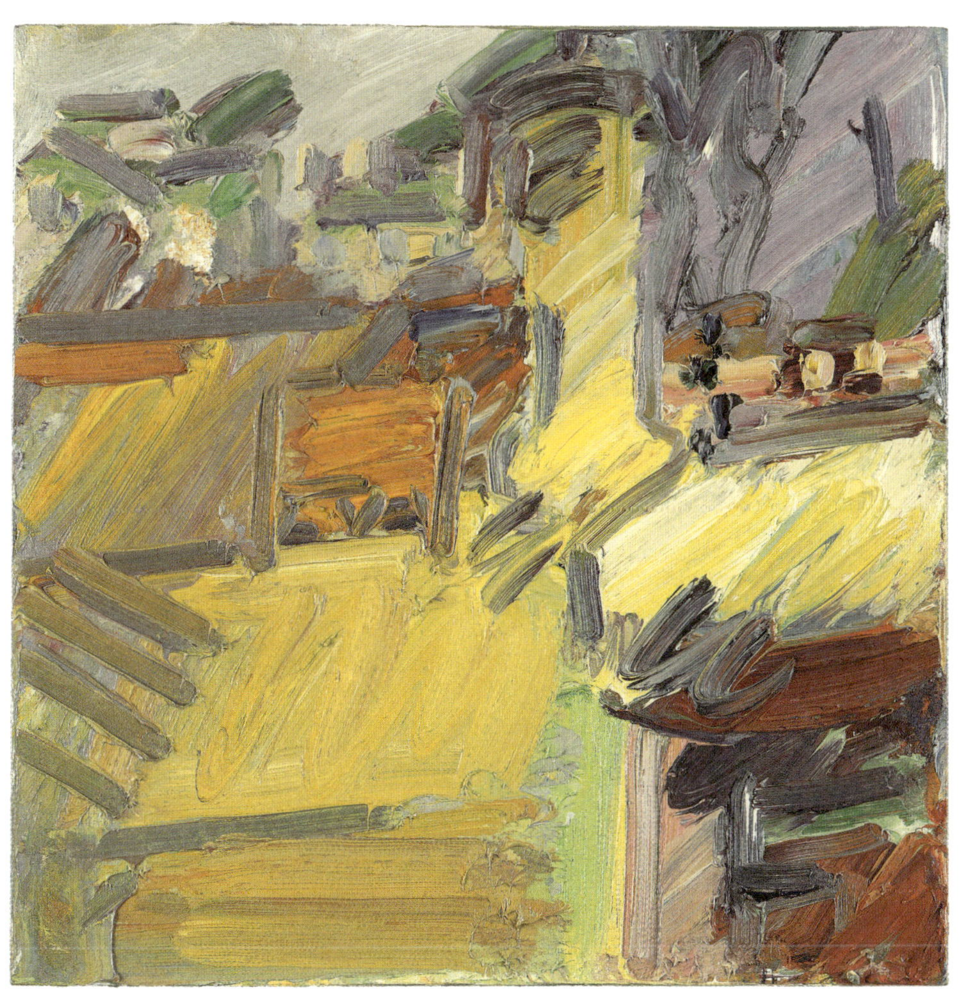

The Pillar Box, 2010–11

[Sickert's locales] are grubby miserable bedrooms: well, those bedrooms with girls in them, where the sheets smell of human congress, they don't look in the least depressing to me – they seem to be really very jolly places. I recognize my life in those streets and in those bedrooms! I felt at home in Sickert's world ... Those Mornington Crescent bedrooms, with plump sweaty nudes in beds, seem to me extremely desirable places to be in.'[24]

One of the flats Sickert rented, 6 Mornington Crescent, is around the corner from Auerbach's studio. However, in Frank's pictures no one is leaning on a dresser, or reaching for their clothes, almost never do a man and woman share a space. Back in 1978 I wanted to know whether this was deliberate. Frank claimed he would not exclude such daily acts on principle, 'But I wouldn't put a model into a situation of pretending to be combing her hair or in fact having a bath – although God knows, Degas did enough good paintings of people presumably pretending to have baths for hours on end – simply because it seems to be a false situation and I think I should feel to some extent uncomfortable.'[25]

The direction in which Auerbach's art might go with respect to painting naked figures was tested in the 1960s through the use he made of J.Y.M. Her availability was 'a piece of blind luck' and specific to her. 'She was brought into the world to be a model, she came and sat and it was not quite like anything else. It wasn't like painting Stella or painting Julia, because it was just that ... She took poses that were natural to her, and then I sometimes suggested things and one would go on. It became like a central spine of what one was doing.'

Across forty years, 1957–97, J.Y.M. grows older. Drawn in charcoal and pastel, sitting on the chair in 1960, her body is spectral, her legs thin and tapering (see p. 90). By 1963, when the focus is often on her head and neck, she is identified as J.Y.M., and can just about be recognized by a curious defiance that is actually a sense of complicity. Lying on the bed in the studio, with the paraffin stove in the foreground, her body is both graphic and curvaceous; during the 1980s five or even eight small paintings might be done in succession. In the same period, when Auerbach begins isolating J.Y.M.'s head, especially lying down or in profile, dark sweeps of the brush convey tenacity and a person who is clearly older and less steady. 'At some time I thought it wasn't relevant to ask her to pose nude.'

After J.Y.M. the women Auerbach engaged were younger, and for them modelling was a temporary job. The experience of Deborah Ratcliff, an Australian who was earning money in the life-room at the Slade in 1983, suggests the incompatibility of Frank's need to shed inhibitions with the presence of strangers. When she arrived, Auerbach seemed shy and impatient to get started, asking her to undress and lie on the bed in a relaxed position. 'The only way I could cope with this was to lie facing away from him. For the next forty minutes or so I listened to the canvas being attacked. There was grunting, groaning and rattling and lunging. Paint was obviously being sloshed about, then scraped and blotted with paper. All this energy was disconcerting. I couldn't see it but I could feel it and there was something quite sexual about it. At the end of the two-hour session, Frank thanked me and gestured at the money, my earnings, underneath one of three clocks on a table against a paint-splattered wall ... My next session with Frank was on the Thursday, same time at 5 p.m. This time Frank asked me if I didn't mind keeping my clothes on. Didn't mind? I was thrilled. The studio was far from warm and I was to sit on a chair facing him.'[26] Three austere, unusually vertical portraits of this future writer resulted, her name in the titles, all shown in Venice in 1986.

Auerbach continued to contact art colleges to find models, telephoning those on a list, until one answered. 'It is a bit like roulette ... '[27] There was an Israeli woman, and one with lots of make-up who came two weeks and not the third. Frank told Hughes, 'I feel uncomfortable painting people nude with whom I haven't had physical relations.'[28] One might identify as a mini-series the several half-length pictures of Julia, all begun in 1987, that describe her naked upper body. Writing in 2001, I saw them as terrifying and protective: 'Each image has the totality of a shrine filled with ex-voto tokens. Descriptive parts sometimes seem to be applied rather savagely, like handfuls, scooped up and thrust onto the surface, forced into new disharmonies by the thinner skin and acidity of acrylic, with its resistance to tonal palpability.'[29]

Subjects: Sitters

During the decade *c.* 1971–81, some eighteen sitters came to the studio to sit for one or two pictures. There was no logic in the choice of people; Auerbach insists he acted then, as always, more by instinct. For example,

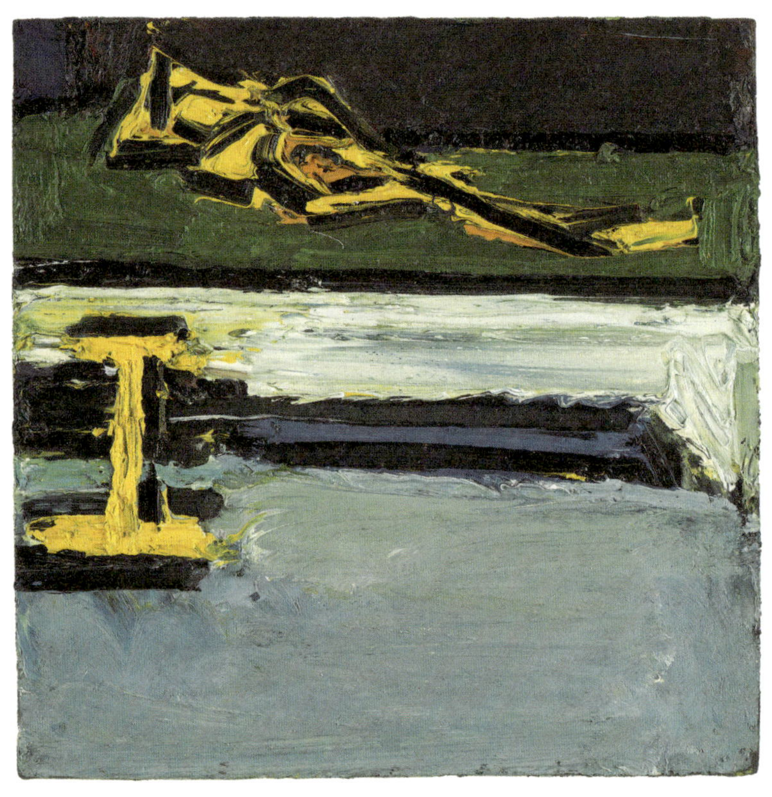

Figure on Bed, 1968

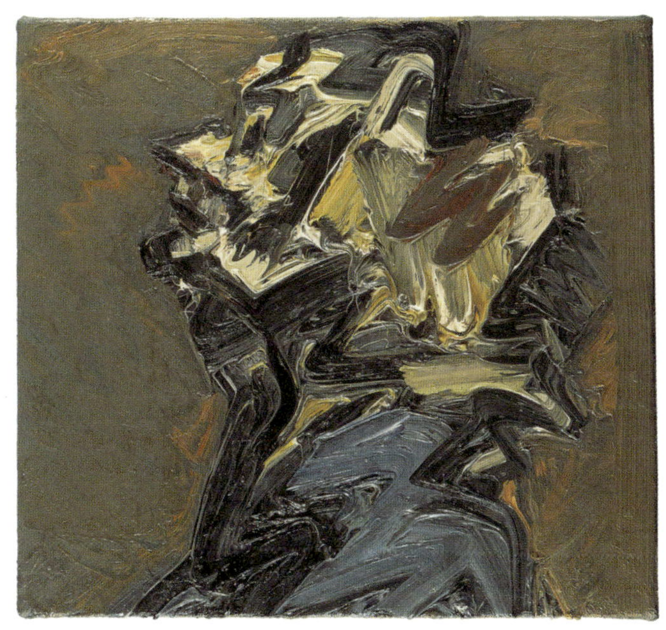

Head of J.Y.M. – Profile II, 1987

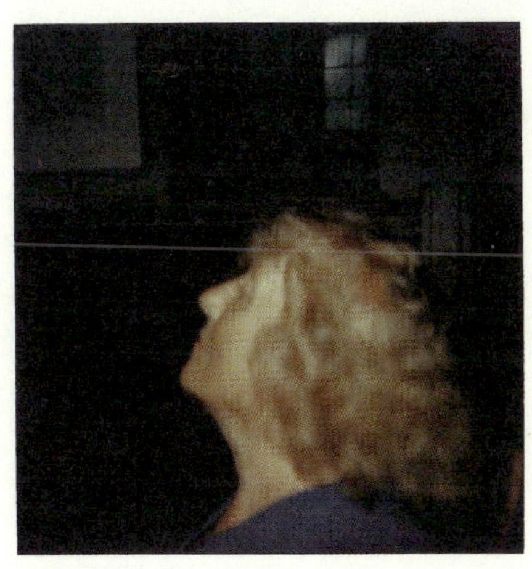

Polaroid photograph of J.Y.M. in pose, *c.* 1987

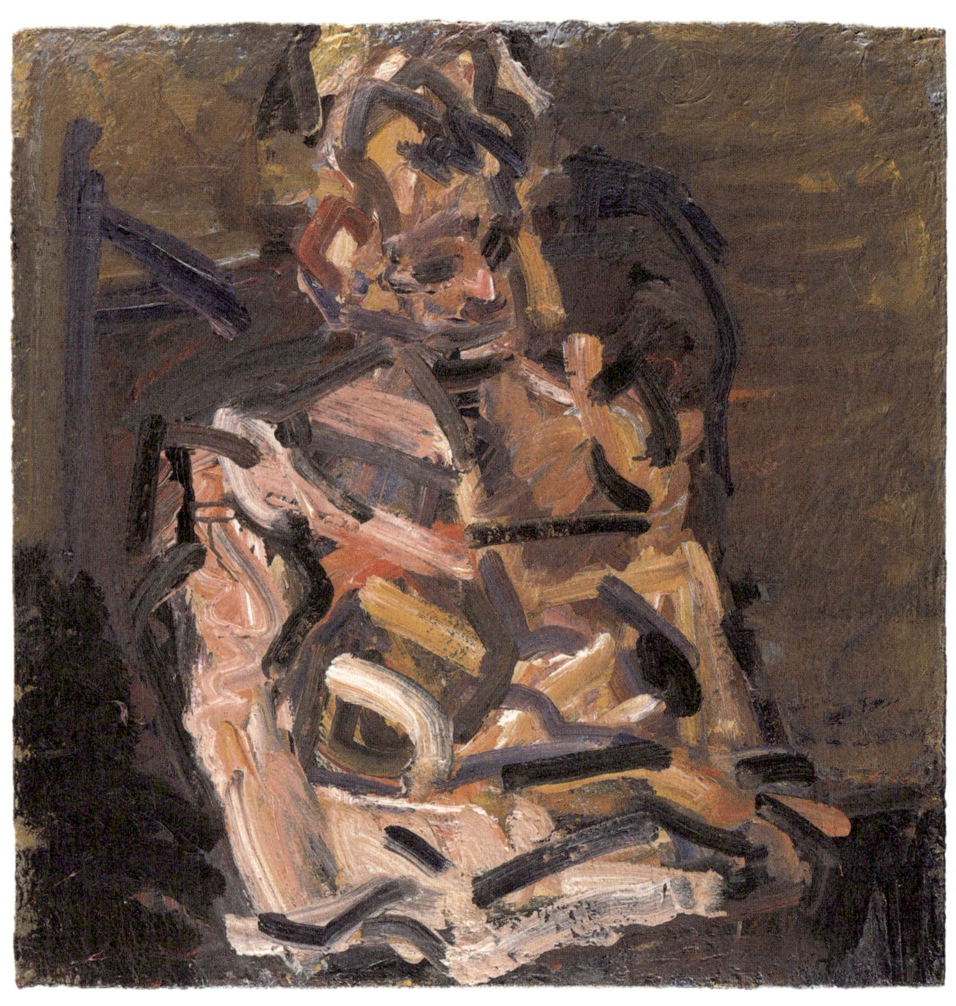

Julia, 1988–89

he met the artist Stephen Finer in the French Pub and thought he would like to paint him; his ex-student Christopher Couch was stopped when he passed by on a bicycle. Francesca Bewer and Shane Dunworth were friends of David Landau. Several sitters had Marlborough connections, such as Christopher Dark, James Kirkman and Geoffrey Parton; others were long-standing friends, Michael and Charlotte Podro, Margaret Schuelein, Ken Garland, Sandra Fisher and Bruce Bernard; as well as a few who asked to pose, such as Jill and Tom Phillips, or did so to have an opportunity to talk, as was the case with Robert Hughes. In most instances he began with drawings, which normally take dozens of sittings and as many months as paintings. They might begin in charcoal and be realized by adding ink and chalk marks. On one occasion, in 1980, on a visit to Joe Tilson's studio in Somerset he tried a new technique, drawing a portrait of the artist on a plate that was made into an etching. In London he continued with five more heads of other artist friends (Kitaj, Kossoff and Freud) or relatives (Julia and Gerda Boehm), using a dart as his implement, and experimented with different acids and inks at the Palm Tree Studios. The etching of Freud was printed from four plates, with the tonal effect coming from mixed blacks and greys.

Hughes sat in 1986 and described the primitive conditions in the studio, 'a troglodyte's den of internalization', and the agitated artist: 'Auerbach works on the balls of his feet, balanced like a welterweight boxer, darting in and out ... He recites from memory long runs of Yeats, George Barker and Auden ... He hisses and puffs. He darts back to consult the reflection of the drawing in a mirror on the wall ... Now and again he fumbles out a book from the nearby shelf, opens it to a reproduction – Giacometti's *Woman with her Throat Cut*, Cézanne's *Self-portrait with Cap* – and lays it on the floor where he can see it, "to have something good to look at," a purpose not kind to the sitter's vanity, until one understands that Auerbach is hoping for osmosis.'[30] From the perspective of the artist, given the constrictions of having a sitter who was a busy writer living in New York, it was a relief to finish on a Monday morning after just fourteen sittings. Auerbach reported to Hughes, what 'appeared in front of me' was a 'rather dark and laborious' drawing that 'was of a sort that I hadn't predicted and which I hope is finished'.[31]

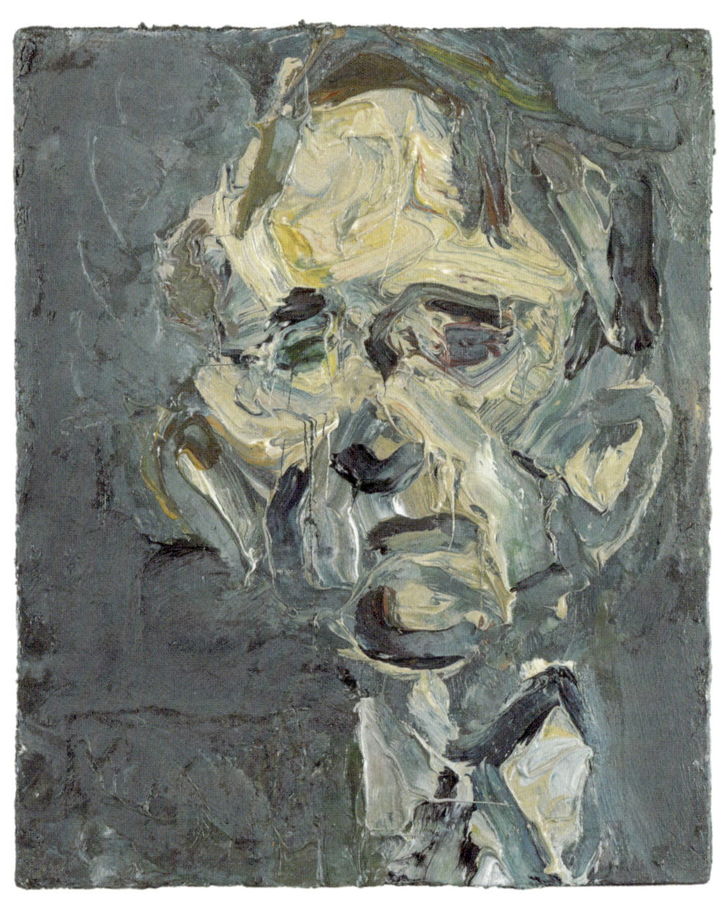

Head of Michael Podro, 1981

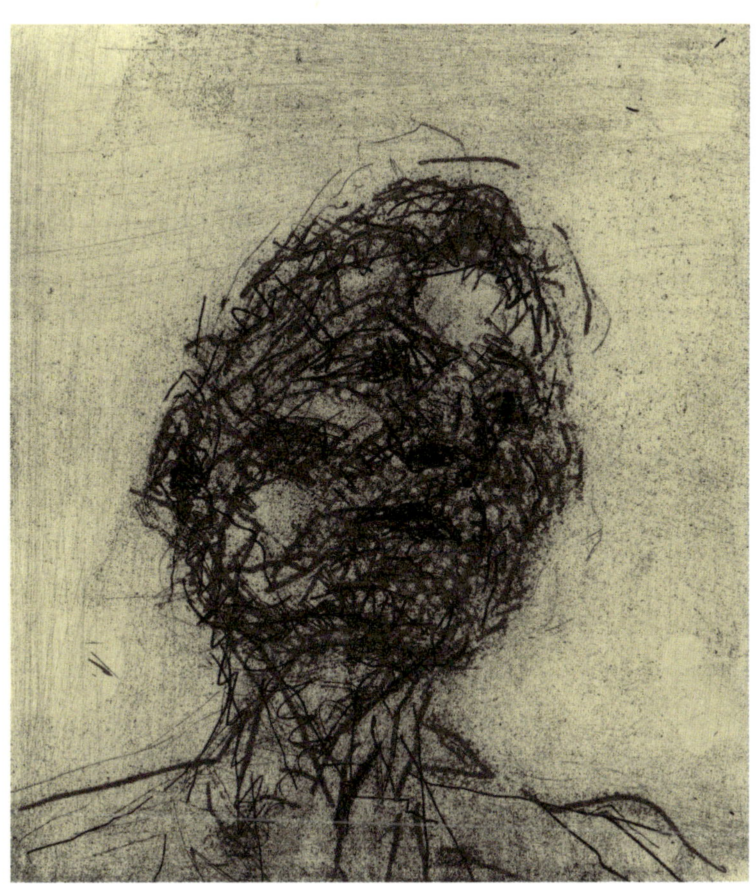

Lucian Freud, 1980–81

During a conversation that was held at the Prince's Drawing School in 2007, William Feaver asked Auerbach whether the talking with sitters that went on in the first hour posing was a response to the sitter's interest in chatter or something useful. 'For many years, for the first twenty-five years, I didn't talk at all, and it produced a certain sort of painting of which I'm not ashamed. But gradually it seemed to me just a little bit as though one was part of this fancy-dress party of art where people came in one costume. There was stripe man or the splash man or the painting-of-the-greenhouse-in-a-particular-way man. And it seemed to me that there was something about people and their movement, and talk and so on, that perhaps had slightly slipped away in these hieratic heads, and – maybe it's simply weakness – I gradually found myself talking. But I talk more with you than with anybody else.'[32]

With the paintings of Jake, Julia and myself, sitters who began in the 1970s, Frank started going from picture to picture without a break until it became accepted that the arrangement might continue indefinitely and thus it became part of one's whole life. David Landau began sitting in 1982; Ruth Bromberg posed from 1992 until she became too ill in 2008; William Feaver began in 2003; thus Auerbach now works from five people, in all cases these are two-hour sessions except for Julia who poses on an evening and the following morning in Finsbury Park.

If I try to recall Auerbach at 47, the age he was when I began modelling for him, I believe he was behaving in an even more zealous, reckless, sort of extemporizing way, not just in the studio, than he does now. When younger I would plunge into daydream scenarios, and there is one painting from 1986 where my tears and scrunched face coincided with the last minutes when the picture emerged. After sixteen years, I volunteered to alter my pose, suggesting that instead of always sitting looking forward, merely changing outfits when a new picture began, I would stand or lie down. Frank thought about this and before I arrived the next week wrote to explain why he rejected the idea. 'I have got a sort of foam rubber thing: a KARRIMAT (used successfully at 28,000 feet on Everest) and I was going to get a little cushion – but I do not really take to the whole idea. If I put down the Karrimat, and you were to "pose" on it, the whole thing would turn into an activity that would be inimical to everything I am trying to do.

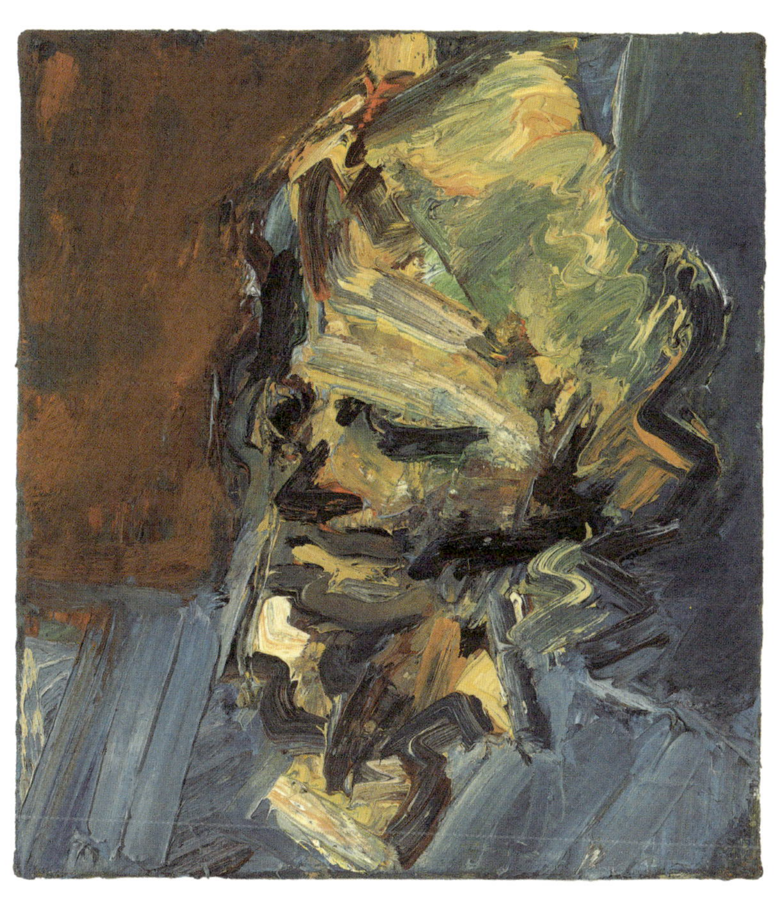

Head of Catherine Lampert, 1986

All sorts of artists, perhaps most of the good ones, have painted "models" "posing", but I am interested in recording things, not models posing, but *people* who come to the studio as it exists. I could quite understand, if after all these years of heroic effort in posing for me, and with everything that you have to do, you simply found coming, and sitting, on Monday evenings too much for you. I would quite understand if you called a halt. I have a photograph of the drawing we finished a week ago on Saturday, and would like more than anything to have another go at another drawing – but you will obviously have to finish *sometime*.'[33]

As it happened, this was an unusually confusing period for me: as well as my job as director at the Whitechapel Gallery, I was looking after a young daughter, had a new love and was facing a life-threatening disease. These circumstances actually made me, like the other sitters, who are each dealing with their own issues, wish even more eagerly to continue posing.

Auerbach underplays the stamina, mental and physical, required to paint non-stop for hours on his feet, in the course of which his hands and clothes become increasingly covered in paint. To suggest it is frenetic would be misleading, there are times when Frank is standing quietly, fairly close to the easel and then moving back. A good deal of the action is reaching for paint from the tins and tubes; the jar of white spirit is next to a cluster of spatulas on a small trolley where basic colours are laid out in blobs; the brush mixing and sloshing, picking up what is needed – the painting sounds hint at how things are going. Other movements include blotting areas with squares of newspaper, scraping, looking at the picture from different angles, changing the orientation on the easel and seeing what is happening to the painting from its reflection. One of the most impressive things to watch is how Auerbach juggles four or five brushes in his left hand, splayed, each available for immediate use. What might have seemed dramatic to Hughes, is rather more normal and not a method; it belongs to the studio where the atmosphere is somehow sacrosanct.

Conversation might resume while the painting goes on, with Auerbach perhaps speaking almost involuntarily, the way someone driving a car might initiate topics and then lapse into concentration and silence. In any case, the sitters also prefer to be silent at times, focusing on trying to keep still, even when their thoughts might be fretful or turbulent, or blown away by a few minutes sleep. The relationship with each sitter is different, but we all know by far the greater pressure is on the artist. Jake's observation is true for all the long-term models: 'Frank feels very strongly the responsibility of taking someone else's time. Not just for himself. Part of both of our feelings is about punctuality. He does feel that time is precious, when someone is under the weather, perhaps he pushes himself harder.' Julia paints, going to Norfolk one week a month to do just this, and especially understands that he is having to hold something visual in his head: 'it is a thing that's alive', he has to go with it, 'it has to come out of what's happening to you'.

At each sitting, the first session lasts nearly an hour, followed by a few minutes break, then another hour. You might be looking across the room at the heap of plastic bags and newspapers in the corner, but as Auerbach has commented, the information he is gaining is more than about a model posed against a static backdrop: 'Because if you're drawing anything, even a person, your head goes up and down and swivels. What you're seeing is in fact lots and lots of different linear perspectives that interpenetrate. So you've got to invent ... the irrational marks actually seem a better record than the literal ones. They suggest things, and suddenly in a corner of the picture you get a little bit of truth, which might actually expand into a whole truth ... What happens is that the painting begins to speak back to one.'[34]

A narrative about the experience of sitting, even one as sympathetic as Martin Gayford's *Man with a Blue Scarf: On Sitting for a Portrait by Lucian Freud* (2010), could not describe what happens in Mornington Crescent. In later years Freud was inclined to engage his subjects on impulse, prompted by curiosity about how they might look naked or what it was like to be a business tycoon, taking, as Gayford says, 'a novelist's attitude to people'.[35] His sitters were able to observe paintings gradually realized, even if the pace felt interminable. He kept them on tenterhooks, seeking his approbation. Most were wrapped into his life outside painting, as companions for dinner, as children, as lovers, but then relatively speaking ignored. I have known both artists and watched them work, and from what I have seen nothing that happens in Auerbach's studio grows organically; the emotional and physical temperature is more desperate. Frank, as he has remarked, feeds on 'the conflict between reality and its awkward edges', which drives him

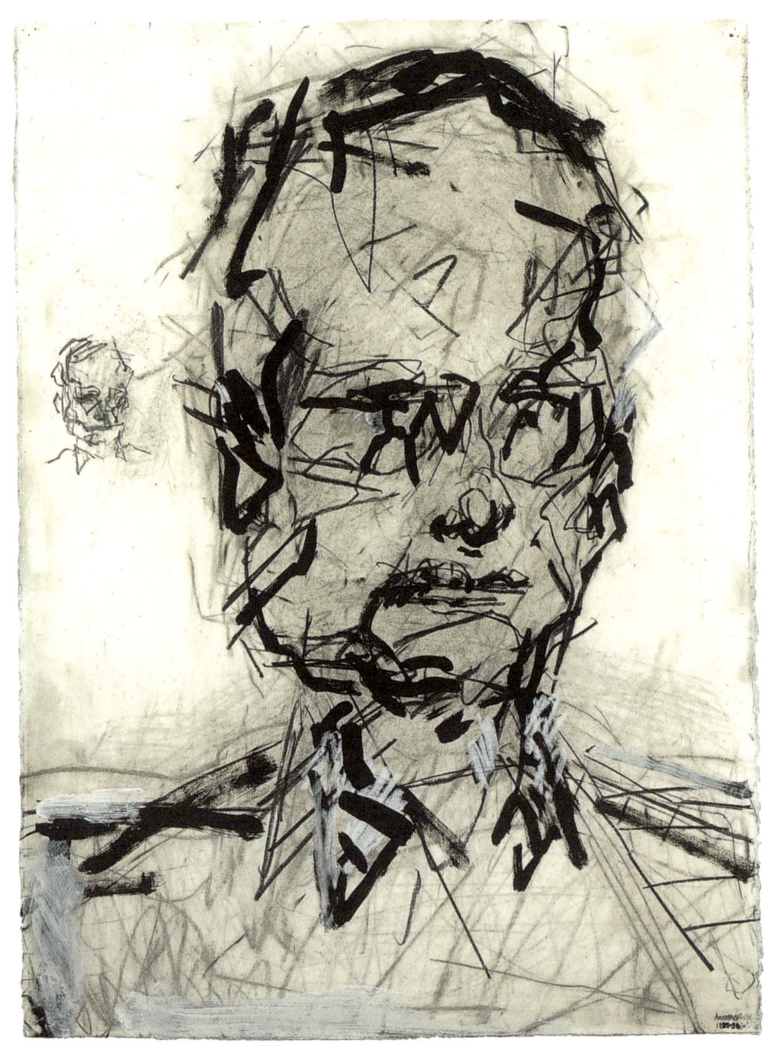

Head of David Landau, 1995–96

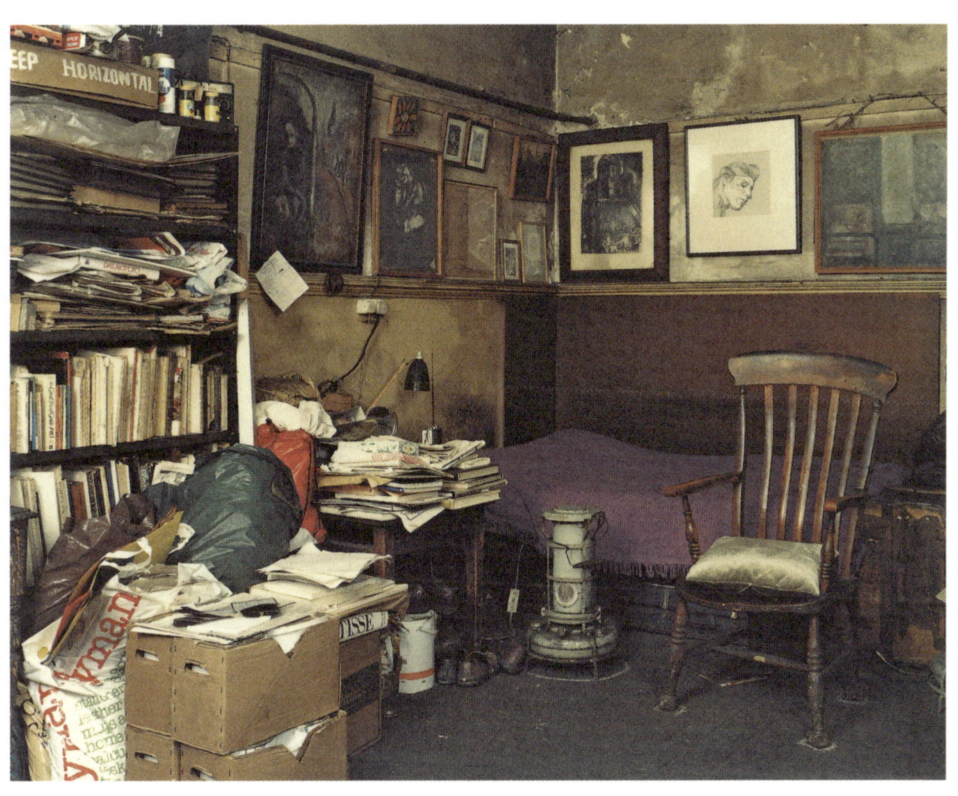

Studio interior, May 1985

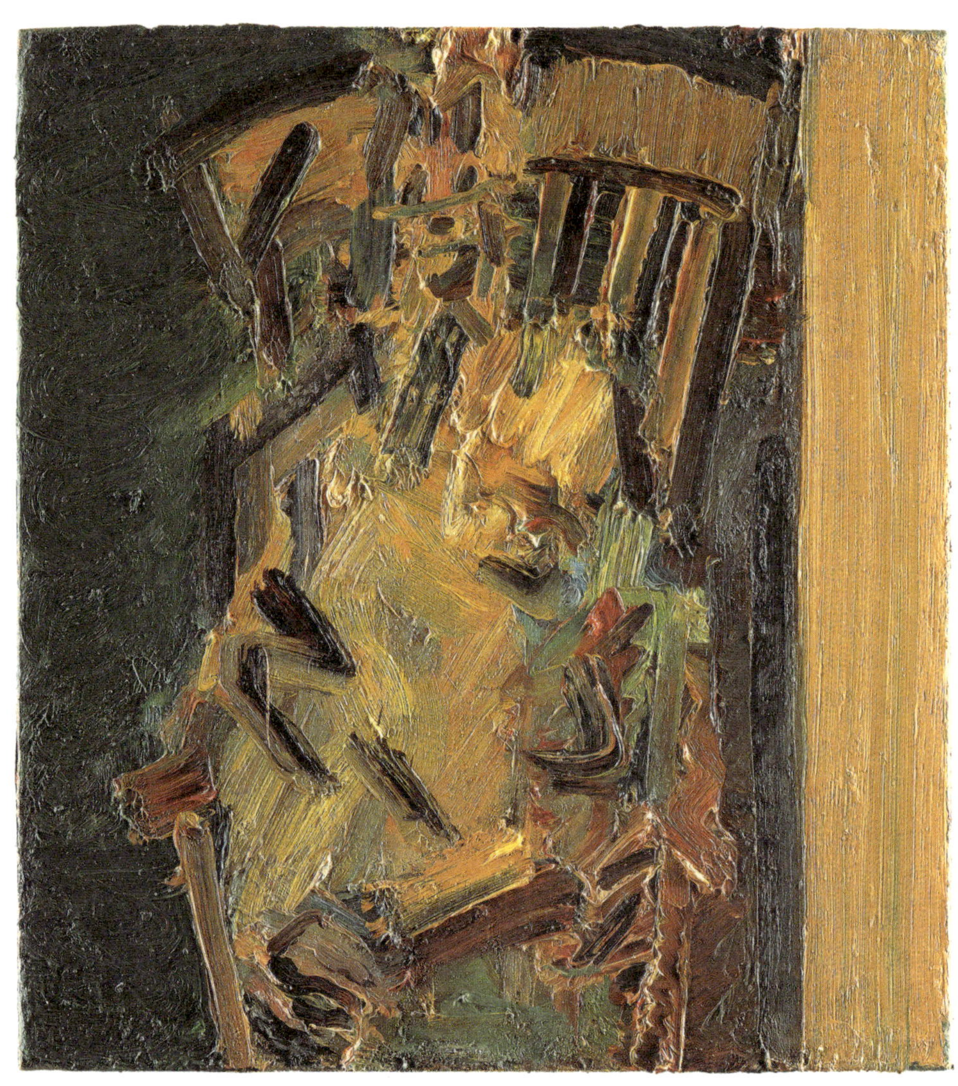

Ruth Bromberg Seated, 2002–03

'to get something sheer and complete – something trapped rather than arranged'.[36] But perhaps there is greater underlying trust and normality, certainly since he began to have sitters come on regular days, decade after decade, the friendships and routines each distinct. 'The way I work with different people who sit for me is the way I work when *they're* there. I'm affected by their mood, certainly. I'm aware that sometimes they're impatient: it affects me. I'm aware that something may have happened to them: that affects me. But it's all part of the process of keeping a lively activity going. But the living activity is not pure recording. The living activity is something that feeds into an architecturally separate form.'[37]

A beacon of integrity

Viewed over a lifetime, Auerbach's intentions compare less to his contemporaries and more to Giacometti's paintings and sculptures of Diego, Annette, Caroline and others who came routinely to his Parisian studio in the rue Hippolyte-Maindron. It could be, as Auerbach puts it, 'because one recognizes an individual likeness by the deviation from a norm. The deeper the portraiture, the deeper the deviation. This can be sensed as an absolute quality but I also, briefly, met Annette and was confirmed in my feeling that the likenesses are totally convincing.'[38]

David Landau flies to London specially in order to sit, to discuss art, to know he is understood. In his view, Frank is 'a beacon of integrity, generosity, humility and a constant source of joy and fun'.[39] Landau's wife thinks no one knows this businessman and art historian as well as Auerbach does. Jake has observed that Frank loves company when he (increasingly rarely) encounters it: 'When I sit there is usually a bit of discussion or chat in the first half which then gutters and dies as momentum decreases and the work takes over. My partner, Lizzy, sometimes collects me from the studio at which point Frank's talk will burst back into flame as the oxygen of a new person enters the room ... Lizzy is an actress which helps, Frank is still in love and awe of all actors.'[40] Each of his sitters feeds in information about art and artists, different generations, their current preoccupations. Frank is curious about the tribulations and adventures of his small group of friends and their families. There are drawings of escapades and machines by Landau's 9-year-old twins pinned to the wall above the desk in the studio, and Frank remarked recently, 'I'm sorry I won't be around to see what Max and Mia Landau do.'

From today's perspective it is unthinkable that one of the five remaining sitters should stop. When Frank says things like, 'one's trying to get some work done before one dies' (that was in 1998), we take it as another way of suggesting that mortality is just something so obvious, so linked with sentimentality for those remaining (not an Auerbach weakness) that time is wasted by public mourning or by worrying continuously about ill health. When I ask Frank why he keeps the same sitters, he answers, 'Because I'm interested in them, and I know that includes you, and because it takes so long, by the time I've finished a picture, the person has changed and also there is a certain security in knowing that they are able to sit, and ....'. I add, 'And they are so keen to sit!' Over time he gets more engaged, as the models grow older and change: 'You've done certain things, and you hope to do something else, and you hope it will go out further in some direction. I know it's only a factor but it gives one some sort of gauge, one's done that, so one's not going to do these things again, so I'm going to go into new territory.'

I wondered about the self-portraits, done on occasion in the early years: two drawings (1958–59) and one painting (1961–65), and a later picture in the collection of the National Portrait Gallery made over seven years, 1994–2001. Now they happen regularly. He told Jackie Wullschlager, writing in the *Financial Times* in 2012: 'When I was young, my head seemed bland: I never had the narcissism of Courbet or Dürer, who obviously thought themselves marvellous-looking chaps. As I got more wrinkly, with bags under the eyes, the whole landscape became more interesting. But I also partly started doing them because people were talking more when I painted them, and there's something refreshing about going back to silence.'[41]

If you stare at or pass by one of Auerbach's pictures day after day, the image changes with the angle of approach and the light, as most paintings do, but more so. Many have a comic aspect, top-knots and bird-like eyes, heads on stalks, features that are more readable and naturalistic if you squint. Sometimes the effect is animalistic, the scale jumping from telescopic to amplified, picture to picture, the thin line of the lips both characteristic and nuanced to catch a split-second's expression.

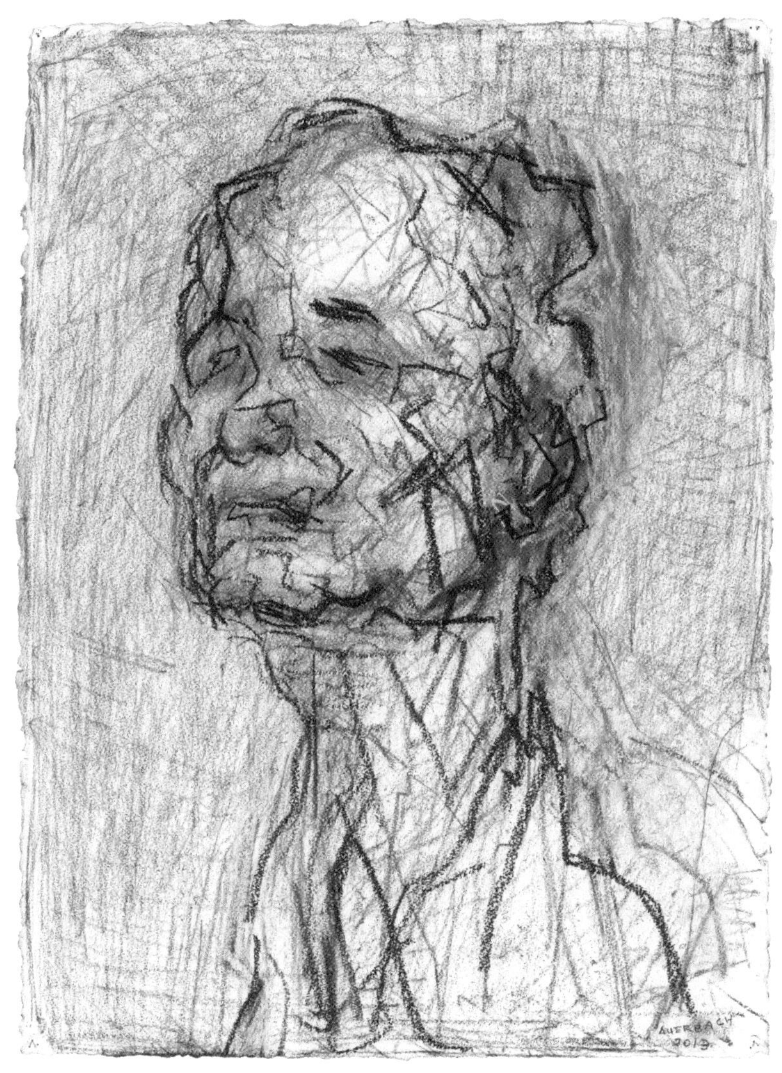

Self-Portrait II, 2013

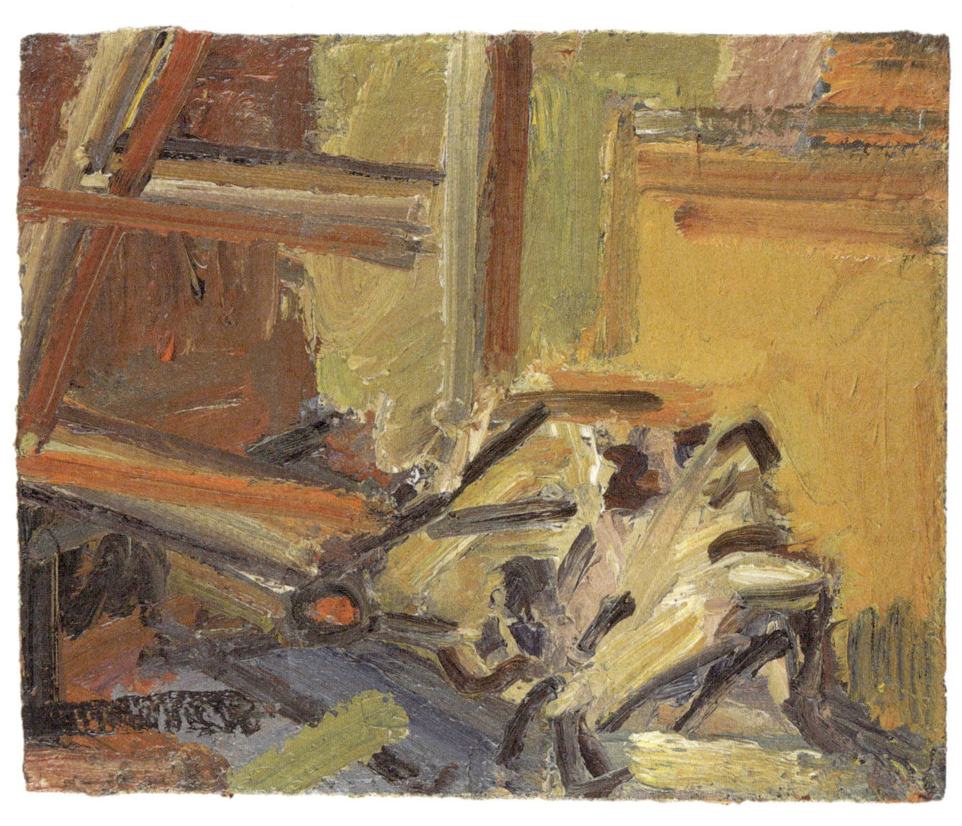

Reclining Head of Julia II, 1996

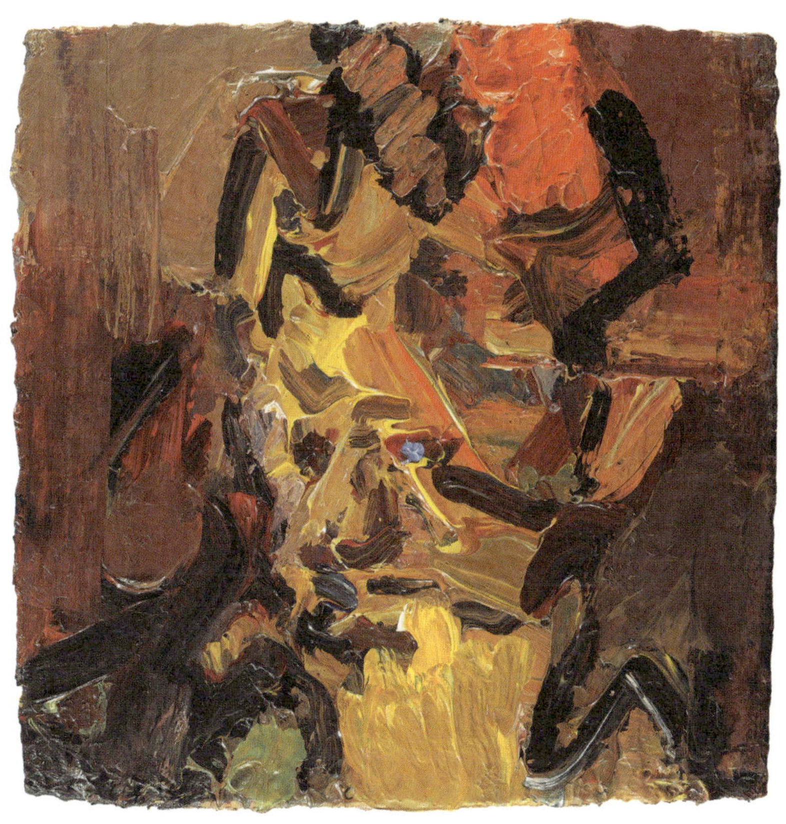

Head of Julia II, 1999

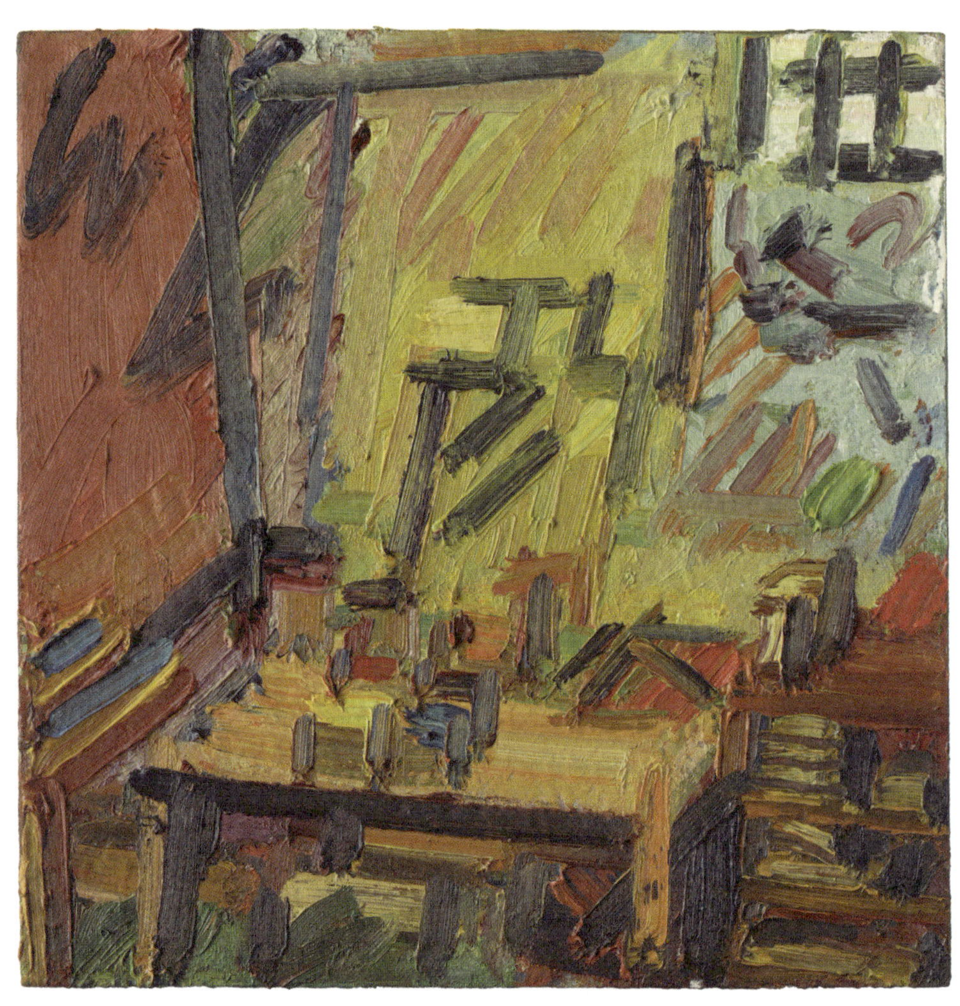

In the Studio, 2013–14

The large landscapes are too awkward to move off the easel and turn to the wall, so the sitters watch them progress, week by week, which is thrilling and a privilege. In 2013–14, the 'landscape' is a corner of the studio, in which the focus is on what is on the easel, but the view takes in the pots of paint, brushes and the blue plastic that protects the wall. The creator hovers on the right, a large head reflected in the mirror. Judging by one of the small versions (see opposite) of the larger *In the Studio* (2013–14), there might, unusually, be vivid bright cylinders and cubes – the materials on the workbench. By the end, however, the palette was cool and the detail reduced. 'It's never recording, it's never topography, and it's always using the material in order to make an image that has a character of its own ... All good painting is abstract in a sense that good painting is abstraction, the better you are painting, the more it feels like dealing with nameless formal things, but non-figurative painting is only for people who believe there is a secret reality beneath, a human will, as Philip Larkin wrote, "To bring to bloom the million-petalled flower/Of being here".'

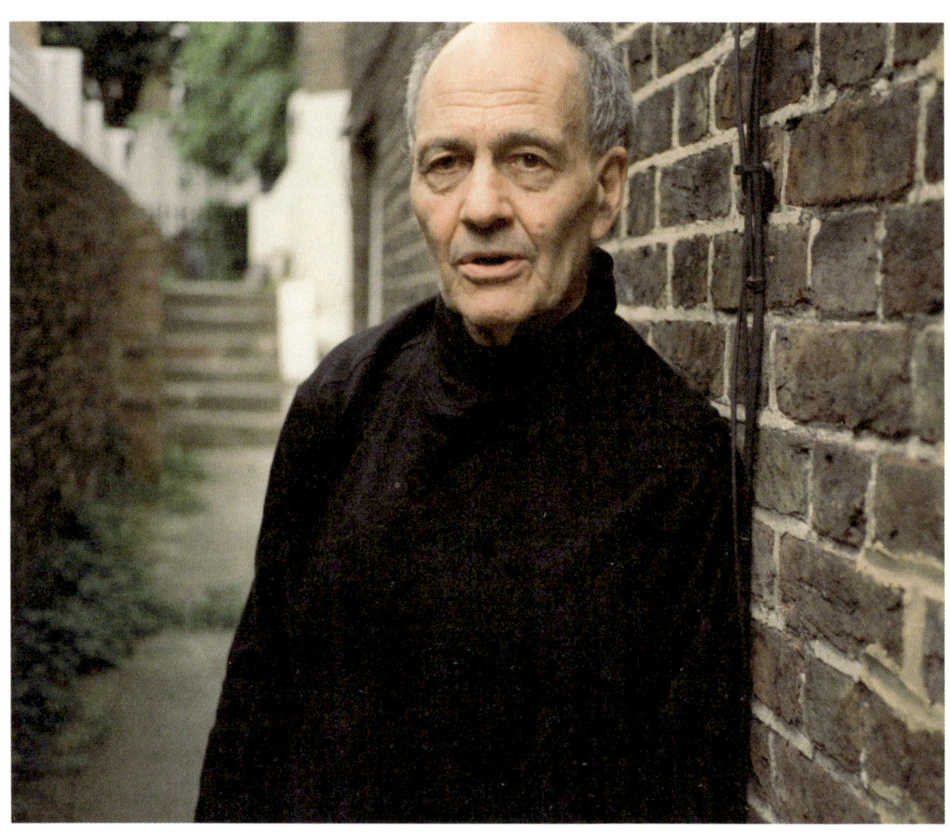

DAVID DAWSON, Frank outside the studio, 2009

Conclusion

The book of life

'There's a phrase of Sickert's where he speaks somewhere about something succeeding in that it is like a page torn from the book of life. I'd like what I do not to be Art with a capital A, although it may or may not be incorporated into that concept. What I'd like it to be is a page torn from that book of life, even though it's an abstracted image.'[1]

Auerbach has said he hopes his art will reach 'the misfit in the backroom', and as far as audience goes, in his experience, 'people who are responsive to painting are a particular set of people who respond to painting. I don't think there's any other classifying equality about them.'[2] An extreme example of how Frank's pictures strike unexpected chords happened during the retrospective of his work at the Royal Academy in 2001, beginning with the opening reception on 11 September. I remember viewers looking at the crusted images of postwar bomb sites, the Camden Town scenes where rough, burnt-black 'girders' indicate the hard man-made matter on the streets, the artist's extreme response to pointed chimneys, metal gates and tower blocks and to buildings tapering upwards in window-filled storeys. Some were clearly thinking of what had happened to the Twin Towers and their occupants that morning. For visitors over the next three months, Auerbach's portraits also spoke to 'Rembrandt's Women', the other exhibition in the RA's main galleries that autumn; after all, even the title conjures up women who still seem alive, especially Hendrickje Stoffels, bathing in a stream, wrapped in fur, or, perhaps, as Bathsheba at her toilet. Frank's pictures of Stella and, stretching now for four decades, of Julia, are similarly sensuous, particular to the person and to the fragility of life.

A postcard always visible in Frank's studio is of Matisse's *Head, White and Rose* (1914–15), a portrait of his daughter, Marguerite. It began, as an X-radiograph confirms, naturalistically, with her rounded jaw lines and the neck ribbon with pendant, though according to Marguerite, Matisse said during a working session: 'This painting wants to take me somewhere else. Do you feel up to it?'[3] Striped bands describe her dress, and a black angular armature is imposed across the face and neck that locks the pink tones of her skin into the whole scheme. The result is nominally geometric, with the nod to Cubism, yet it is also so dependent on the relationship and ultimately so believable – as Auerbach put it, she 'looks back at us with a gaze as direct and human as Rembrandt in his self-portraits'.[4]

Art historians and critics discussing Auerbach's work often exhort their audience not to be 'parochial' and place the artist only in a British context. Michael Kimmelman, reviewing Frank's New York exhibition in 2006, designated Auerbach as one of the 'best painters around'. He described charcoal drawings where the faces made of 'hooks, crotchets and scrawls' were pushed even further than Giacometti's to 'the edge of coherence while still registering as characters', and he suggested that many of his fellow Americans were 'natively uneasy with any art that's so frankly self-serious and indifferent to novelty'.[5]

Relatively few parallels or contrasts have been drawn between Auerbach and outstanding painters of the same age working in other countries, such as Jasper Johns (b. 1930) and Gerhard Richter (b. 1932). Those two artists are commonly associated with signs specific to their times and culture: Johns's bronze tins of Ballantine Ale or his paintings of the American flag, and Richter's work based on blurred photographs of terrorists or family snapshots. In the 1960s and today they are commended by curators for their brilliance in defining strategies and inventing a process to return painting to relevance in an age of lens-based images, to accommodate paradox, irony and art history.

However, these art historical distinctions can be too crude. In 2012, Johns began working with a torn photograph *c.* 1958 of Lucian Freud by John Deakin reproduced in an auction catalogue for the sale of a Bacon

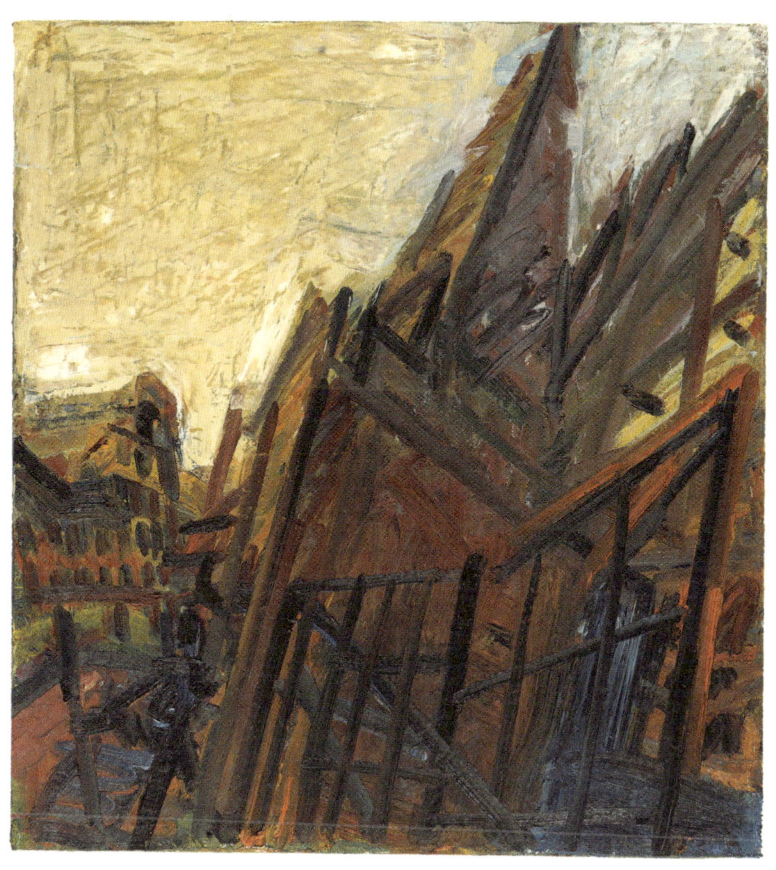

Chimney in Mornington Crescent – Winter Morning, 1991

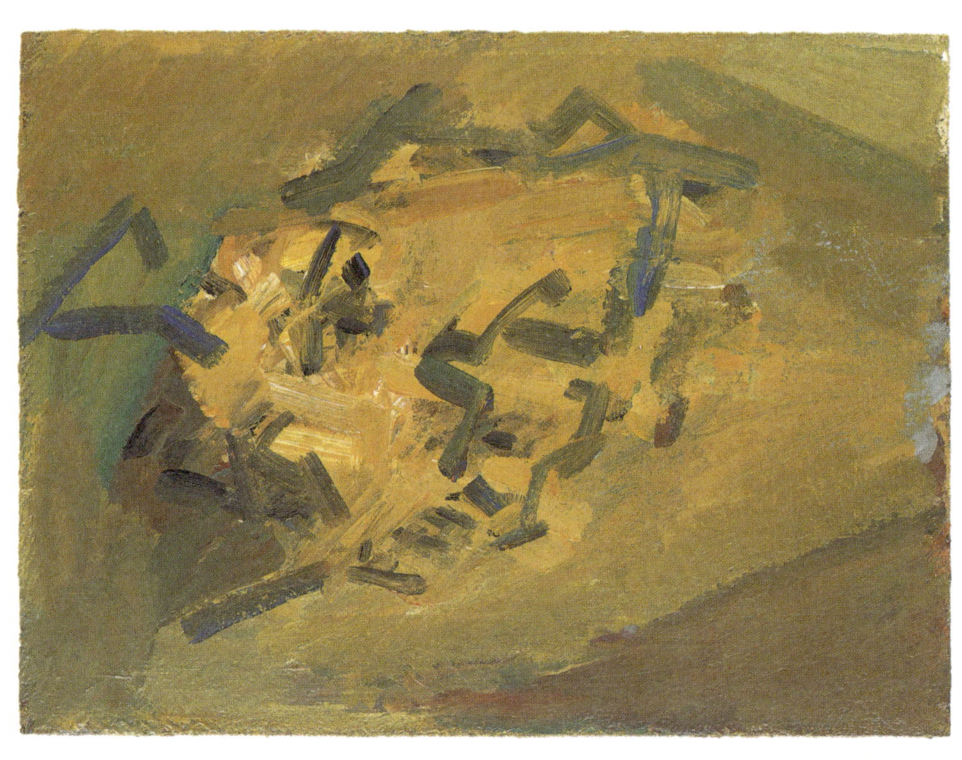

Reclining Head of Julia II, 2007

painting. In various drawings, paintings and etchings he traced it, inverted the seated figure so that it is conjoined with its mirror image, added colour and translated details from the source into sometimes puzzle-like pieces. In the empty centre something like his own jowly, aged face in a skull-like format presides, an allusion to memories of fraught relationships and ebbing passion, strongest in the large oil realized in muted greys. The series is named *Regrets*.[6] Looking at the catalogue Auerbach responded not just to Johns's weeks and years of patient preparation, but also to his ability to get to the point where something truthful emerges.

Although Auerbach has shunned such hybrid tactics, nonetheless he too has changed the genres within which he works. With respect to portraits, given the practice of working with the same people over long periods, the genre has once again proved capable of a subtle argument about what it is to place yourself and the subject in an environment, where in a way there is a mutual, performative resolution that is momentarily final, while in the artist's mind the next work is germinating. His urban landscapes respond to the undisciplined reality of life in London, but one also senses that the inhabitants – and Frank is one – have become fond of their refuse-strewn pavements and routines. Cumulatively, they constitute a half century of readings, a kind of weathervane, a suggestion of time-travel.

In the studio, waving his arm with the gusto of a conductor, he captures on the surface of the painting myriad and precise inflections of this world. The mind taking in the image is entranced, jostled and buffeted, with the eye alighting on streaks and globules. However, on occasion this improvisation has resulted in a kind of gaiety and force that comes close to caricature: the stick figures walking away, rings of pigment around the eyes, a reclining head made of broken brushstrokes. But Auerbach is never trying to mock nor to persuade the viewer of anything and such variety and daring makes his work so thrilling to those on the other side of the footlights, and so universal.

Lately Frank has mentioned that Delacroix is present in his mind and has said Picasso is always 'exhorting me to be naughtier'. A reproduction of a head of Dora Maar with a funny headdress is pinned to the wall, not unlike the paintings of her in the 1946 Barr monograph. 'When I see a Picasso, it feels like an owl blinking, its eyes coming into the light.' Time and again, 'he's made this thing in his imaginative private mind and there it is and it's captured the world. That's what people want to see, they don't want to see something they know about already, they don't want to have a programme presented to them of something they believe in or approve of, they want this amazing thing they haven't thought of before.'[7] Auerbach believes traditional art history misunderstands the way artists think, it is not like the history of science where after one discovery previous theories fall away. Rather than think in a linear way, most artists choose what they want to study and steal from; he mentions Picasso returning to African sculpture, El Greco or Ingres, and Matisse's interest in Persian or Indian painting. They behave in similar ways: 'When you read the biographies of painters you discover what they did was no different to the way painters behave now. When Titian writes to someone to say "I'm sorry I haven't finished this" and then spends a further seven years doing it over and over again until he feels he has got it right, it is very like what I know of painting.'[8] In his seventies Matisse looked back and reminded his interviewer that artists 'don't work for fame and glory, they work to express themselves' and are aware reputations are in flux: 'We've seen people with great qualities remain obscure for a long time; sometimes they're forgotten for centuries. Look at El Greco. It needed our epoch to bring him out, to extol him; it needed the advent of Cézanne for El Greco to find his place.'[9]

Frank remembers that Francis Bacon used to say, 'if you can think things clearly you can say them clearly'. But, he argues, expository language fails to cover the complex way artists orient themselves and offers a better analogy: 'Ballet dancers think clearly, carpenters think clearly, and they don't think in words, they don't think of saying; they do. They act directly according to their sensations and there's no interposition of words at all, so it is a wordless zone.'[10]

In the conversation with Auerbach at the Prince's Drawing School in 2007 William Feaver asked Frank whether lines of poetry or drama ran through his head: 'Sometimes – occasionally – in the way that other people use Benzedrine, because I'm excited by it. Recently ... I had a really intelligent thought to do with a poem. I'd just read some of Tony Harrison's, and I was struck by the fact that in one of them the scansion was incorrect because he had a simple thing to say plainly, and while I was working

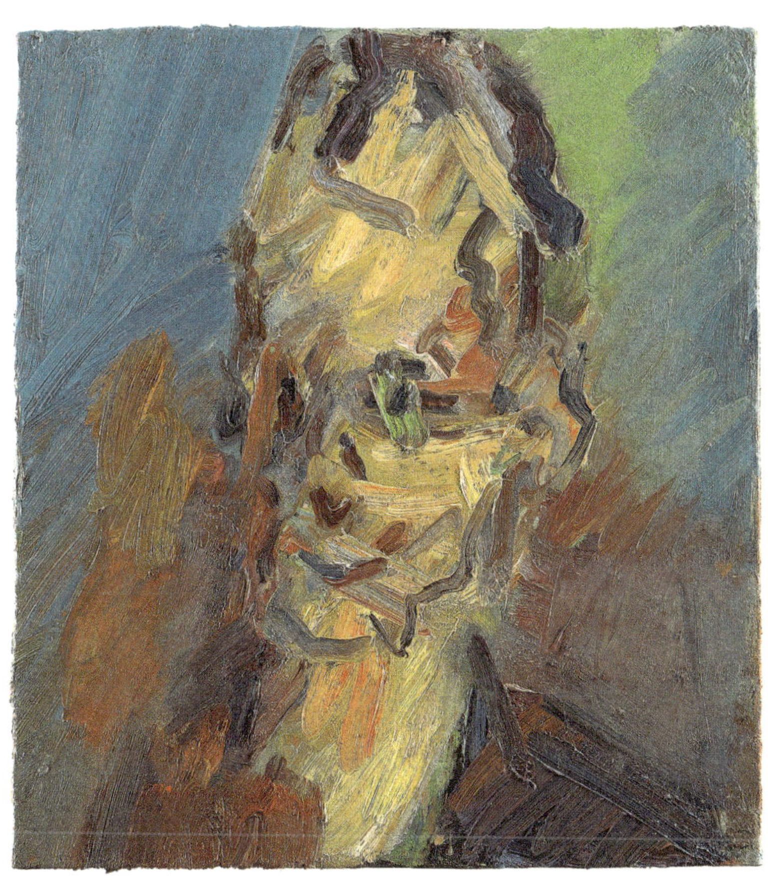

Head of William Feaver, 2008

I thought that, actually, the geometry doesn't have to be that coherent, I can break it here because that's what Tony Harrison did with this poem. If the truth is there, the architectural coherence can be broken or shifted. Sometimes the lines go round in my head as I'm painting because they are so exciting.'[11]

Auerbach used to recite, incant, very long passages of poetry, but now does so less frequently. He knows Keats's Odes from studying them for his Higher School Certificate. 'I forget things, but I was very affected by verse and like everybody else I know, I wrote poems, quite a few of them. They are a succinct expression of what is finally an artistic impulse. If you have them in your head, you are affected by their purity and force. They do come into my head.' I remembered hearing him recite 'Lapis Lazuli' by W. B. Yeats. 'Yes, I absolutely love it, but I didn't think of it for a subject. I knew 'The Second Coming' by heart – "And what rough beast, its hour come round at last,/Slouches towards Bethlehem to be born?" It is probably not common to everybody but certainly common to old Cézanne who knew Latin poetry, which I suspect is the basis of all poetry, and quoted great swathes of Virgil. It is one of the things that painters do. Like a telegram, it is shorthand, just for seeing the secret pattern in life and expressing it with specifics. I love that poem by Thomas Hardy when he has lists.'[12]

This poem, 'An Ancient to Ancients', carries something of how Auerbach, and other artists of similar habits and determination, might feel when they reach their eighties. A sense of wanting to justify his existence was there when Auerbach was still a student, and soon was coupled with a desire to leave behind a substantial *oeuvre*, have exhibitions and maybe to hand 'on the torch a bit': 'Obviously when I was young the glamour of it appealed, and the hedonism and a bit of fame, but as I have got older it is just the doing of it that is the fun.' And, as in the last verse, after the waning of romance and sport, these older men thinking back across the centuries are upbeat that people will understand what was going through the artists' minds as they responded to the motifs and their materials, addicted to the 'best game' – painting.

An Ancient to Ancients

Thomas Hardy

Where once we danced, where once we sang,
    Gentlemen,
The floors are sunken, cobwebs hang,
And cracks creep; worms have fed upon
The doors. Yea, sprightlier times were then
Than now, with harps and tabrets gone,
    Gentlemen!

Where once we rowed, where once we sailed,
    Gentlemen,
And damsels took the tiller, veiled
Against too strong a stare (God wot
Their fancy, then or anywhen!)
Upon that shore we are clean forgot,
    Gentlemen!

We have lost somewhat, afar and near,
    Gentlemen,
The thinning of our ranks each year
Affords a hint we are nigh undone,
That we shall not be ever again,
That marked of many, loved of one,
    Gentlemen.

In dance the polka hit our wish,
    Gentlemen,
The paced quadrille, the spry schottische,
"Sir Roger." – And in opera spheres
The "Girl" (the famed "Bohemian"),
And "Trovatore," held the ears,
    Gentlemen.

This season's paintings do not please,
    Gentlemen,
Like Etty, Mulready, Maclise;
Throbbing romance has waned and wanned;
No wizard wields the witching pen
Of Bulwer, Scott, Dumas, and Sand,
    Gentlemen.

The bower we shrined to Tennyson,
    Gentlemen,
Is roof-wrecked; damps there drip upon
Sagged seats, the creeper-nails are rust,
The spider is sole denizen;
Even she who read those rhymes is dust,
    Gentlemen!

We who met sunrise sanguine-souled,
    Gentlemen,
Are wearing weary. We are old;
These younger press; we feel our rout
Is imminent to Aïdes' den, –
That evening's shades are stretching out,
    Gentlemen!

And yet, though ours be failing frames,
    Gentlemen,
So were some others' history names,
Who trode their track light-limbed and fast
As these youth, and not alien
From enterprise, to their long last,
    Gentlemen.

Sophocles, Plato, Socrates,
    Gentlemen,
Pythagoras, Thucydides,
Herodotus, and Homer, – yea,
Clement, Augustin, Origen,
Burnt brightlier towards their setting-day,
    Gentlemen.

And ye, red-lipped and smooth-browed; list,
    Gentlemen;
Much is there waits you we have missed;
Much lore we leave you worth the knowing,
Much, much has lain outside our ken;
Nay, rush not: time serves: we are going,
    Gentlemen.

NOTES

Quotations in the text without a reference number are taken from conversations with the author in the period 2008–13. The word 'revised' indicates where Frank Auerbach has slightly changed quotations cited in published interviews. MA = Marlborough Fine Art, London, Archives.

Chapter One, pp. 10–53

1   The apartment block is 'Berlin' before 1914 when most of Wilmersdorf was built. The front was redone in the 1930s. The so-called 'Bauakten' survived the war in most cases (information from Juergen Kraue and Tanja Pirsig-Marshall).

2   John Tusa, *The John Tusa Interviews*, 'Frank Auerbach,' BBC Radio 3, 7 October 2001, revised by Frank Auerbach.

3   William Feaver, *Frank Auerbach*, New York, 2009, p. 8.

4   Early on in the war, the Origos took in twenty refugee children fleeing the bombing of Genoa, and for the next five years protected partisans and escaped Allied prisoners of war hiding in the grounds of their estate, even while the house was occupied by German soldiers, as recounted in *War in Val d'Orcia: An Italian War Diary 1943-1944* (London, 1947). Other books include *The Merchant of Prato*, a biography of Byron and *A Need to Testify* (four short biographies).

5   Field Marshal Erwin Rommel's family lived in the Landschulheim buildings in Herrlingen during the war and that is where he was detained in 1944. See Harold Jackson's article http://www.theguardian. com/education/2003/jul/18/schools.uk1.

6   Auerbach's arrival in England was not part of the *Kindertransport* as mistakenly reported elsewhere.

7   Leslie Bellew, 'Watched over by angel', www.kentonline.co.uk, 9 August 2013. Badsworth died in 2014.

8   Tusa 2001.

9   Dr Fridolin Friedmann became the headmaster for a brief period. See Leslie Baruch Brent's book, *Sunday's Child,*

A Memoir (New Romney, 2009), and Anthea Gerrie, 'Revealed: the wartime school that saved lives', *Jewish Chronicle*, 11 August 2011. Other alumni include Martin Lubowski, the documentary filmmaker; director Martin Sarne who had a hit with 'Come Outside' and directed among other films *Myra Breckinridge* (1970); Peter Morley (formerly Meyer), documentary filmmaker, whose *Women of Courage* (1948) is a story from the Nazi era; and David Edwards, writer of (and actor in) the first TV soap, 'The Appleyards' (1952–57).

10   The *Stolpersteine* commemorative brass plaques placed at the last address of choice are a project of the artist Gunter Demnig. The first one was installed in Kreuzberg, Berlin, in 1997: http://www.stolpersteine. eu/en/. In their records Charlotte was deported 3 March and Max 1 March.

11   Vikram Seth, *Two Lives* (New York and London, 2005), p. 200.

12   Ibid., p. 253. W. G. Sebald created a fictional character who had a close resemblance to what he knew about Auerbach's past, which he combined with features of his Mancunian landlord. Auerbach felt the story was invasive and misleading and conveyed his objections to the British publisher. In the English edition of *The Emigrants* (1996) the character's name was changed from Max Aurach to Max Ferber and an illustration of one of his drawings was removed.

13   Geordie Greig, 'The constant painter', *London Evening Standard*, 10 September 2009, p. 32, revised by Frank Auerbach, February 2014.

14   Michael Peppiatt, 'Frank Auerbach. Camden Town London 1998' and 'Frank Auerbach. Camden Town London 1999', in *Interviews with Artists 1966-2012* (New Haven and London, 2012), pp. 39–40. *Everyman* is a late fifteenth-century English morality play, author unknown.

15   Richard Cork, 'Frank Auerbach: An interview by Richard Cork', *Art & Design*, 4:9/10, 1988, p. 16. During the war, Marckwald took Auerbach to London to see a production of *King Lear* starring the

famous actor-manager Donald Wolfit. The former teacher and pupil last met in 1955 for dinner at a Chinese restaurant, by which time Marckwald had moved to Hull as county drama director, where he also taught at the university. He was in London to see Joan Plowright (whom he had launched in Hull, as he did John Hurt). She was playing Pip in Orson Welles's *Moby Dick - Rehearsed*.

16 Robert Hughes, transcript of interview with artist, March 1986. MA. The Sword of Stalingrad was a gift to the 'steel-hearted citizens of Stalingrad' from King George VI 'in token of the homage of the British people'. It was presented to Stalin by Churchill at the Tehran conference in 1943.

17 Geordie Greig, 'Hidden talent', *The Times*, 12 December 1998, p. 38.

18 Patrick O'Connor, 'Frank Marcus and the ITG in the 50s', *London Magazine*, April/May 2000, p. 84.

19 Ibid., p. 86.

20 Peter Ustinov, *House of Regrets* (London, 1943), pp. 65–66. The date of the production has been given elsewhere inaccurately as 1947. In Stella West's copy of the play, she added in pencil the first names of the twelve actors, apparently Frank as the General and someone called 'Sydney' as Strukhov.

21 O'Connor 2000, p. 87. *The Broken Jug* is by Heinrich von Kleist.

22 Tusa, 2001. The myths around Bomberg continue to be related in an especially dramatic fashion; the undeniable hostility and neglect he suffered is transferred to stories. For example, Auerbach points out that Bomberg did destroy the drawings he did at the Slade. Those shown in the 2011 BBC series 'British Masters' were done after the war. He was stroppy and hit someone at art school, which is why he was asked to leave, not because his work was too avant-garde.

23 Hughes 1986.

24 Tusa 2001.

25 Hughes 1986.

26 Unedited transcript of interview with Catherine Lampert, 1978.

27 Tusa 2001.

28 Robert Hughes, *Frank Auerbach* (London and New York, 1990), p. 28.

29 Stuart Jeffries, 'Gustav Metzger: "Destroy, and you create"', *Guardian*, 26 November 2012.

30 Hughes 1990, p. 31.

31 Ibid. Bomberg left the Borough Polytechnic in 1953 and Metzger asked his fellow students and staff to give money so they could buy Bomberg the multi-volume set of Bishop Berkeley's theories as a leaving present. Leavis and his ideas were discussed at Bunce Court although the teaching of English literature was fairly erratic.

32 Hughes 1986.

33 Hughes 1990, pp. 26–27.

34 Martin Gayford, 'Auerbach's London', *Apollo*, October 2009, p. 59.

35 Hughes 1986.

36 Catherine Lampert, 'A conversation with Frank Auerbach', in *Frank Auerbach* (Arts Council, London, 1978), pp. 20–21.

37 Hughes 1986. FA explained to CL, September 2014, that he became attached to the black-and-white reproduction of the 1907 *Head* and although the picture was in London in the collection of E. S. T. Mesens he did not see the original.

38 There were other opportunities to see Picasso's work in postwar London, including *Demoiselles d'Avignon* (1907), which was shown in the '40 Years of Modern Art' exhibition in 1948 (at the Academy Hall) that was put together by Roland Penrose on behalf of the new ICA before it had its own premises.

39 Hughes 1990, p. 87.

40 Ibid., p. 88.

41 Ibid., p. 33.

42 Judith Bumpus, 'Frank Auerbach', *Art & Artists*, June 1986, p. 24.

43 Ibid.

44 Coldstream was associated with the Euston Road School, the studios that took in students wishing to study drawing and painting. Its structure resembled the French atelier system where practising artists could visit to draw and paint from the model. Claude Rogers, Victor

Notes

Pasmore and Coldstream were the principal teachers, first at 12 Fitzroy Street and then 214 Euston Road, in the period 1937–39. Before the war Moynihan had experimented with Objective Abstraction, a short-lived group of artists who exhibited at the Zwemmer Gallery and attempted to record 'the artist's response to the motif by a sequence of brushstrokes devoid of conceptual or idealistic style,' and for whom 'the painting is simply an object'. Lawrence Gowing, *Rodrigo Moynihan: A Retrospective Exhibition* (Royal Academy of Arts, London, 1978), n.p.

45 Barnaby Wright (ed.), *Frank Auerbach: London Building Sites, 1952–62* (Courtauld Gallery, London, 2009), p. 80.

46 Tusa 2001.

47 Ibid.

48 Unpublished text sent by Andrews to Bruce Bernard. Courtesy of Virginia Verran.

49 Andrew Forge, 'Helen Lessore and the Beaux Arts Gallery', in *Helen Lessore and the Beaux Arts Gallery* (Marlborough Fine Art, London, 1968), p. 6.

50 Ibid., p. 9.

51 Undated letter, TGA 8922/4/50. Reply from Coldstream 7 October 1953 explaining there were no vacancies but suggesting Bomberg come to the Slade later in the month for lunch with him and Claude Rogers, TGA 8922/4/8.

52 Frank Auerbach, 'Seven Portraits', *Ark*, 23, 1958, p. 28.

53 Stella West, transcript of interview with Robert Hughes, Malvern, 1 March 1986. MA.

54 For some time Wilde worked (erratically) at a petrol station that Wauchope ran next to Duloe Mill, a curious building where he was living. This non-functioning windmill faced the Great North Road at Eaton Socon on the border of Bedfordshire and Cambridgeshire. O. S. Wauchope's landlord was Dr Patterson, who also rented rooms in the house he owned in The Cut, 22a Lower Marsh, near Waterloo station. A number of artists associated with Camberwell School of Art and the Slade were resident, among them Craigie Aitchison, Myles Murphy and Patrick George, and when Os, as he was called, sometimes stayed there he kept them up all night in philosophical discussion.

55 FA to Sarah West, 24 May 2011.

56 Hannah Rothschild, 'The sitter's tale', *Sunday Telegraph Magazine*, 28 October 2001, p. 35.

Chapter Two, pp. 54–83

1 Gayford 2009, p. 60. A few drawings from St Martin's survive, but all the building-site pictures Auerbach did there were destroyed.

2 Barnaby Wright, 'Creative destruction: Frank Auerbach and the rebuilding of London', in Wright 2009, p. 15.

3 Ibid., p. 19.

4 Ibid., p. 94. Kossoff also tackled the Shell building site before going on to locations north of King's Cross station, such as the viaduct adjacent to York Way and the train-line-crossed territory near Willesden Junction.

5 Gayford 2009, p. 59.

6 Paul Moorhouse, 'A human universe: Auerbach's building site paintings and existentialism', in Wright 2009, p. 67.

7 Ibid., p. 52.

8 Wright 2009, pp. 14–15.

9 Richard Cork in conversation with Frank Auerbach, BBC Radio 3, 18 November 1985.

10 Tim Adams, 'Frank's other half', *Observer, The New Review*, 21 September 2014, p. 18.

11 The exhibition was the newspaper publisher Lord Beaverbrook's initiative and the first prize was shared between Geoffrey Banks's *Departure for Cythera* (1955) and Bryan Kneale's *Pony in the Snow* (1954). Lady Caroline Blackwood, Freud's second wife, is the blonde woman in *Hotel Bedroom*.

12 Leon Kossoff, 'The paintings of Frank Auerbach', in *Frank Auerbach* (Arts Council, London, 1978), p. 9.

13 Peppiatt 2012, p. 5.

14 Unedited transcript, Lampert, 1978.

15 David Sylvester, 'Young English painting', *Listener*, 12 January 1956, vol. 55, p. 64.

16 Ibid.

17 According to the catalogue, the Summer
Exhibition, 22 July–16 September 1955, had
a portrait of Bacon by Lessore, works by
Edward Middleditch and Jack Smith, a
Kossoff drawing, *Weeping Figure*, figurative
work by Tilson, Cunningham and
Whishaw, but nothing by Mike Pope.

18 Helen Lessore, *A Partial Testament: Essays
on some Moderns in the Great Tradition*
(Tate Gallery, London), 1986, p. 55.

19 Sylvester 1956, p. 64.

20 Richard Cork, 'Two old masters', *Times
2*, 3 May 2006, p. 4 (revised). A number of
the portraits were on canvas but, as Freud
remembered, most of the thickly painted
works were on board.

21 Ibid., p. 4.

22 Forge 1968, p. 5.

23 David Sylvester, *Critic's Choice* (Arthur
Tooth & Sons, London), 1958, n.p.

24 David Sylvester observed the painter
Patrick George coming into Tooth's
wearing a scruffy raincoat and asking the
man at the desk the price of Coldstream's
Study from Two Models (1953–54), and was
told, as if he would be shocked, £300.
George bought and lived with this
intriguing, beautifully painted work until
2011 when he gave it to the Fitzwilliam
Museum in Cambridge.

25 John Berger, 'A stick in the dark', *New
Statesman*, 28 November 1959. The *Observer*
critic reviewing the same exhibition felt
less moved: 'he may peer down into the
building craters, as Auerbach does, and
so bulldoze his thick, glutinous pigment
across the canvas as to convey an exact
sense of the intractable mound of clay,
and the thrust and strain of tackle.' Anon.,
Observer, 29 November 1959. Berger argued
that those who called these original works
'muddy, churned-up failures' were those
'familiar only with styles as they are filed
in the sales-catalogues of modern art'.

26 Wright 2009, p. 30. *The Times*, 30 November
1959.

27 David Sylvester, *Sunday Times Colour
Magazine*, 2 June 1963.

28 Alan Bowness, 'At the galleries', *Observer*,
11 February 1962.

29 Andrew Forge, 'Auerbach and Paolozzi',
New Statesman, 13 September 1963, p. 329.
Not all reviews were positive; there was
a complaint about the 'heaped-up paint'
and the repetition of subjects. Discussing
Auerbach's 1961 exhibition on the BBC
radio programme 'The Critics', Basil Taylor
was so negative he provoked a strong
objection from Stephen Spender who
wrote to the *Listener* on 27 April 1961: 'In
my ignorance I think that Mr Auerbach is
one of the two or three most interesting
young painters in England. He is perhaps
unique in showing in his work a completely
serious, utterly absorbed devotion to the
objects he paints, which have tended to
be a few square yards or Primrose Hill, or
building sites, or one model ... The chorus
of disapprobation was altogether too pack-
like to do credit to this programme, and
it must have pained listeners who feel as I
do that an exceptionally scrupulous young
painter deserves better treatment.'

30 Auerbach letter, dated 4 December 1963,
a reply to 'A letter from Michael Peppiatt',
was published in *Cambridge Opinion* (special
issue: *Modern Art in Britain*), 37, January
1964, p. 51.

31 Lampert 1978, p. 21.

32 She contacted Auerbach after seeing the
Royal Academy exhibition in 2001, letter
dated 7 December 2001. MA.

33 After some of the students graduated,
Auerbach told Lampert, 'Colburn who
was sort of a visionary, instead of chucking
them out, found an abandoned nursery
school, and gave them conditions which
they would never have again, each with a
studio, only four of them, and a life model.'

34 Frank Auerbach, 'Fragments from a
conversation', *X: A Quarterly Review*, 1:1,
November 1959, pp. 32–33.

35 Geoff Hassell, *Camberwell School of Arts
& Crafts: Its Students and Teachers, 1943–1960*
(Woodbridge, 1998), p. 31.

36 The foreword Frank contributed for an
exhibition of Christopher Couch's was
short: 'I admire these paintings and find it
hard to say anything about them, perhaps
because they are so clear. Since I do not

care about idiom it must be their spirit I value. There is a desire to celebrate organic experience and there is an inner need for coherence. Here both these impulses seem urgent and precise and neither is betrayed. I wish I could have expressed this more simply, but I believe Christopher has done so in his work.' MA, undated.

37 John Wonnacott to Catherine Lampert, e-mail, 9 February 2014.

38 John Christopher Battye, 'Frank Auerbach', *Art & Artists*, 5:10, January 1971, p. 55.

39 Paul Bonaventura, 'Een Benadering van Frank Auerbach', *Metropolis M, 2*, Summer 1986, p. 4. Coldstream, along with Sylvester, Robert Melville, Kitaj and Hamilton had taken part in a conversation with Duchamp the day after the show opened. Duchamp had claimed to have abandoned making art even though he confessed he liked manual execution; he would no longer designate readymades nor paint in oil as it required 'the selfsame process and material', 'the mark is a personal problem'. Duchamp papers, 3:2, Philadelphia Museum of Art.

40 Greig 2009, p. 32.

41 Tusa 2001.

42 Marcel Reich-Ranicki, *The Author of Himself: The Life of Marcel Reich-Ranicki* (London and Princeton, 2001), pp. 14–15. Auerbach thinks 'distinguished' is a more accurate description of the neighbourhood than 'aristocratic'. The story of Jakob continues, 'the family who had kindly received me, the son of a bankrupt businessman from a small Polish town, did not live in the fashionable west of Berlin, or in Dahlem or Grünewald, but on Roonstrasse, immediately next to the Reichstag.' Long-term Marcel was the host of 'The Literary Quartet' television programme, which became a popular pastime, and until his nineties he was a contributor to the *Frankfurter Allgemeine Zeitung*.

43 Ibid., p. 15. Jakob hid in Holland during the war and after moving to London became a tenant in one of the flats at 35 Belsize Avenue, Hampstead, built by Fritz Hess, a Jewish businessman and building contractor who employed Ernst Freud, Lucian's father, to convert a garage into a dwelling. Fritz Hess was something of a tycoon, and with his second wife, Ann, began collecting German Expressionist pictures and then works by Freud, as well as three paintings by Auerbach, one of which was the beautiful black-and-white *Head of E.O.W. III* (1961).

44 Ibid., pp. 29 and 63.

45 Ibid., pp. 63–64. Andrew Ranicki knew his father was familiar with *Stolpersteine* but he did not suggest that one should be put in place for his parents, Helene and David Reich, whose last address of choice was 53 Güntzelstrasse. On 12 September 2014 one was installed: 'I am fairly sure that he [Marcel] would have had the same attitude as he had some twenty years ago, at the time of the discussion regarding plans for the Holocaust memorial here in Berlin: "I am neither for nor against it. I do not need it, and my father, my mother, my brother and the many other members of my family who were murdered do not need it either. I have not uttered even one word in this matter."' From Ranicki's speech, entitled 'Here in Berlin, which he loved so much, against all the odds', at the dedication. Information from AR to CL, e-mail, 24 September 2014.

46 Ibid., p. 66.

47 Greig 1998, p. 38.

48 A second, square version *Study after Rembrandt I* (1961) was destroyed, a decision he later regretted. In fact, the surviving painting was made 'after' this version rather than directly from the Rembrandt.

49 Auerbach speaking to Wiggins. Colin Wiggins, 'Rembrandt: The Lamentation over the Dead Christ', in Colin Wiggins (ed.), *Frank Auerbach and the National Gallery: Working after the Masters* (London, 1995), p. 28.

50 Ibid, p. 29.

51 Ibid., p. 28. The big painting was then titled *After Rembrandt's The Lamentation over the Dead Christ II* (1961).

Chapter Three, pp. 84–117

1 Forge 1968, p. 9. Forge wrote, 'He must work unprotected in any way by the general

milieu' (the protagonist is always male, although Sheila Fell was one of the Beaux Arts Gallery artists referred to). Auerbach identified with the 'absoluteness' and 'puritanical thoroughness' of these artists but he and the others felt uncomfortable with Lessore's preoccupation with what she called 'The Great Tradition'. Her thesis claimed a two-thousand-year lineage in Western art connected to the 'imitation of natural appearances', and in her book *A Partial Testament: Essays on Some Moderns in the Great Tradition* (London, 1986) she described 'a huge chasm' between the last great age and the situation now: 'It was the void left by the vanishing of belief.'

2   The 'Situation' exhibition was held at the Royal Society of British Artists (RBA) gallery, London, in September 1960. An exhibition addressing this movement at Tate Liverpool in 2003, 'Formal Situations: Abstraction in Britain 1960–1970', described the premises: 'The powerful influence exercised by the American painters is manifest in two common threads, which the organisers expressed as conditions for inclusion in the *Situation* exhibition. The first condition was that the work shown should be abstract. This rejected the literal representation of recognisable subjects and also abstraction from nature – a stipulation that pointedly excluded the earlier generation of St Ives painters whose work was rooted in observation. *Situation* emphasized the importance of working with purely pictorial elements without explicit reference to outside phenomena. The second criterion for inclusion was that the paintings should be large in scale: no work was to be less than thirty square feet.' http://www.tate.org.uk/whats-on/tate-liverpool/exhibition/formal-situations-abstraction-britain-1960-1970. As to the possibility of these individuals being regarded as a group or movement (or, by the late 1970s, mistakenly elided with the invented 'School of London'), Auerbach has cautioned, 'Francis had a show there [the Beaux Arts Gallery], Lucian almost did, and

they used to visit the gallery. I think the situation of people who are, as it were, in the same ambience is very much like that of a political party, where the tensions between them are greater than they are with those in another party. If people have a programme here, they tend to keep it to themselves.'

3   Battye 1971, p. 55.

4   After 1977 Freud began working in Holland Park in a flat with more comfort, and after the early 1990s had an assistant to help. The other artists remained in the same studios, unaided except by their galleries.

5   Doris von Drateln, 'Malen ist nicht wie Husten oder Spucken' ('Painting is not like coughing or spitting'), *Kunstforum*, 87, January/February 1987, kindly translated by Tanja Pirsig-Marshall and rephrased in English by Frank Auerbach.

6   David Sylvester, *Looking at Giacometti* (London, 1994), reprinted re-edited versions of earlier texts, such as 'Perpetuating the Transient', the catalogue introduction for the Arts Council Giacometti exhibition, 1955. The Swiss artist's direct connections with London flourished through those who got to know him in Paris: Isabel Rawsthorne, then Freud, Raymond Mason, David Sylvester, Euan Uglow and William Turnbull. This was a different group from those he knew in the 1930s, such as Winifred and Ben Nicholson and F. E. McWilliam.

7   Alfred H. Barr, Jr., Introduction, *The New American Painting* (Tate Gallery, London, 1959), pp. 10–11.

8   Feaver 2009, p. 233. David Sylvester confessed to a 'Damascene conversion' to American painting after seeing the exhibition 'Modern Art in the United States' at the Tate in 1956. 'Hommage à Nicolas de Staël' was held 6–31 March 1956 at Arthur Tooth & Sons.

9   Conversation between Frank Auerbach, Taco Dibbits, Geoffrey Parton and Pilar Ordovas, *Raw Truth: Auerbach–Rembrandt* (London, 2013), p. 25, catalogue for exhibition at Ordovas London and the Rijksmuseum, Amsterdam.

Notes

10 David Sylvester, *About Modern Art* (London, 1997), p. 338.
11 *de Kooning: A Retrospective* (Museum of Modern Art, New York, 2011), p. 271.
12 Ibid., p. 278.
13 John Elderfield, 'Woman and landscape', in *de Kooning: A Retrospective*, 2011, p. 282.
14 Two pictures from 1970 of Renée Fedden, an assistant to the cookery writer Elizabeth David, were commissions made at the request of her friend the Hon. Rosemary Peto, who collected works by Auerbach.
15 Hughes 1990, p. 166.
16 Wright, who was stone deaf, wrote his poems in absolutely regular meters; Swift, in Auerbach's view, was a much better writer than painter, writing in this issue a good polemical article about the state of painting at the time, which Wright thought completely dire. It was published under the pseudonym James Mahon, 'Official art and the modern painter', *X: A Quarterly Review*, 1:1, November 1959.
17 Auerbach 1959, p. 32.
18 Bumpus 1986, p. 25.
19 Auerbach 1959, p. 34.
20 Jackie Wullschlager, 'Lunch with the FT: Frank Auerbach', *Financial Times*, 6–7 October 2012, p. 3.
21 Nevile Wallis, 'The arts', *Spectator*, 13 September 1965, p. 318.
22 Lawrence H. Bradshaw, 'Frank Auerbach', *Arts Review*, 17, 20 February–6 March 1965, p. 17, quoted in *The Tate Gallery 1984-86: Illustrated Catalogue of Acquisitions*, London, 1988, pp. 91–92.
23 Sarah West to CL, 7 November 2013.
43 Unedited transcript, Lampert, 1978.
25 Lampert 1978, p. 17.
26 Unedited transcript, Lampert, 1978.
27 John O'Mahony, 'Surfaces and depths', *Guardian*, 15 September 2001, p. 7.
28 Hughes interview with E.O.W., 1986. MA.
29 In Stella's last home in Malvern visitors recognized objects from the Brentford sitting room: a three-tiered table, the lamp and the pictures on the wall. During the making of the 2001 film, *Frank Auerbach: To the Studio*, the director Hannah Rothschild asked Stella, 'Why did you put up with this?' She replied: 'Why did I put up with it? Well, that's puzzled me. I loved him, I suppose. I used to think, "Well, why am I doing this? I've got three children, I've got a demanding job and I'm doing this." What was the answer? I just loved him, and I did it for him.' Rothschild 2001, p. 35. The producer was Jake Auerbach and the film was made by the company Rothschild Auerbach.
30 Ibid.
31 Hughes interview with E.O.W., 1986. MA.

Chapter Four, pp. 118–165
1 Hannah Rothschild, 'Man of many layers,' *Telegraph Magazine*, 28 September 2013, p. 33.
2 Gayford 2009, p. 61.
3 Support for making the film came from the BFI Experimental Film Fund. Mazzetti's professor, Coldstream, was then chairman of the BFI. The film was shot in 1954 and completed in January 1956 shortly before the screening; it won acclaim at the Cannes Film Festival that year.
4 Michael Peppiatt, 'Frank Auerbach', *Tate*, 14, Spring 1998, p. 15, revised by Frank Auerbach, February 2014.
5 David Sylvester commented on the relationship in *Looking at Giacometti* (London, 1994), pp. 157–58, and it is also described by Pilar Ordovas in *Crossing the Channel: Friendships and Connections in Paris and London, 1946-1965* (Gagosian Gallery, London, 2010).
6 When Bacon saw this work, now in the Scottish National Gallery of Art, at Auerbach's Hayward exhibition in 1978, he regretted he had not kept the painting. 11 November 2008. FA to Valerie Beston, MA.
7 Andrew Billen, 'Portrait of an artist at 81', *The Times Magazine*, 6 October 2012, p. 49.
8 Francis Bacon, in David Sylvester, *Interviews with Francis Bacon* (London, 1989), p. 105.
9 Martin Harrison, *In Camera: Francis Bacon*, (London, 2005), p. 76. See also Martin Hammer, '"Mainly Nourishment", Echoes of Sickert in the work of Francis Bacon and Lucian Freud', *Visual Culture in Britain*, 14:1, 2013.
10 Frank Auerbach, Foreword, *Late Sickert:*

Paintings 1927 to 1942 (Arts Council, London, 1981), p. 7.

11 Valerie Beston to Richard Cork, 27 October 1977. MA.

12 Michael Peppiatt, 'Frank Auerbach. Going against the grain', *Art International*, 1, 1987, pp. 24–26.

13 H. R. Fischer to FA, 2 May 1964. MA.

14 FA to John Synge, 1 January 1965. MA.

15 H. R. Fischer to FA, 4 December 1964. MA. Freud had begun painting with a loaded brush, making portraits of less attractive subjects such as John Deakin; moreover, his work was not selling. In 1972, Freud left the Marlborough to be represented by James Kirkman and Anthony d'Offay.

16 FA to John Synge, 7 February 1965. MA.

17 FA to Valerie Beston, April 1967, and FA to James Kirkman, 20 April 1966. MA.

18 FA to H. R. Fischer, 2 August 1966. MA.

19 FA to James Kirkman, Brentford, Monday 10 p.m., no date [August 1966]. MA.

20 Valerie Beston to FA, 11 September 1972. MA. Quite often in future years sales did not cover the artist's advance, and to compensate pictures were taken into the gallery stock.

21 Valerie Beston to FA, 1 January 1966, and FA to Valerie Beston, 13 April 1966. MA.

22 The father of his first wife, Ellen, the nineteenth-century Liberal politician Richard Cobden.

23 John Russell, 'Millais: How art avenged success', *Sunday Times*, 1 January 1967, review included Richard Diebenkorn at Waddington.

24 Lawrence Alloway, *Listener*, 10 April 1958, n.p.; Nevile Wallis, 'Freud and Colquhoun', *Observer*, 30 March 1958, n.p.

25 Greig 2009, p. 32, revised by Frank Auerbach, February 2014. Of course, over the years Frank met Lucian's friends. Lady Jane Willoughby acquired outstanding paintings by Freud, Andrews, Bacon and Auerbach; her constancy and capabilities continuing to be impressive. Auerbach is one of many admirers of Celia Paul's work and he is curious how her son by Lucian, Frank, also an artist, develops.

26 Feaver 2009, p. 18.

27 Quoted in Robert Hughes, 'On Lucian Freud', *Lucian Freud: Paintings* (British Council, London, 1987), p. 18. This is the catalogue for the touring show that began at the Hirshhorn, Washington, DC, and finished in Berlin, reprinted by Thames & Hudson.

28 Bruce Bernard, 'Frank Auerbach – painter in the grand manner', *Sunday Times Magazine*, 30 April 1978, p. 43.

29 Freud began acquiring Auerbach's work – by gift, loan and purchase – in the 1980s. Fifteen paintings plus drawings and one print were accepted in lieu of taxes by the UK government in 2014.

30 Lucian Freud, 'Frank Auerbach's paintings', in Wiggins 1995, p. 5. Auerbach and Freud gave each other artist's proofs of the prints they did (Auerbach donated most of those by Freud to the Courtauld Gallery, London).

31 Billen 2012, p. 49.

32 Ibid.

33 'Painting 1961', *London Magazine*, new series, 1:4, July 1961.

34 Peppiatt 1987, p. 24.

35 Lampert 1978, p. 16.

36 R. B. Kitaj, Introduction, *The Human Clay: An Exhibition Selected by R. B. Kitaj* (Arts Council, London, 1976), n.p.

37 He expressed regret for coining the phrase. See R. B. Kitaj in Alistair Hicks (ed.), *Art Works: British and German Contemporary Art, 1960–2000* (Deutsche Bank, London, 2000). The show included paintings borrowed from the Arts Council collection and elsewhere. To some extent this return of figurative painting coincided with a broader international trend, as marked by 'A New Spirit in Painting', the exhibition at the Royal Academy in London in 1981.

38 Michael Peppiatt, 'R. B. Kitaj: The diaspora in London', *Art International*, 1, Autumn 1987, p. 34.

39 Undated letter to Katia; her questions were sent in 2008. MA.

40 Ibid.

41 Lawrence Gowing, *Michael Andrews, Frank Auerbach, Francis Bacon, William Coldstream,*

Lucian Freud, Patrick George, Leon Kossoff and Euan Uglow. Eight Figurative Painters (New Haven and Santa Barbara, 1981), p. 24.

42 Bonaventura 1986, p. 14.

43 Bacon interviewed by Andrew Forge on BBC Radio 3, 4 March 1972.

44 David Wilkie (1921–1992) was a quiet man who worked as a clerk in the City office of an insurance company. His collection, displayed in the rooms of his modest suburban home in Brentwood, Essex, included a painting, a sculpture and two decorated boxes by John Lessore, a couple of paintings each by Winifred Nicholson, Craigie Aitchison and Peter Snow, as well as works by Michael Andrews, John Bratby, Heinz Koppel and his own portrait by Helen Lessore. Wilkie's solicitor advised him to leave these pictures to Auerbach with instructions that they be presented to the Tate, which they were.

45 Paul Moorhouse, 'David Wilkie', in *The Wilkie Gift. Contemporary Art from the Collection of David Wilkie, 1921–1992* (Tate Gallery, London, 1994). *The Origin of the Great Bear* (1968) was about a theme, another myth in Ovid's *Metamorphoses*, Titian might have painted. However, no particular work by Titian formed the starting point (he had painted an earlier episode in the story). Auerbach began with drawings done on Hampstead Heath.

46 Richard Wollheim, 'Titian and Auerbach', *Listener*, 4 October 1973, p. 466. Wilkie had a special interest in existentialism and the philosophical potential of art, and accumulated a large library. As a last commission he suggested that Auerbach make a painting based on Bernini's marble group *Saint Teresa in Ecstasy* in the Cornaro Chapel of Santa Maria della Vittoria in Rome, perhaps using a live model. Learning that Auerbach was disinclined to do so, he proposed a portrait of Arthur Rimbaud, and in the end Auerbach, working from photographs, fused these sources, and created four images of the unlikely combination – a large Rimbaud 'banner' seems to be enshrined, or perhaps rests, in the chapel before being carried in a procession. See Moorhouse, *The Wilkie Gift*, 1994.

47 Ibid.

48 Frank Auerbach, 'The Paintings', *Frank Auerbach,* University of Essex, Colchester.

49 Michael Podro, 'The sense of composure', *Times Literary Supplement*, 5 May 1978. The Tate painting just preceded the bright blue and yellow *Primrose Hill* (1968) that Podro and his wife, Charlotte, owned.

50 FA to Penny Marcus, 16 March 1972. Also discussed in FA to Anne Seymour, 15 March 1971.

51 FA to Norman Reid, 30 December 1972. A summary of these remarks was published in a description of new acquisitions, *The Tate Gallery 1970-72*, for T1270, pp. 76–77.

52 Colin Wiggins, 'Rubens: Samson and Delilah', in Wiggins 1995, p. 20.

53 Although Auerbach began drawing from paintings in the National Gallery while a student, most of these sketches were thrown away. A group, the majority dating from 1981–93, from a larger donation by James Kirkman, was displayed for years in rows on the red walls of the learning-resources centre on the National Gallery's lower floor.

54 Unedited transcript, Lampert, 1978.

55 JA to CL, 25 January 2014.

56 Enjoying New York, Auerbach checked in with Miss Beston before extending the trip by forty-eight hours, and she reassured him by telegram that Stella approved of the plan, the gallery could change the ticket, and, most importantly, reported that 'All is well with Studio. Nothing has happened to it'; adding, 'How does the Exhibition look. Love Beston'. VB to FA, telegram, 19 September 1969. MA.

57 Postcard to CL, 27 March 1982.

58 Bumpus 1986, p. 26. He returned to the Barnes Collection in 1994 with Julia and Jake.

59 Unedited transcript, Lampert, 1978.

60 Ibid.

61 These were nos 34, 78, 87, 118, 143 and 170 in Feaver 2009.

62 FA to CL, 1986.

63 FA to Andrews, 3 January 1984. MA.

Auerbach composed a five-page letter to Miss Beston defining the groupings, each picture identified by a stamp-sized sketch, date, collection if known; the information was taken from the black binders filled with black and white photographs kept in the studio. The plan was chronological (covering 1953–84) and by type, sets of three to six works in running order: compositions, heads, nudes, paintings of Primrose Hill, paintings of heads, reclining heads, drawings of different people, paintings of the studios, three paintings of Deborah Ratcliff and, to finish, seated figures. In 2001, for the exhibition at the Royal Academy, the selection was mine with Norman Rosenthal, Isabel Carlisle and Frank making suggestions. To understand what might be there, again the artist broke down the proposed list into large and small landscapes, advocating double the number of paintings and drawings of people, and pointing out that three of the best images of David Landau were drawings. The first paper plan for the installation seemed rather too spacious: 'One does want an exhibition to be something of a feast (rather than a slimming diet)', letter to CL, 2001. Since then Auerbach's inclination has been to go for more sparse hangs and to emphasize the dissimilarities between works.

64 Tusa 2001, revised by FA. Auerbach regards the contemporary way of valuing art by the gigantic sums some works reach as artificial and most likely unsustainable; once a painting leaves the studio its ownership is of little interest.

65 Bumpus 1986, p. 26.

66 Auerbach went to Essen as well but did not travel to Madrid. The Spanish showing of the Venice exhibition in the spring of 1987 happened in the first year of the Centro de Arte Reina Sofía (as it was then called) when Carmen Giménez was the director of the National Center for Exhibitions for the Spanish Ministry of Culture. The painter Antonio Saura wrote 'Auerbach o el espacio coagulado', an introduction to the catalogue.

67 Von Drateln 1987.

68 Cork 1988, p. 15.

69 Bumpus 1986, p. 23.

70 Greig 1998 (revised by Frank Auerbach from 'three' to 'five' days).

71 JA to CL, 25 January 2014.

Chapter Five, pp. 166–205

1 Peppiatt 2012, p. 11.

2 James Elkins, *What Painting Is* (New York and London, 1999), p. 74; statement 11 April 1998.

3 The artist Jenny Saville told me that for a while she used Stokes paint because she so admired Auerbach's work, but it was too much of a struggle and she changed when she could afford a brand intended for fine art.

4 Peppiatt 2012, p. 9.

5 Cork 1988, p. 20.

6 Andrew Lambirth, 'Living in the moment', *Spectator*, 24 October 2009, p. 52.

7 Michael Peppiatt, 'Talking to Frank Auerbach', in *Frank Auerbach: Recent Works* (Marlborough, New York, 1998), pp. 6–7.

8 Peppiatt 2012, p. 10.

9 Feaver 2009, p. 230.

10 *Raw Truth: Auerbach-Rembrandt* (London, 2013), p. 24.

11 Bumpus 1986, p. 23.

12 Auerbach letter, dated 4 December 1963, published in *Cambridge Opinion* (special issue: *Modern Art in Britain*), 37, January 1964, p. 51. *The Last Art Film* (2012) was directed by Jake Auerbach.

13 Feaver 2009, p. 230.

14 Wullschlager 2012, p. 3.

15 Tusa 2001.

16 Lampert 1978, p. 11.

17 William Feaver, Introduction, *Frank Auerbach, Recent Paintings and Drawings*, (Marlborough Fine Art, London, 1987), p. 5.

18 Lambirth 2009, p. 52.

19 Feaver 2009, p. 230.

20 Adams 2014, p. 18.

21 I was the curator and asked for these. However, the Royal Academy budget would not stretch to loans from Montreal and Japan.

22 Rothschild 2013, p. 33.

Notes

23 Hughes 1990, p. 89.

24 Ibid.

25 Lampert 1978, p. 17.

26 E-mail exchange, CL with Deborah Ratcliff, April–May 2001.

27 FA to Valerie Beston, 8 June 1984. MA.

28 Hughes 1986.

29 Catherine Lampert, 'Auerbach and his sitters', in *Frank Auerbach: Paintings and Drawings 1954-2001* (London, 2001), p. 30.

30 Hughes 1990, pp. 15–16.

31 Letter to Robert Hughes, undated. MA.

32 'Frank Auerbach in conversation with William Feaver', in Feaver 2009, p. 231.

33 FA to CL, letter dated 22 December 1994.

34 Peppiatt 2012, pp. 45–46.

35 Martin Gayford, *Man with a Blue Scarf: On Sitting for a Portrait by Lucian Freud* (London and New York, 2010), p. 58.

36 Wullschlager 2012.

37 Feaver 2009, p. 230.

38 Auerbach, draft introduction to Giacometti exhibition, 1986 (unpublished).

39 'David Landau & Oliver Barker in conversation, May 2012', in *A Dialogue in Paint: Frank Auerbach's Portraits of Ruth Bromberg*, Sotheby's, auction 26 June 2012, p. 21. Auerbach was commissioned to paint the first portrait of Ruth Bromberg, and was attracted to the idea of working from a stranger. When the portrait was finished, she urged him to continue letting her sit. They became friends but it might be going too far, as this auction catalogue does, to describe the sequences of pictures of one person as following a trajectory or 'navigating an evolution' and reaching a 'finale', or as 'unprecedented and enhanced by the accompanying provenance'.

40 JA to CL, e-mail, 25 January 2014. Being reminded of mutual friends, such as Bruce Bernard, Euan Uglow and Lucian Freud, is part of sitting.

41 Wullschlager 2012.

Conclusion, pp. 206–215

1 Greig 2009, p. 32.

2 Catherine Lampert interview with Auerbach, *Connect* (British Council staff magazine), 9, March 1986, p. 7.

3 Stephanie D'Alessandro, *Matisse: Radical Invention, 1913-1917* (Museum of Modern Art, New York, 2010), pp. 238–39.

4 Auerbach, in Simon Grant (ed.), *Personal Reflections on Art by Today's Leading Artists* (London, 2012), p. 29.

5 Michael Kimmelman, 'Recent works by Frank Auerbach in an exhibition at the Marlborough Gallery', *New York Times*, 4 April 2006.

6 See Christophe Cherix and Ann Temkin, *Jasper Johns: Regrets* (The Museum of Modern Art, New York, 2014). The photograph was taken in 1958 as Bacon prepared to make portraits of Freud (revised date courtesy Paul Rousseau). It records an intense friendship that ultimately disintegrated, as did Johns's own relationship with Robert Rauschenberg, to whom he was close from 1954 to 1961. The Auerbach Hayward show in 1978 ended on 2 July but for the last four days overlapped with the Jasper Johns exhibition in the lower galleries – the shows were discussed together in Lynda Morris, 'Double bill', *Listener*, 6 July 1978.

7 Jay Elwes, 'Interview: Frank Auerbach', *Prospect*, 197, August 2012, pp. 75–76.

8 Adams 2014, p. 18.

9 Ninth Conversation, *Chatting with Henri Matisse: The Lost 1941 Interview*, Henri Matisse with Pierre Courthion, ed. by Serge Guilbaut (Los Angeles and London, 2013), p. 134.

10 Elwes 2012, p. 74.

11 Feaver 2009, p. 232.

12 Thomas Hardy, 'An Ancient to Ancients', *Late Lyrics and Earlier* (London, 1922), pp. 282–84.

SELECTED BIBLIOGRAPHY

Monographs

Feaver, William, *Frank Auerbach*, Rizzoli, New York, 2009

Hughes, Robert, *Frank Auerbach*, Thames & Hudson, London and New York, 1990

Exhibition catalogues

1969 *Frank Auerbach*, Introduction by Michael Podro, Marlborough-Gerson Gallery, New York, September–October

1976 *Frank Auerbach, Paintings and Drawings 1954–1976*, Introduction by William Feaver, Marlborough Galerie, Zurich, May

1978 *Frank Auerbach*, Foreword by Leon Kossoff, Hayward Gallery, Arts Council of Great Britain, London, May–July; Fruitmarket, Edinburgh, July–August

1982 *Frank Auerbach, Recents Paintings and Drawings*, Introduction by Stephen Spender, Marlborough Gallery, New York, April

1986 *Frank Auerbach*, Foreword by Catherine Lampert, XLII Venice Biennale, June–September, British Council, London; with additional texts by Karl-Egon Vester and Paul Bonaventura, Kunstverein, Hamburg, October–November, and Museum Folkwang, Essen, January–March 1987; and by Antonio Saura and Paul Bonaventura, Centro de Arte Reina Sofía, Madrid, April–May 1987

1987 *Frank Auerbach, Recent Paintings and Drawings*, Introduction by William Feaver, Marlborough Fine Art, London, January–February

1989 *Frank Auerbach, Recent Work*, Introduction by Mel Gooding, Rijksmuseum Vincent van Gogh, Amsterdam, September–December

1990 *Frank Auerbach, Recent Work*, Introduction by Mel Gooding, Marlborough Fine Art, London, September–October

1990 *Frank Auerbach. The Complete Etchings 1954–1990*, Introduction by Michael Podro, Marlborough Graphics, London

1994 *Frank Auerbach, Recent Works*, Introduction by Peter Ackroyd, Marlborough Gallery, New York, April

1995 *Frank Auerbach and the National Gallery: Working after the Masters*, Colin Wiggins (ed.), National Gallery, July–September

1995 *Frank Auerbach*, Foreword by Richard Wollheim, Campbell-Thiebaud Gallery, San Francisco, November–December

1998 *Frank Auerbach: Recent Works*, 'Talking to Frank Auerbach' by Michael Peppiatt, Marlborough Gallery, New York, September–October

2001 *Frank Auerbach: Paintings and Drawings 1954–2001*, Essays by Catherine Lampert, Norman Rosenthal and Isabel Carlisle, Royal Academy of Arts, September–December

2009–10 *Frank Auerbach: London Building Sites, 1952–62*, Barnaby Wright (ed.), Essays by Margaret Garlake, Paul Moorhouse and Barnaby Wright, Courtauld Gallery, London, October–January

2012 *Frank Auerbach: Next Door*, Foreword by John Wonnacott, Marlborough Fine Art, London, October–November

2012 *Frank Auerbach, Early Works 1954–1978*, Introduction by Paul Moorhouse, Offer Waterman & Co., London, November–December

2013 *Raw Truth: Auerbach-Rembrandt*, Pilar Ordovas (ed.), Conversation between Frank Auerbach, Taco Dibbits, Geoffrey Parton and Pilar Ordovas, Ordovas, London, October–December; Rijksmuseum, Amsterdam, December 2013–March 2014

Interviews, writings and statements by the artist

Adams, Tim, 'Frank's other half', *Observer, The New Review*, 21 September 2014

Auerbach, Frank, 'Seven Portraits', *ARK*, 23, 1958

—, 'Fragments from a conversation', *X: A Quarterly Review*, 1:1, November 1959

—, Letter dated 4 December 1963, a reply to 'A letter from Michael Peppiatt', *Cambridge Opinion* (special issue: *Modern Art in Britain*), 37, January 1964

—, 'Homage to Sickert', *Listener*, 89:2307, 14 June 1973

—, Foreword, *Late Sickert: Paintings 1927 to 1942*, exh. cat., Arts Council, London, 1981

Selected Bibliography

—, Statement dated June 1975, *Frank Auerbach: Paintings and Drawings 1954–1976*, exh. cat., Marlborough Galerie, Zurich, 1976

—, 'The Golden Lion and other stories', *Bamboo*, 13, Summer 1987

Battye, John Christopher, 'Frank Auerbach talks to John Christopher Battye', *Art & Artists*, 5:10, January 1971

Billen, Andrew, 'Portrait of an artist at 81', *The Times Magazine*, 6 October 2012

Bonaventura, Paul, 'Een Benadering van Frank Auerbach', *Metropolis M*, 2, Summer 1986

Bumpus, Judith, 'Frank Auerbach', *Art & Artists*, June 1986

Cork, Richard, 'Frank Auerbach: An interview by Richard Cork', *Art & Design*, 4:9/10, 1988

—, 'Two old masters', interview with Lucian Freud and Frank Auerbach, *The Times*, 3 May 2006

—, *Face To Face: Interviews with Artists*, Tate, London, 2015

Elwes, Jay, 'Interview: Frank Auerbach', *Prospect*, 197, August 2012

Fernand, Deirdre, 'Alone is where his art is', *Sunday Times Magazine*, 6 December 2009

Frank Auerbach: Paintings and Drawings relating to Titian [commissioned by David Wilkie], exh. cat., University of Essex, Colchester, 1973

'Frank Auerbach', *Bamboo*, 14, Autumn 1987

'Frank Auerbach, Der Endpunkt ist der Punkt, an dem das Problem gelöst zu sein scheint', a conversation with Mona Körte and Judith Elisabeth Weiss, *Kunstforum*, 216, July–August 2012

Gayford, Martin, 'A master at seventy', *Daily Telegraph*, 1 September 2001

—, 'Auerbach's London', *Apollo*, October 2009

Greig, Geordie, 'Paint or die, meeting Frank Auerbach', *Modern Painters*, 11:3, Autumn 1998

—, 'Hidden talent', *Times Magazine*, 12 December 1998

—, 'The constant painter', *London Evening Standard*, 10 September 2009

Lambirth, Andrew, 'Living in the moment', *Spectator*, 24 October 2009, 311:9452

Lampert, Catherine, 'A conversation with Frank Auerbach', *Frank Auerbach*, exh. cat., Arts Council, London, 1978

—, 'Frank Auerbach in his own words', *Telegraph*, 3 November 2012

Peppiatt, Michael, 'Frank Auerbach: Going against the grain', *Art International*, Autumn 1987

—, 'Frank Auerbach', *Tate*, 14, Spring 1998

—, 'Frank Auerbach, Camden Town London 1998', 'Frank Auerbach, Camden Town London 1999', *Interviews with Artists 1966–2012*, New Haven and London, 2012

Rothschild, Hannah, 'Man of many layers', *Telegraph Magazine*, 28 September 2013

Tusa, John, *John Tusa on Creativity: Interviews Exploring the Process*, London, 2003

Von Drateln, Doris, 'Malen ist nicht wie Husten oder Spucken', *Kunstforum*, 87, January/February 1987

Wullschlager, Jackie, 'Lunch with the FT: Frank Auerbach', *Financial Times*, 6–7 October 2012

TV and Radio

Front Row, 'Raw Truth–Auerbach–Rembrandt', BBC Radio 4, 4 October 2013

The John Tusa Interviews, 'Frank Auerbach', BBC Radio 3, 7 October 2001

In Pursuit of Change, 'Frank Auerbach in conversation with Richard Cork', BBC Radio 3, 18 November 1985

Omnibus, 'Frank Auerbach: To the Studio', Hannah Rothschild and Jake Auerbach Film Productions, BBC 2, 10 November 2001

South Bank Show, 'Frank Auerbach', directed by Tony Cash, London Weekend Television, 20 May 1978

CHRONOLOGY

1931
On 29 April Frank Helmut Auerbach is born in Berlin, son of Max Auerbach and Charlotte Nora Borchardt.

1939
On 4 April, Auerbach, sponsored by the writer Iris Origo, sets sail from Hamburg for school in England. He attends Bunce Court at Lenham, near Faversham in Kent, a school founded by Anna Essinger, a German Jewish-Quaker. She had relocated her school from southern Germany to England in 1933. Many of the children and teachers are Jewish refugees. The school is evacuated to Wem, Shropshire, in the period 1940–45.

1943
In March Auerbach's parents are sent to Auschwitz, where they subsequently die.

1947
Auerbach leaves school with a Higher School Certificate and on 16 July receives a document of naturalization. In the autumn he attends art classes at the Hampstead Garden Suburb Institute. He begins (into 1948) to act in small parts in plays with the International Theatre Group, at the Torch Theatre, the 20th Century Theatre and the Tavistock Theatre.

1948
In January Auerbach enrolls at the Borough Polytechnic Institute in south London for two terms. One of his tutors is David Bomberg. During Frank Marcus's production of *House of Regrets* by Peter Ustinov at the Torch Theatre he meets Estella Olive West (E.O.W.). In September he begins a National Diploma in Design at St Martin's School of Art (to 1952), where he later befriends Leon Kossoff. He continues to attend evening classes given by Bomberg until 1953.

1952
Auerbach does not pass his army medical and is exempted from National Service. He enters the Royal College of Art (graduating in 1955 with a silver medal and first-class honours). In September he experiences a 'breakthrough',

realizing *Summer Building Site* and the first resolved portrait of E.O.W., a nude figure.

1954
In March Auerbach takes over the studio near Mornington Crescent, Camden Town, previously rented by Leon Kossoff. He begins painting Primrose Hill.

1956
One-person exhibition at the Beaux Arts Gallery in January. Auerbach continues to exhibit there through 1963, the year before Helen Lessore's gallery closes. Teaches at various art colleges, including Sidcup, Bromley, Camberwell, Ealing and the Slade (until 1968). J.Y.M. (Julia Yardley Mills) begins posing in 1957.

1958
Marries Julia Wolstenholme, a painter who also studied at the Royal College. Their son Jacob is born in March.

1961
Auerbach paints two versions of Rembrandt's *Deposition* in the National Gallery. Paintings of his neighbourhood begin with the Carreras cigarette factory and extend to the streets behind and around the Underground stations, Camden Town and Mornington Crescent.

1965
David Wilkie, an insurance clerk in the City, commissions Auerbach to paint a work based on Titian, and this relationship results in other works. The Wilkie works are later donated to the Tate. In February Auerbach has his first exhibition at Marlborough Fine Art, London. The gallery continues to represent and show his work, also at its associated galleries in Europe and New York (at the latter from 1969).

1978
The Arts Council of Great Britain organizes a retrospective that opens at the Hayward Gallery, London, and tours to the Fruitmarket Gallery, Edinburgh. The catalogue includes a foreword by Leon Kossoff and a conversation between Auerbach and Catherine Lampert, the exhibition's organizer.

Chronology

1981
'A New Spirit in Painting', a widely discussed review of figurative painting selected by Norman Rosenthal, Nicholas Serota and Christos M. Joachimides opens at the Royal Academy of Arts (five paintings by Auerbach are included).

1986
Auerbach represents Britain at the XLII Venice Biennale, June–September, where he shares the Golden Lion prize with Sigmar Polke. The exhibition travels to the Kunstverein, Hamburg, the Museum Folkwang, Essen, and the newly opened Centro de Arte Reina Sofía, Madrid, in 1987.

1987
Begins working in a studio in Finsbury Park for part of each week.

1989
Exhibition of recent work at the Rijksmuseum Vincent van Gogh in Amsterdam.

1990
Publication of Robert Hughes's monograph *Frank Auerbach* (Thames & Hudson). Marlborough Graphics shows 'The Complete Etchings 1954–1990'.

1990–91
A focus exhibition around the version of *To the Studios* acquired by the Saint Louis Art Museum is shown in the museum and with the addition of twelve paintings at the Yale Center for British Art, New Haven.

1995
The exhibition 'Frank Auerbach and the National Gallery: Working after the Masters', July–September, is built around the drawings he made over a thirty-year period from paintings in the collection, together with his versions of paintings by Rembrandt, Rubens and Titian.

2000
A room of Auerbach's paintings owned by the Tate is presented in the first display at Tate Modern in May. Auerbach is included in the National Gallery's 'Encounters', one of the millennium exhibitions.

2001
Retrospective in the main galleries of the Royal Academy of Arts, September–December; the catalogue has essays by Norman Rosenthal and Catherine Lampert, the curator. *Frank Auerbach: To the Studio,* the first film about the artist, directed by Hannah Rothschild and produced by her and Jake Auerbach, is built around interviews with the regular sitters going back to E.O.W. and J.Y.M., and the current ones: Julia Auerbach, Jake Auerbach Catherine Lampert, David Landau and Ruth Bromberg (until 2008). William Feaver begins sitting in 2003.

2006–07
Shows with Lucian Freud at the Victoria & Albert Museum in 2006. The artist's etchings and drypoints are shown at the Fitzwilliam Museum, Cambridge, 2007; the museum owns a complete set thanks to donations by Ruth Bromberg, James Kirkman and the artist.

2009
'Frank Auerbach: London Building Sites, 1952–62' opens at the Courtauld Gallery; the catalogue is edited by Barnaby Wright. *Frank Auerbach* by William Feaver is published (Rizzoli) with a complete catalogue of images compiled by Kate Austin.

2013–14
Six paintings by Auerbach are shown with several Rembrandts at Ordovas, London, and then at the Rijksmuseum, Amsterdam, in the Dutch Gallery of Honour. By now, Auerbach's work is in British public collections and ones in Australia, Brazil, Denmark, France, Israel, Mexico, Norway, Portugal, South Africa, Spain and USA, and in private collections worldwide.

2014
The works by Auerbach that were owned by Lucian Freud and acquired for the nation through the Acceptance in Lieu scheme are shown at Manchester City Art Gallery and Tate Britain.

2015
Major exhibition, the first six galleries selected by the artist, the last two by Catherine Lampert, opens in June at the Kunstmuseum, Bonn, and at Tate Britain in October.

Measurements are given in centimetres, followed by inches, height before width. Marlborough = Marlborough Fine Art, London, a = above, b = below.

List of Illustrations

Museum, Jerusalem, Anonymous gift through British Friends of the Art Museums of Israel, in memory of Lily Sieff, B12.0254. Courtesy Marlborough

p. 197 Studio interior, May 1985. Photo Prudence Cuming Associates. Courtesy Marlborough

p. 198 *Ruth Bromberg Seated*, 2002–03. Oil on board, 61 × 56.2 (24 × 22⅛). Private collection. Courtesy Marlborough

p. 201 *Self-Portrait II*, 2013. Graphite and chalk on paper, 77.5 × 57.5 (30⅝ × 22⅝). Marlborough Fine Art. Courtesy Marlborough

p. 202 *Reclining Head of Julia II*, 1996. Acrylic on board, 50.8 × 63.5 (20 × 25). Private collection. Courtesy Marlborough

p. 203 *Head of Julia II*, 1999. Acrylic on board, 30.5 × 30.5 (12 × 12). Louisiana Museum of Modern Art, Humlebaek, Denmark. Acquired with support from The New Carlsberg Foundation. Courtesy Marlborough

p. 204 *In the Studio*, 2013–14. Oil on board, 50.8 × 50.8 (20 × 20). Private collection. Courtesy Marlborough

p. 206 Frank Auerbach outside the studio, 2009. Photo David Dawson. Courtesy David Dawson

p. 209 *Chimney in Mornington Crescent - Winter Morning*, 1991. Oil on canvas, 143.2 × 133 (56⅜ × 52⅜). Private collection. Courtesy Marlborough

p. 210 *Reclining Head of Julia II*, 2007. Acrylic on board, 55.9 × 76.2 (22 × 30). Private collection. Courtesy Marlborough

p. 213 *Head of William Feaver*, 2008. Oil on canvas, 55.9 × 51.1 (22 × 20⅛). Private collection. Courtesy Marlborough

p. 235 Frank Auerbach, Catherine Lampert and Leon Kossoff, dinner after the opening of 'The Mystery of Appearance' exhibition, December 2011. Photo David Dawson. Courtesy David Dawson

PERMISSIONS

ACKNOWLEDGMENTS

The images, documents and memories of those close to Frank Auerbach over many years have allowed the book to have an 'inside' feeling, and I am extremely grateful to Julia Auerbach, Jake Auerbach, Sarah West, Andrew Ranicki, David Landau and William Feaver in this regard. Kate Austin at Marlborough Fine Art has been an irreplaceable collaborator throughout the process, and the Marlborough records and images as well as the encouragement of Geoffrey Parton have been essential. As is obvious from the quality and empathy of the photographs, those who have made the records of Frank in his studio have been on his wavelength, and Virginia Verran, Frances von Hofmannsthal and the photographers Marc Trivier and David Dawson have been especially helpful. The same generosity is true of those who have interviewed him, several on multiple occasions, and I have drawn upon these records of life in the studio as well as comments by friends of Frank's, many of them artists, over time.

Jacky Klein, formerly commissioning editor at Thames & Hudson, persuaded me to begin the book, and Roger Thorp extended the invitation. The contributions of the whole team at Thames & Hudson have been very valuable. At home I depend upon Andrew Dempsey as a reader and on him and Susana Lampert as supporters as I struggle to write.

Frank has sharpened the anecdotes and opened up with memories, participating in this book even when anything that is 'looking back' must seem unwanted; and he has understood that my desire to bring out a book that was accurate and used his words might enhance the pleasure people take in his art. I am lucky to have been sitting since 1978. It is an important part of my life.

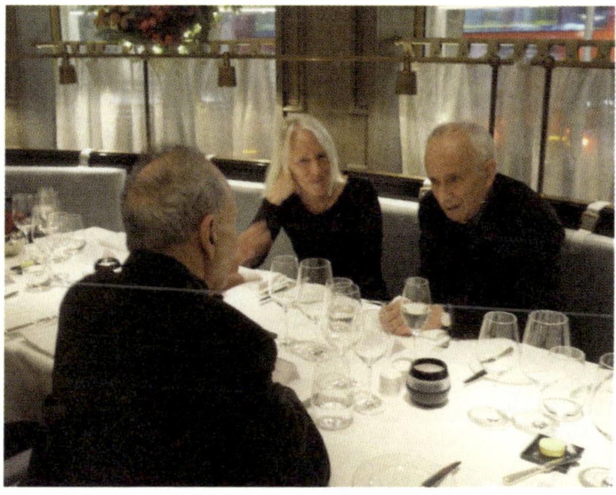

DAVID DAWSON, Frank Auerbach, Catherine Lampert and Leon Kossoff, dinner after the opening of 'The Mystery of Appearance' exhibition, December 2011

INDEX

Index

Index